Shrapnel from
a Writing Life

Ⓑ

Other Books by Ian Gouge

Novels and Novellas

On Parliament Hill - Coverstory books, 2021
A Pattern of Sorts - Coverstory books, 2020
The Opposite of Remembering - Coverstory books, 2020
At Maunston Quay - Coverstory books, 2019
An Infinity of Mirrors - Coverstory books, 2018 (2nd ed.)
The Big Frog Theory - Coverstory books, 2018 (2nd ed.)
Losing Moby Dick and Other Stories - Coverstory books, 2017

Short Stories

Degrees of Separation - Coverstory books, 2018
Secrets & Wisdom - Paperback, 2017

Poetry

The Homelessness of a Child - Coverstory books, 2021
The Myths of Native Trees - Coverstory books, 2020
First-time Visions of Earth from Space - Coverstory books, 2019
After the Rehearsals - Coverstory books, 2018
Punctuations from History - Coverstory books, 2018
Human Archaeology - Paperback, 2017
Collected Poems (1979-2016) - KDP, 2017

Anthologies

New Contexts: 1 - Coverstory books, 2021
Triple Measures - Ian Gouge, K.M.Miller, Tom Furniss, Coverstory books, 2020
Oak Tree Alchemy - Coverstory books, 2019
Play for Three Hands - Tom Furniss, Ian Gouge, K.M.Miller, pamphlet, 1981

Non-Fiction

Shaping the IT Organization - Springer-Verlag, 2003
e-Management - Springer-Verlag, 2003
On the 7th Day - Management Books 2000, 2001

Ian Gouge

Shrapnel from a Writing Life

Coverstory
books

First published in hardback format by Coverstory books 2022

ISBN 978-1-8382321-4-6

Copyright © Ian Gouge 2022

www.iangouge.com

www.coverstorybooks.com

Contents

Foreword

I don't think I can say precisely when I first became aware of him. It would have been in childhood certainly, given we attended the same school, took the same classes; but aware of him as a 'person'? That's a different matter altogether.

For a number of years it might be said that we 'rubbed along together'. It was an episodic relationship which defied labelling and categorisation. I can only assume there must have been moments of synergy, but ask me when they occurred or how they manifested themselves and I would have to admit defeat. It might be safest to describe me as an historically disinterested observer. I watched him stumble and fumble his way through life with horror and approbation in equal measure - though even as I write that, I wonder if the statement is true, whether or not there might just have been a shade more of the former. In any event, it doesn't really matter. He was not, after all, a man of any note, at least back then. Indeed, he may still not be one now, but something has changed; there has been a shift - in him or in me - which, either way, has reduced the degree of apathy in which I traditionally held him. Is it possible to put a label on the status in which we now mutually exist or to pin down the catalyst for the shift? Not definitively.

You might ask when I began to take him seriously. Relatively recently, I would suggest. Can you accept the last ten years or so as 'recent' in a timespan of, what, over fifty? It is a period which certainly feels fresh enough. And even if it is impossible to locate the source of our changed relationship, there is a more recent event which allows me to bring it into focus.

"I would like you," he said in that almost silent voice of his, "to examine my notebooks, my scribblings. There are a few I must warn you, and they go back - what? - to somewhere in the early eighties. And although I suspect, deep down, they are ultimately of little worth, you might be able to conjure something of merit from them. I would be interested to see what you can come up with."

Surprised, I wanted to understand what he was expecting. He laughed, again silently.

"Frankly, I have no idea! Perhaps filter out all the dross and see what you are left with. Or counterpoint my musings - my desires for and forecasts of the future - with what actually happened; that might be worth something. Or throw the whole lot up in the air and see how it falls. I am - as they say - in your hands."

Blessing or curse, I had no clear idea; but it was a responsibility of sorts. Might there be any value in the exercise? For him? For me?

As some of you may know, he professes to be a writer. Or, in his vocabulary, a 'Writer'. The capital letter does - I believe - make all the difference. A writer of what, you may ask? Fiction and poetry in equal measure - though not if that measure is judged on the basis of the number of printed pages devoted to each. On that basis, let us say he's a novelist who dabbles in poetry; that's a garment with a better fit than one cut the other way around. His notebooks and their hundreds of pages are - if this mixed metaphor is not too fanciful - akin to the mortar between bricks. And if you were in the mood to be cruel, you might argue that there was often too much 'mortar' and not enough 'brick', the result of his notebook entries tending to be the most prolific when he was 'between' things, looking back at the last brick and anticipating the next. Once I had managed to corral all the relevant words and sifted through them, their overwhelming preoccupations - angst, repetition, hopes, doubts, plans, ideas - became all too clear; the simmering of a minestrone that had been on the hob for far too long. Did he expect, I wondered, a biography, something that was all about him?

"Not at all." That laugh again. "It should be about the journey, the adventure; it should tell the story of the ideas, mapping out the stepping stones that took me from one place to the next. Me? I'm almost insignificant in all of this. If you end up with a biography we're both lost."

All of which was - if I'm honest - of very little comfort.

Is there a beginning to go back to? Undoubtedly; but this is not where the notebooks start. How could they? Would you expect a five-year-old - however precocious - to start drafting missives about an obsession upon which they had yet to consciously settle? I could have delved, pushed him for the backstory, the foundations upon which to build the edifice; but he would surely have rejected my request, having already made it clear that he did not want a 'life'. It is, of course, impossible to extract one from the other - the writing life from the lived life - yet this was the task he had ostensibly set me. And there was something in his request - to "see what you can come up with" - which seemed to presuppose failure, as if the challenge I had been set was doomed from the outset.

Therefore, in terms of a beginning, I had no choice other than focus on a vague point just before 1983. That there is no attributable date to the earliest record found is both a critical date missing from the entry concerned and an indication of how ill-disciplined he often was when making them. Where they were dated, it became possible to visualise them coming rat-a-tat in quick succession over a few days - or, conversely, to expose barren tracts of months when nothing was said. In the most extreme case I was staring into a vast desert which spanned eight years. Many entries do allude to a month or are specific to a single date, yet in the case of the former it became abundantly clear that often one 'single' entry was indeed no such thing but rather a collection of thoughts tagged one onto the other with no clue where any calendar boundaries might lie - other than a change of pen, perhaps! He had made time fluid and indistinct.

Taking all of this into account, I had no option other than to start in what was effectively the 'middle'. I could still have unilaterally chosen to customise my brief somewhat and go back to that five-year-old and the first story he ever wrote, to attempt to fill-in the considerable gap between then - 1963 - and that initial "pre-1983" entry; but I would have been doing so without permission or authority, and I would be telling the tale not 'live' but in self-conscious retrospect, glasses rose-tinted or otherwise. The one thing the notebook entries do have, of course, is authenticity. They are his, rooted in the moment in which they were written, essentially unsullied by hindsight and the knowledge of what happened next. I am obviously in possession of such understanding because I know what followed, and it may therefore be legitimate to occasionally qualify the original text in some way to take advantage of such knowledge; but anything I might transcribe to cover the earlier undocumented period - the 'lived life' - before that first entry could be nothing but supposition, focussed not on "the journey, the adventure...the story of the ideas, the words...the stepping stones" but on an imagined or second-hand existence and surely invalid on that basis. At least in the context of the contract made.

Yet in a way even the 'authorised' beginning taken from the earliest entry found is no such thing. Not only is it in the middle of his life but, more importantly, it is evidently in the middle of an idea which must have originated sometime earlier. It is as if one has eaves-dropped on a conversation when it is half-way through: you are conscious something must have come before and so are always playing catch-up, fighting to avoid the impulse to re-construct something, even if you've no idea what that might be. Yet, when all's said and done, perhaps on balance it is part of my job to try and fill-in where I can, to ease the transition, to smooth the road.

I asked him if there had been something before.

"Oh, undoubtedly! Isn't there always? But don't ask me where it is because I couldn't find it. Decomposing at the bottom of a box in a dusty cupboard there may be a few pages of something which might be relevant and pre-date the first;

but if so, I've no idea where it might be, what it might look like, or what it might say."

He was unapologetic in a factual way, as if unreservedly recognising both my request and the potential importance of those missing jigsaw pieces - yet doing so with a shrug of the shoulders. I suspected he had a better view than that, an inkling formed from a half-forgotten image, a fading snapshot from his past. It was, I suppose, to his credit that he chose not to elaborate, not to fill in the blanks himself. He could very easily have conjured up something out of thin air, or planted a seed - but this would have been to corrupt the whole enterprise. Even I could see that.

Is it significant - or mere coincidence - that the first word in that initial entry is 'mirrors'? Full capitals, underlined. Not only was this was to be the title of a novel he was to publish some thirty years later - a long gestation period and a difficult birth - but it surely also describes both his relationship to his notebooks and the enterprise in which I am currently engaged. What are the notebooks but a reflection of his contemporary thoughts? And what is this - 'book' - but my historical reflections upon those?

Apt, don't you think?

Part One - to 1991

pre-1983 (CON)

<u>MIRRORS</u>

"It was a lottery…"

Story concerning seeing oneself and others.
Perspectives of view.   (internal exploration)

* (i) purchase of mirror as wedding gift
      (scene: relationship between Mark + Julia)
      suggest? basic flaw in harmony* (its perfection?)
          some corrupting disquiet

(ii) disruption / disagreement
      awakening of Mark to potentialities + limitations**
      breaking of mirror as physical exposure;
          fragmentation of his image of himself
              his relationship with Julia

(iii) breaking of mirror must accord with the breaking of Mark's philosophy
and the relationship with Julia.
      ? by showing former, implication of future consequences sufficient

* would there be a 'flaw' in the mirror too? ∴ sense of imperfect
representation of "the real" ('flaw' is the 'perfection'; unreal presentation)

** ∴ awakening possibilities + limitations of mirrors

★ Novel needing to possess (internally) a mirror image

~~~

Do you see what I mean? Hardly the very genesis of an idea; the notions and characters already seem semi-formed, some way along their journey. He already has an intimacy with the mirror to which he refers and which is clearly central; he knows when it will be procured - and that it will be broken. The presence of an underlying theme - about the novel, what it needs to tackle - undoubtedly points to this not being the first time the proposition has come to him.

As you may also gather - strictly from a practical, reader's perspective - there are difficulties in the text. In its raw form the words are not necessarily coherent or neatly arranged; at this distance they are subject to what might appear random indentations, side notes, marginalia, arrows and symbols, all of which would have been entirely meaningful at the time, yet now - divorced from that precise moment - may require interpretation. Of course, their layout and structure are further abstracted from what they actually signified at the time because they are being interpreted by a third party - or multiple third parties, you and I. A double-whammy: not only are these words from years ago, we can have no idea exactly what they were intended to mean when they were written. This will be a constant challenge.

More than that, how can one possibly recreate the dynamism of thought on a printed page? This would have been his challenge at the time as much as it is the rubicon we must now cross. In some places the words are written in a slightly larger hand, or imply greater emphasis based on how they have been scribed. How do I convey that on a page of printed text without access to an authentic facsimile? You see part of my problem.

And knowing what I know, what should I do with a simple annotation like "(its perfection?)"? There is nothing 'perfect' about the relationship Mark and Julia share - or is that me overlaying my own interpretation on that fiction now that I have read the final work? Of course at this stage, years before they actually come into being as fully-formed characters, perhaps he had been assuming their relationship would somehow be perfect and therefore ripe for destruction; but given what I know about Mark - and what you will hopefully come to find out - should that side-note not be "(its imperfection?)"? How much is that judgement - my judgement - even valid?

~~~~

'Rotten Row'

(i) couple in Hyde Park
      physical situation could be taken as the opposite of what it actually is
      (i.e. open to interpretation)
      comfort / protection against / from…

(ii) ? dip into history; an attempt to answer some questions

(iii) man (reflecting - pun! - in park) meets girl.
      knowing the girl will be unfulfilling, not stimulating,
          he wins her (i.e. not for her own sake)
    consequence: into an impossible relationship =>
        reflection on a previous one

| Link with <u>Mirrors</u>? i.e. how Mark met Julia.
| - beginning of <u>Rotten Row</u> is Mark + Lesley
| transgression into the past
| a; into mirror (symbol of present) => thoughts of past
| b; how Julia met (immediate past) =? how Lesley lost
| c; Lesley + how Lesley met

to be left open ended, with relationship beginning (conclusion unsatisfactory - nothing forthcoming or particularly evident, like the relationship itself).

Mark 'loses' Julia + himself again.

~~~~

Proof - as if proof were needed - that we are explorers. At this stage 'Rotten Row' was potentially a discrete story, standing apart. If it were not, why would the question "Link with Mirrors?" even be asked?

It is good to get an example like this early on. We will be able to see how his thinking develops; how, in this instance, the second idea - 'Rotten Row' - not only becomes linked with 'Mirrors' but eventually an integral scene within it. (Or does that recognition only truly come when you read the novel itself?) There is much of this too-ing and fro-ing in the notebooks as notions bounce around, sometimes germinating, sometimes not. In the context of my arrangement with him, I can only see these as examples of 'the journey'; a unique opportunity for us to examine narratives as they coalesce, before they become the finished article - though, as we will discover, in some cases they fail to do so. No matter how hard he tries to work up an idea it can still prove illusive, insubstantial, as if built on weak foundations. If you asked him, I suspect he would say that there were far too many of these (though in my final assessment I might be prepared to argue that the underlying failure to do so may have resided elsewhere).

~~~~

Novel constructed around a mirror. (Parallels; reflections suggesting opposites)

Thus:

Present	Past
Mark + Julia	Mark + Lesley
Meeting of Julia	<= Splitting up in Hyde Park
(Change in immediate feeling of impossibility of satisfaction. This original response the flaw in their relationship?)	
∴ ultimately no sense of loss?	∴ ultimately a sense of loss?

(Pivotal event)

the breaking of the mirror (paradoxically a revelation)	perhaps distortion - discovery of a flaw; noticing that their mutual reflection is false, incorrect, imperfect

(outcome)

exposing of self; attitudes etc. removal of facade (as if the mirror provided only an inaccurate vision) idea of a flaw intrinsic in the mirror	(beginning) - relationship as a forming / finding of self. Each seeing other as a picture / reflection of themselves incompleteness (naivety) of vision (simplistic vision?)

✿

Mirror; Parallel ; Reflection; (revelation)

MIRROR:	vb	pass for; reflect; imitate; portray; echo; mime; mimic; represent; parody; caricature; copy; translate; counterfeit; (re-present)
	n	copy; reproduction; imitation; image; form; effigy; transfer; glass; looking-glass; hand-mirror; (re-production)

PARALLEL: vb   compare; confront; juxtapose;
                                contrast; match; correlate;

           n   equivalent; match; mate; twin; double;
                                companion; pair; complement;
                                counterpart; reflection; duplicate;
                                correspondence; (counter-part)

REFLECTION: scattering; polish; gloss; sheen; lustre;
                                mediation; consideration; inspection;
                                embodiment; representation; realisation;
                                manifestation; (re-presentation)

REVELATION: discovery; finding; exposure; illumination;
                                authenticity; accuracy; reversal;
                                disclosure; communication; (dis-covery)
                                (dis-closure)

                                [co____ ; dis____ ; re____]

~~~~

Scanning a thesaurus for a list of words associated with his core theme would seem to serve two purposes: the first, the prosaic one of providing alternatives or equivalents to be used in the drafting of the book; the second, as a potential springboard to other ideas.

Spoiler alert: as you will see, some of these words will pop-up later and be repeated in his notes. Repetition is a recurrent theme in the notebooks, with ideas, notions, and suggestions at times played back pretty much in exactly the same way and at others morphing into something else.

But this is, I fear, already giving too much of the game away. I tell myself that I do so in order to give you a grounding, a running start at his text, rather than throwing you in at the deep end and seeing if you will swim. Perhaps the provision of arm-bands is not the best approach; it almost certainly isn't the most 'authentic'. Should I stop?

~~~~

Character Listing: provisional

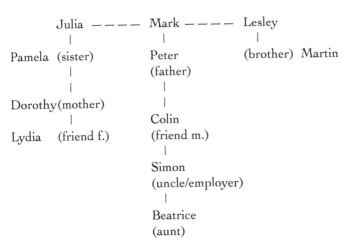

Pamela is to be married, hence the mirror as gift (never received).
Dorothy - possibly over-obliging, uncritical woman.
Lydia, a hypocritical 'feminist'; unmarried (<u>not</u> unwanted);
       attractive etc.
Colin; journalist friend of Mark (from University days)
Peter } brothers { of a kind?   attitude to Mark?
Simon }   { at poles?   difficulty of relationship
                                         relative / business
Beatrice; sympathetic figure (to Mark) offering contrast - when needed - to
Simon?
Martin; untalented contrast to Mark

Plot   Importance of old photographs
         Fire - destruction of papers, photos etc.
             ✸ destruction of <u>the past</u>

〜〜〜

There are two common and recurrent subjects in notes on potential fiction projects. The first might be loosely labelled with the heading 'Characters'; the second, 'Plot'. In the sub-entry above (and in what immediately follows) we get the first examples of these, related - of course - to 'Mirrors'.

It is interesting to observe - both here and later - how important it is for him to ascribe names to his characters from very early on in the process, as if that is the first vital step in turning them into 'real' creations. Occasionally the names alter and shift but, as will become clear, as soon as there is a peg on which to hang 'people' - like 'Mark' and 'Julia' in this case - doing so seems to allow him to 'work them out' (my phrase). Before they can become rounded for us, they need to do so for him; an understandable prerequisite. And, if you think about it, this trope is one of the core functions of his note-making process.

It is a pattern repeated with plot lines too. This first example relating to 'Mirrors' - including, as you will soon see, various twists and turns as it is worked through - is typical. Having said that, often the word 'plot' is a misnomer, referring to no more than a loose collection of ideas which may end up being (or needing to be) a plot strand. In the entry immediately below this interruption, "Mark's relationship with..." is hardly a pointer to concrete action, and "Role of Lydia and Colin?" is precisely what it seems to be, a question. Therefore, we should not take all of his 'plot' components - or character components, come to that - as gospel. It is akin to someone sitting a maths exam and showing their intermediate calculations in the margins. Of course one never sees any of that in the final text, merely the culmination of the effort. Which is probably just as well.

And thinking about it, there is a composite component at play here when he takes both of these principals - 'character' and 'plot' - and beings to weave them together, often in a tighter framework; the first step on the way to defining the detailed structure and sequence of the end product.

~~~

plot:

Mirror taken (concealed) at Mark's uncle's house.
Mark working on a book for his uncle:
> research involves the collection of old photographs
> (book: biography of a distant relative; man of letters, but fairly obscure. Importance of book; reflecting on various characters of early C20th lit. etc. etc.)

Mark's concern with finding photos drives him to a reviewing of his own -> a lead into memory of Lesley.
Letter to Mark from Martin concerning Lesley (can he help?)
Mark's relationship with his family: father/uncle/aunt
Mark's relationship with Julia's family: mother
Role of Lydia and Colin?
Fire destroys Uncle's office. Mirror, ruined, is discovered after.
Lydia: possible seduction of Mark or Colin?
What causes split (albeit a subtle one) between Mark + Julia?

scheme:

1	2	3	4
Mirror bought			
Installed at Uncle's Julia/mother Julia/Lydia	Mark's seeking of photos (rediscovery of past) father/uncle uncle/aunt + Colin	Mark + Lesley Martin's letter (+ Lesley now?)	reflection upon Lydia/Colin?
	FIRE		
discovery of mirror ruined (loss of irreplaceable)	(research etc. reduced to dust) loss of the irreplaceable	repercussions of Lesley?	

~~~~

There is another element to call out here, though I hesitate to do so given that my knowledge of what follows (both in the notes themselves and the final work) is so much greater than yours...

Suffice to say it is not only the metamorphosis of plot and character which can be tracked through the notebooks. In some examples we might observe what could be called the 'nucleus' of an idea changing. In 'Mirrors', for example, the role of Mark's book and its subject - "(book: biography of a distant relative; man of letters, but fairly obscure)" - bears nothing more than an embryonic resemblance to the final product. Indeed, not only does Mark's own book become central to the novel [the book within the book], but the books that appear within Mark's book are equally critical [the books within the book within the book - the most significant 'mirror' of them all?]. Indeed, it could be argued that it / they become as important as his narration of Mark's own story.

1. Buying of mirror (Mark, Julia)
2. Leaving the mirror at uncle's house (Mark, Julia, Simon, Beatrice)
3. Mark drives Julia home (Mark, Julia); (Simon, Beatrice); (Julia, Pamela, Dorothy)

4. The evening out (Mark, Colin); (Julia, Lydia); (Mark, Colin, Julia, Lydia)
5. Examination of photographs (Mark, Peter); (Mark)
6. Mark and Lesley - how they had parted
7. Dinner party (Dorothy, Pamela, Julia, Mark, Colin, Lydia, Peter(?))
8. Work (Mark, Simon); (Simon, Peter)
9. Play (Colin, Lydia)
10. Martin's letter (Mark)
11. Engagement party (Pamela, Frank, Dorothy, Julia, Mark); (Julia, Mark)
12. Mark and Lesley - a day out together
13. Advice (Beatrice, Simon); (Mark, Beatrice)
14. The Picnic (Mark, Colin, Julia, Lydia)
15. Inroads (Mark, Martin); (Mark, Julia)
16. Mark and Lesley - how they had met
17. Aftermath of fire (Simon, Beatrice, Mark, Peter)
18. The mirror (Mark); (Mark, Julia)
19. Loss of the irreplaceable (Simon, Beatrice); (Beatrice, Mark); (Julia)
20. Repercussions of Lesley?

★ Mark as arsonist: burning Uncle's house as destruction of the photographs - ∴ his past with Lesley - and the mirror (flawless) - symbol of his future with Julia.
Consequence of a breakdown.

"I" first person narrator as pysch. in interspersed chapters. (an attempt to delve, rediscover what happened).

Scheme 2
1. The mirror (Mark, Julia)
2. At Simon's (Mark, Julia, Simon, Beatrice)
3. Evening party (Mark, Julia, Colin, Lydia)
4. The photographs (Mark, Simon/Peter?)
5. [Mark's photographs (Mark)]
6. The parting (Mark, Lesley)
7. Play (Colin, Lydia)
8. [At work (Mark, Simon, Peter)
9. Martin's letter (Mark)
10. Mark's photographs (Mark)
11. The day out (Mark, Lesley)
12. Family elders (Beatrice, Simon, Peter)
13. The picnic (Mark, Julia, Colin, Lydia)
14. [Julia's family (Julia, Dorothy, Pamela)

15. At work (Mark, Simon) = the acknowledgement in the book. Inroads (Martin, Mark)
16. The meeting (Mark, Lesley)
17. Aftermath (Simon, Beatrice, Mark, Julia)
18. The mirror
19. [Part 2]
20. [Part 3]

Part 2: Mark via Psychologist-type "interview"
Part 3: Witnesses - the external (but not impartial view)

~~~~

Note: it may be entirely superficial to point this out, but in the same way that plot lines and characters can change and be manipulated as he works through his ideas, they also might gain in importance or reduce in significance - even to the extent of disappearing altogether (for example, 'Dorothy' never appears in the final iteration of 'Mirrors').

~~~~

MIRRORS (reappraisal of essential points)

i) 'Harmonic relationship' flawed because of Mark's notion of it, because of its 'perfection'.

ii) ? The mirror is flawed because it is too perfect, its reflection of reality being too real (indistinguishable).

iii) Disruption awakes Mark to his (all) limitations (? and to potentialities and limitations of mirrors).

iv) "Breaking" of mirror as an image of the breaking of a) Mark's philosophy b) his relationship with Julia.

v) Novel needing to possess, internally, a mirror image.

vi) 'Rotten Row' section as a reflection of history, to be held up against present realities (transgression into Past) [a) Mark + Lesley parting , b) Mark + Julia meeting]

vii) Relationship with Lesley as discovery of self, the making of a philosophy; relationship with Julia an attempt to live by that philosophy (but the static position is insufficient to live by, inflexible, inadequate, simplistic, two-dimensional)

viii) People as mirrors, to be looked into (Mark and Lesley looking for images of themselves through the other; things naively "read-in")

ix) Plot should place a high degree of importance on artefacts of the past and make Mark responsible for them. (There must be some real, physical, destruction of the past - its mutability)

x) Mark as instigator; internal -> external breakdown, destruction (thinking that removal of artefacts will clear his own past, that from which he is trying to escape, for which he no longer wishes to be responsible)

Plot ideas:-

X   Mark caught in a confined space (a ship); impossibility of escape; inevitability of confrontation. (a real possibility, this one) - though 'a ship' too confined?

X   He comes into possession of some photographs which bring him in danger (intrusion of past upon the present).

X   'Intrigue and suspense' revolve around the ascertaining of 'the photos' precise significance. Mark's attempts to both reveal and conceal them (and to keep them and himself safe), and the 'jostling' of 'shipmates' (who are they?) to get hold of them.

?   Mark confronted by his own past, Lesley & brother and his photos brings Mark into self-confrontation and doubt. (what is the precise significance of the photos of Lesley to him?)

          Destruction of photos (and self?!) - made public, known? - as self-preservation. Photos of Lesley destroyed too in order to attempt the obliteration of that responsibility.

X   Mark's profession as historian: the voyage ostensibly to allow him the completion of a manuscript (this history as impersonal, a past into which he can freely and easily delve).

          Blackmail (motivation) allowing history to be fixed, for it to be decided 'what happened'. The history Mark becomes involved in is attempting to be made certain - and the danger it carries for him is external, physical; the responsibility, that of being an aide. implying the peril of ??? or attempting fixity.

          Mark's own history (with Lesley) is attempting to break loose, to lose its fixity and authority in Mark's mind; the danger is internal, psychological and self-engendered.

~~~~

As I have already said, the replaying of plans and ideas is a constant theme throughout the notebooks, often giving the same components and lists alternative labels (cf. "essential points", above). Was that, I wonder, just a mechanism to kid himself that he wasn't simply saying the same thing over and over again, to give the illusion of progress? But then perhaps such a judgement is a trifle unfair. In his day-to-day life he is not (to the best of my knowledge) someone who needs to constantly revisit and revalidate a proposal before making decisions - unless it relates to the purchasing of a car over which he can agonise for months.

But I digress.

It is also not uncommon for him to 'score' constituents under consideration though most of the time these assessments are rudimentary rather than scientific in any way. In the example above, the plot ideas are annotated with either a tick, cross, or question mark, and even though these attributions give the impression of being definitive, most often they are not. Oh, at the time they may well have felt decisive and so we should take them at face value and refrain from questioning their integrity; but, as with his workings for plot and character, nothing is 'concrete' until it is committed to the final piece. This leaves us in an ambiguous position; it implies that whilst we must believe what is written in the notebook entries (how can we doubt their veracity?), we must also take what they say with a pinch of salt, a condiment freely available for application thanks to the benefit of hindsight.

The next entry (presumably written later than the one preceding it) shows his mind at work. Having floated an idea, he is clearly utilising the process of 'free thinking' (my term) in order to challenge it. Knowing himself - and the process he is bound to go through - much of this thinking is articulated in the form of questions to himself (as if it were a dialogue of some kind) and all with a self-evident degree of uncertainty. Where these questions are addressed - and in many cases throughout the notebooks they remain unsatisfied - the next entry, the one after that, and so on, become his medium for attempting resolution.

Yet having made that observation, I am immediately persuaded that it is not necessarily correct. Later there will be clear evidence that reaching conclusions - on questions, plot, characters etc. - does not always happen in the notebooks. On multiple occasions entries do little more that surface the challenges; how they play out is often only decided when he is actually 'putting pen to paper' and drafting the work concerned. Does this in any way diminish the value of the questions posed in the notebooks? I would venture not. But what it does suggest is that in order to close the loop on a notion first raised in their pages, one must read the final work.

~~~~~

Is there any need for the confinement / restriction to be physical in the absolute (i.e. on a ship at sea). A mental claustrophobia would seem to be much more threatening.

Mark could make a 'discovery' about someone vis-a-vis the past, the revelation of which could be damaging (in the intangible sense of 'reputation' rather than the tangible threat of imprisonment).

Perhaps letters discovered with old photographs: we see the pursuit in Mark's terms - limitations for it - not as it must unfold itself.

Mark's concern is a transgression upon the past and his responsibility for revealing it as fact, as history. 'How much history is left?' (and his attitude to his own past? i.e. revealing it to Julia)

~~~~~

As you will see for yourself, the relationship between past and present (occasionally bleeding into the future) is not just a preoccupation for 'Mirrors'. It is a recurring topic in virtually all his fiction.

This of course puts an interesting spin on a) the notebook entries - which go from 'present' to 'past' as soon as the next one is written - and b) this endeavour, which throws them all into the past and is an attempt - at his request, remember! - to see what sense we can make of them today.

~~~~~

<u>Mark</u>   Present: Julia   Past: Lesley

Concern is the uncovering (rediscovery) of the past and whether or not it can be divulged to Julia.

Whatever the decision, its irrelevance lies in the fact that the existence of the past is sufficiently disrupting for Mark: without the past's intrusion, it doesn't impinge upon his relationship with Julia (from his viewpoint).

? Delving into history suggests an illegitimacy which has been covered up. Mark's discovery of this threatens the present stability and the regime that has been built upon this weak foundation. Mark faces the repercussions of disclosure; a conflict with that which he considers his duty as a historian. Having the power to create a scandal causes him to question his whole value set, the past's intrusion and the need for re-evaluation. He had never himself been faced with an example of the power of the past i.e. his control of it. History, its making, always seemed an external domain; one to study, not to get involved in.

(cast.)
Mark
Julia
Lesley
Mark's Uncle   Adam; Edmund; Edward; William
Mark's Aunt   Alice; Florence; Martha; Prudence
*(Colin)
(Lydia)
(Julia's sister)   Catherine; Fiona; Laura
(Lesley's brother)   Michael(?)

(Politician)   Alexander; Chester; Donald; Douglas; Kenneth
(his wife)   Belinda; Clara; Linda; Melanie; Penelope; Sophia
(his friends)   Anthony; Conrad; Gavin; Jacob
(his lawyer)   Aaron; Alexander; Roger
(the old lady)   Adela; Camilla; Dinah; Myra
(the reporter)   Amos; Bernard; Evan; Gavin; Martin
(the publisher)   Adam; Bernard; Gregory; Leo

*Colin/Lydia as a subplot is unnecessary. They should be appendages to the story in the sense that they are friends of the protagonists, but nothing beyond that. (Whatever exposes itself naturally is sufficient).

~~~~

I find it interesting that, seemingly having settled on names for Mark's aunt and uncle - 'Beatrice' and 'Simon' - he should suddenly be trying to find 'new' names for them, with those originally chosen not even on the shortlist. Was this because he was looking for the names to 'say' something else?

He penchant for candidate name listing is not unique to the above entry nor this project. In the case of 'Mirrors', some of the characters from the cast above fail to make the cut - and it's interesting to see the names with which the aunt and uncle are ultimately christened. [I resist the spoiler at this point!]

Plot Lines

1 - Mark in stable "pre-marital" relationship with Julia. [datum] Mark receives letter from Lesley's brother triggering Mark's memory. The old photos of he and Lesley. He visits her in the past of his mind, re-living, re-enacting. * Disturbance of equilibrium; questioning of his relationship with Julia. Mark is drawn in, fascinated. Perhaps destroying the photos as an attempt to purge the past. (good) Meeting Lesley again comes to symbolise a confrontation with what he has been, his own past. (Perhaps leave the novel with him facing this prospect(?!) - after all, by the end he will be considerably shaken up by events, a less stable person.)

2 - Y was a fairly successful writer of the late 40s who has recently died; Mark's uncle preparing a biography. Mark as a researcher for his uncle (Historian by profession/academia). Leads to meeting with the Old Lady and a revelation concerning a connection with X, a now successful (rising) politician. [datum] Mark comes into possession of dangerous facts, (letters etc.): dangerous both to X and himself. Meetings with X. Talks, negotiations, threats, bribes. Mark's difficult position. (morally, 'thematically')

? His flat is burgled but nothing of value taken. Uncle's premises destroyed, along with it (the disruption of the present) all the notes, photos, letters etc. connected with Y and X. (! In this case, history is destroyed because it existed only in its mutable form - i.e. non-internal, not subject to personal memory.) (! And the balance of Mark's mind? The plan of him as arsonist, destroying the past in order to free himself - as he cannot free himself from Lesley.)

* there must be something in the plot to be drawn into; a parallel investigation.

1. Purchase of mirror
2. Installation at Uncle's
3. (Julia; Colin/Lydia)
4. Preparation of the book
5. Meeting with Old Lady
6. (Uncle/Aunt)
7. Reporter's interest in X
8. (Julia; Colin)
9. Meeting with X
10. (X's wife/X's lawyer)
11. Meeting reporter (+ Julia)
12. Reporting delving into histories?

13. (Colin; X's friends)
14. Letter from Lesley's brother (+ Julia)
15. Recall of the past (a contract of construct)
16. (Julia)
17. Publisher pressure
18. 2nd interview with X
19. (+ Lydia; X's friends)
20. Reporter's intrusion into Mark's history
21. Recall of the past
22. (+ Julia; X's wife)
23. (Aunt/Uncle; Julia)
24. The burglary
25. (+ Julia; Colin)
26. Reporter's interest
27. (Julia; Colin/Lydia)
28. Lesley's brother (a real/tangible contract)
29. Recall of the past
30. (X's friends; Julia)
31. Attempt on his life
32. (Colin; Uncle/Aunt)
33. (Julia; Uncle/Aunt)
34. The fire
35. Aftermath
36. Going to see Lesley (the confrontation)
37. Truth revealed (though in exactly what format? Parts 2 + 3?)

1 Recall of the past occasioned by external trigger such as a letter, an enquiry, a meeting. Then immediately followed by the present relationship with Julia and how that relationship is affected.

2 Progress toward some sort of event throughout (Concerning Mark/Julia, Colin/Lydia - the wedding, the mirror ∴)

Mark fails to realise that his past is as damaging to himself as is the politician's own.

This plot is not strong enough as a whole, through various parts offer…

~~~~

His final comment in this section of entries is significant a) if you consider some of the more 'thriller-like' aspects of the plot ideas sketched thus far (e.g. "31. Attempt on his life"), and b) where he ended up with it…

When he notes "[datum]" a little way above, I can only interpret this as his intention for the starting point (in terms of the 'now') from which each of the plot lines would then develop.

~~~~

<div align="right">

∂uring 1983 (CON)

</div>

Mirrors '83

? Abandon superficiality of plot.

? Establish an immediate exteriority of viewpoint. Convey the sense of being allowed the all-seeing, all-knowing viewer, removing any sentiment, sympathy for Mark.

Novel become a tale in which the anonymous teller/viewer is constantly aware of his relationship to the tale, the tale's relationship with the history, the overbearing unconcerning of history with all, its quirk-some quality of randomness.

Mark become a subject in a controlled experiment, a tool used by the teller to explore the plot, to involve the reader in his own history.

Dissolving of structure, giving way to a series of random reflections and memories randomly/tenuously connected, set off in a chain by words, essentially: power of language in memory - History as language.

~~~~

Given what has gone before, you might regard this entry from some point in 1983 as a curved ball. How long were these ideas - new or otherwise - in gestation? There are some themes in here - both in relation to 'Mirrors' and in general terms - which not only move his ambitions for that project on, but also will repeat at various points across the years: a focus on '"words", the notion of "History as language". Given what went immediately before, do these sparse comments herald a shift from the "superficial" of the thriller-like towards something far more complex? If that is the case (or was the case when he penned it) then one might see it as the moment when 'Mirrors' made the most critical step from embryo into its final form - not merely in terms plot, character, and structure, but in the philosophy that was to underlie it.

Whether the end product meets the intention behind the entry above is a moot point. How can we know? Asking him what he meant when he wrote those words could never provide us with a definitive answer - even if he were prepared to tackle the question. Surely he would be guessing just as much as we are.

And just how significant - in the most profound of senses - is the word "superficiality" in the dated entry below, whether or not it came before or after that which we have just read? Is "superficiality" valid? Does it apply, accurately, to where 'Mirrors' was heading or where it finished up? And how much does it apply to the rest of his oeuvre - indeed, to anything written by anyone?

~~~~

24ᵗʰ August 1983 (CON)

Idea of a plot for which there is a solution. A question is posed - both externally in the sense of 'what happened', and internally in the sense of relationship to one's own past - but never answered conclusively. The plot offers, eventually, the superficiality of answer.

(i.e. there must be a who? what? where? why? element)

A 'stable' beginning is necessary <u>only</u> in terms of mind vis-a-vis situation; non-relationship specific[1].

✱

'An Unceremonious Departure'

1. 1982 - The Story: Prescott
2. 1982 - The View: Jordan, Smith
3. 1948 - The Ship: Prescott, *Marcus, *Gisella
4. 1951 - The U.S.: Prescott, *Marcus, *Gisella
5. 1982 - The Interview: Jordan, Smith, Prescott
6. 1982 - The Letter: Prescott
7. 1975 - The Affair: Prescott, Lesley
8. 1982 - The Meeting: Prescott, Lesley's brother
9. 1982 - The Interview: Jordan, Smith, Prescott
10. 1982 - The Visit: Smith, Lesley
11. 1982 - The Threat: Marcus, Prescott
12. 1975 - The Recall: Prescott, Prescott

---

[1] This is exactly how the entry was written. Unable to fathom its meaning, I reproduce it in its original construction.

13. 1982 - The Conference: Jordan, Smith
14. 1982 - The Discovery: Prescott, Anna
15. 1982 - The Capture: Jordan, Smith, Lesley's brother
16. 1982 - The Confrontation: Prescott, Anna, Marcus, Smith, Jordan
17. 1982 - The Epilogue: Prescott, Lesley

* different name

~~~

This is an interesting one, if only because the commercial leaning of the 'thriller' is still very much in evidence. Not merely in evidence, but significantly enhanced perhaps. Is the structure above 'new' or something - perhaps triggered by the notion of 'Lesley' and 'Lesley's brother' - that makes us want to draw a direct line between it and 'Mirrors'? And is that link made stronger if we see 'Prescott' as a direct replacement / parallel for 'Mark'? There are other associations too, such as the ship in '3' vs. the idea of Mark being confined on a ship as enunciated earlier for 'Mirrors', or the plot points of 'threat' and 'confrontation'.

What then are we looking at? Was 'An Unceremonious Departure' on one level an attempt to "abandon superficiality of plot" as far as 'Mirrors' was concerned? Or, conversely and somewhat obtusely, is this a complete acceptance of plot superficiality, the shallowness of the thriller against something far more intellectual?[2]

Clearly the idea didn't immediately evaporate...

~~~

15th & 17th October 1984 (CON)

1. 1982 - Prescott's introduction
2. 1982 - Jordan + Smith's reaction to Prescott's introduction
3. 1948 - Prescott Snr., seeing Marcus + Gisella aboard US ship
4. pre '45 - Prescott + Marcus meet under wartime conditions
5. pre '45 - Marcus + Gisella meet in Italy
6. 1982 - Jordan + Smith interview Prescott (where is the key?)
7. 1951 - Marcus + Gisella giving party in US
8. 1951 - Prescott Snr. in US; the origin of the file

---

[2] It also begs the question as to the sequence in which the last two entries were written. Would we have ended up with a different conclusion had we presented and analysed them the other way round?

9. '51-'57 - Births: Prescott Snr. marries; Prescott Jnr.; 'Investigator'; Lesley's brother; Anna; Lesley
10. 1982 - Prescott receives the letter
11. 1975 - University: Anna + Lesley preparing
12. 1975 - Lesley's brother: leavings and beginnings + Marcus
13. 1975 - Prescott and Lesley meet, and their affair
14. 1976? - Marcus + Lesley's brother. Prescott Snr. takes note again
15. 1976? - Lesley's breakdown. Her brother's reaction
16. 1982 - Prescott meets Lesley's brother
17. 1982 - Jordan + Smith interview Prescott again
18. 1982 - Jordan + Smith visit Lesley
19. 1982 - Marcus threatens Prescott
20. 1975 - Prescott recalls his father
21. 1982 - Jordan and Smith hold conference
22. 1982 - Prescott discovers Anna's role
23. 1982 - Jordan and Smith capture Lesley's brother
24. 1982 - The confrontation: Prescott, Anna, Marcus, Smith, Jordan
25. 1982 - Prescott and Lesley

❀

1. Prescott's intro
2. Jordan / Smith
3. Prescott, Marcus, Gisella - the boat to the US (48)
4. Anna, Lesley, Michael - University comings and goings (75)
5. Jordan / Smith, Prescott - the interview
6. Prescott receives Michael's letter
7. Marcus, Gisella - the US party (51)
8. Prescott Snr. the origins of the file (51)
9. Jordan / Smith, Prescott - more talking
10. Prescott meets Michael
11. Prescott, Lesley - the affair (76)
12. Prescott, Lesley - the breakdown (76)
13. Marcus threatens Prescott
14. Jordan / Smith interview Lesley
15. Prescott Snr., Marcus - the interview (45)
16. Marcus meets Gisella in Italy (45)
17. Prescott Snr., Prescott Jnr. (75)? year?
18. Jordan / Smith - a conference
19. Marcus and Michael (76)
20. Prescott, Anna - Anna's true identity revealed
21. Jordan / Smith - close on Michael
22. Births - the backgrounds of the characters (51-54)

23. Climax - Prescott, Anna, Marcus, Jordan, Smith
24. Prescott meets Lesley again

~~~~

Without doubt, "the affair" and "the breakdown" only succeed in heaping fuel on the argument that 'AUD' is a fresh incarnation of 'Mirrors' but based on an entirely different premise, theme and outcome.

His process - of reworking and refining plot components - is one with which we are beginning to become familiar. In the second breakdown above, I can only conclude that the numbers in brackets relate to the years in which those events / chapters would be set, aligning as they do with the immediately preceding list. What are we to make of this proposal? Do we have enough here to assess whether AUD would have been viable or not? Unlikely, I suggest. And there are two further factors which contribute to this assessment.

The first is that, although a few pages were drafted, they came to represent the final extent of his pursuit of this project. I recognise I am benefiting from hindsight here, but given this is the last we shall see of 'An Unceremonious Departure' (if memory serves me correctly) then it feels an acceptable transgression.

*The second - and much more significant factor - is that the next notebook entry I could find was dated nearly **five years** later! And it began with a revisit of 'Mirrors'.*

Just what caused such a period of silence? Was he writing nothing at all during the period or simply not making any notes? And what might have been going on the background - in 'Life' - that would have either fuelled or prevented such activity / inactivity? I am tempted to ask him or to insert what I understand to be historically correct - but we've already been through that! Even though I know some of the detail myself, we have agreed not to implant a third-person perspective of his history into this analysis (if that's what it is).

In any event, what will be the most interesting - and this to whet your appetite - will be to see what the passage of time has done to his ideas for 'Mirrors'. Or indeed, what it has done to him, and in consequence, where that left him in relation to his first 'great idea'...

~~~~

MIRRORS

- ❖ purchase of mirror as wedding gift
- ❖ breaking of mirror as physical exposure
    - fragmentation of his image of himself
    - fragmentation of his philosophy
    - fragmentation of his relationship with Julia
- ❖ flaw in mirror?
    - imperfect representation of 'the real'?
    - perfect reflection of partial picture?
- ❖ novel needs an internal mirror image
- ❖ 'Rotten Row' - situation could be taken as the opposite of what it is (love/hate)
- ❖ Mark/Lesley relationship as a finding of self; each seeing other as a picture, reflection of self (simplistic vision)
- ❖ Mirror: imitate, represent, translate, counterfeit, re-present, re-production, looking-glass
- ❖ Parallel: juxtapose, contrast, match, counter-part, reflection
- ❖ Reflection: gloss, lustre, representation, manifestation, re-presentation
- ❖ Revelation: exposure, reversal, dis-covery, dis-closure
- ❖ Importance of old photographs
- ❖ Fire - destruction of papers, photos etc. destruction of the past
- ❖ Mirror taken (concealed) at Mark's uncle's house
- ❖ Mark working on a book for his uncle - research involves the collection of old photographs (importance of book)
- ❖ Mark's concern with finding photos drives him to a reviewing of his own -> a lead into memory of Lesley
- ❖ Fire destroys uncle's office: mirror, ruined, is discovered after
- ❖ Mark as arsonist: burning uncle's house as destruction of the photographs - his past with Lesley - and the mirror - symbol of his present/future with Julia
- ❖ Consequence of breakdown
- ❖ People as mirrors, to be looked into
- ❖ Mark's philosophy (gained via Lesley + lived by with Julia) is insufficient to live by; inflexible, inadequate, simplistic, two-dimensional
- ❖ Importance of artefacts of the past; Mark responsible for them
- ❖ Photos of Lesley destroyed in order to attempt the obliteration of that responsibility
- ❖ Mark's own history (with Lesley) is attempting to break loose, to lose its fixity and authority in Mark's mind: the danger is internal, psychological & self-engendered

- We see Mark's pursuit of history within his own terms + limitations for it - not as it must unfold itself
- Mark's concerns are a transgression upon the past and his responsibility for revealing it as fact, as history. 'How much history is left?'
- Mark faces the repercussion of disclosure
- He visits Lesley in the past of his mind, re-living, re-enacting
- Thinking about Lesley disturbs the equilibrium: ∴ questioning his relationship with Julia
- Destroying photos as attempt to purge the past
- Fire causes disruption of the present: + history (for the book) is destroyed because it existed only in its mutable form - i.e. non-internal, not subject of memory
- Destroying the past in order to free himself - as he cannot free himself from Lesley

~~~~

Although this appears a superficial revisit of much that has gone before - a sifting and filtering of the ideas he has had up to this point - it is so much more than simple restatement; it is also something of a reset. Having been through the process of reviewing all his old notes - just as we have done, placing ourselves in his shoes! - he must have sat back and looked at this bulleted list and thought "I have something worthwhile here". And after a gap of five years, how could it not be a reset?

Surely how he responded to this honed-down list will have been informed by all that had happened to him in the intervening period (including a new job, a move of cities...). But not only that, there must have been a new motivation, a fresh momentum, for him to even consider digging out his old notes and plug himself back into the process. Remember, the last time he tried to engineer a narrative from the skeleton of those early 'Mirrors' ideas he came up with 'An Unceremonious Departure' - which was a failure. Where did this new impetus come from if not as a result of all that had happened in his recent past and the beginning of a fresh outlook on his writing? More than that; perhaps also a deep-seated belief that he had really been on to something five years earlier. Although the gap to the next entry is shorter (six months rather than half a decade) when he eventually gets there not only is he still banging the 'Mirrors' drum but he is getting closer to how the novel will eventually look.

~~~~

<u>Plot Strands</u>

1   <u>Present</u>
     Mark working on book; relationship with Julia; instability; fire

2   <u>Immediate Past</u>
     Previous relationship (?) about which Mark feels guilt; threat of
     history

3   <u>Distant Past</u>
     As mirror of present / immediate past; Mark by association; threat too

Research into book about relative; clever, insane, murderous.
Mirrors (parallels) across plot strands.

❋

3   Man; clever, mercurial - a writer (of?)
     Weakness for gambling.
     Wife with money ∴ conflict, friction.
     Kills wife to inherit money; murder, fire.
     Lives; spends; suicide.

2   Mark with dominant mother, unstable (family trait).
     Interfering - evidence?
     Has her committed (or kills her?) to give himself freedom.
     ∴ guilt

1   Mark - writer - in stable relationship
     Searching into the past awakens history, instability.
     Mark's desire to blank out the past.
     (His aunt reminds him of his mother too - sisters!)

So - what sends Mark over the edge? Too much self-examination? Some kind
of dramatic revelation - or the writing of it?!
(we see 3 unfold as Mark writes about it ∴ his writing about the fire is the
trigger.)

Unbeknown to Mark, his aunt writing his mother's story... (Famous family.)

❋

Mark used to live with his aunt (father's sister) - explains why he still has a room in the house.

Uncle as father-substitute.

Guilt - because of Lesley; his father; his imagined affair with Lydia

✱

Purchase of mirror -
      establish: Mark
                        relationship with Julia
                        relationship with mirror
                        his 'philosophy'
                        sense of strangeness of character

Return to house -
      establish: Edward + Alice
                        relationship to them
                        history with house
                        Edward's 'function'
                        Alice's 'function'

      (must establish passing of time)

Evening out (days later) -
      establish: Colin & Lydia
                        relationships -
imagined + 'real'   Julia & Lydia
conversations in   Mark & Colin
parallel?   Mark & Lydia

Edward's book (over a period)
      establish: Mark's role
                        relationship with book
                        relationship with history
                        relationship with artefacts

Julia & Alice shopping (preparation for Mark's birthday)

Mark & Edward discuss book - difference of opinion viz use of 'history'.

Mark & Colin play squash - Mark loses; unusually. Colin senses something "wrong".

Mark & Julia (situation?) - unease

↓

Introduce   Lesley
                Mark's father
                imagined relationship with Lydia

Establish guilt: cause + effect in each (Lydia, Lesley, Julia confusion)

Establish trigger - sense that something (related to Edward's book) will spark Mark into action.

Birthday?

"How much history is left?" - climax

Critical events
1. Purchase of Mirror
4. Discovery of old photographs
3. Imagined affair with Lydia
2. Remembering of / revelation about father
5. The fire

Sequence?
1. Purchase of mirror / return to house (1)
2. Evening out
3. Mark working at home (2)
4. Julia and Alice shopping
5. Mark & Colin play squash
6. Mark at house (3)
7. Mark & Julia (situation?)
8. ?
9. Mark & Edward (4)
10. Preparations for Mark's birthday
11. ?
12. Mark
13. Fire (5)
14. ???

~~~~

So finally, eight years after his first musings, Mark's father makes a first significant appearance in the notes on 'Mirrors'. I raise it not to point out the obvious, but to highlight it in the context of what follows. Firstly, a subsequent gap of another two years until the next entry; presumably another example of 'Life' getting in the way again - which once more begs the question as to what he had been doing in the intervening period, as all large time-gaps between notebook entries must do.

Secondly, there is no material mention of 'Mirrors' for another four years - some twelve years after the very first notebook entry. I call this out more to manage expectations than anything else, just in case you have been lulled into believing you are now going to see the ongoing development of 'Mirrors' as a smooth progression from this point through to birth. This gap begs other questions too - and ones we cannot answer based on what can be found in the notebooks ('the evidence') - such as: during the period to 1994 did he continue to think about or work on 'Mirrors' and simply not record that process? Or did he, perhaps, start to draft some parts of the novel to test out his ideas? It would surely be naïve to assume that, after all the work that had gone into it thus far, he simply stopped thinking about it. The absence of any evidence of that may - or may not - be significant. How can we tell?

What we have established, of course, is a degree of insight into how his mind works; how he plots and theorises, questions and posits; how he surfaces ideas either to dismiss or build on them. And the same for his characters too. As we have also seen, the way he reviews and tests his notions - for plot, place, and character - clearly demonstrates a level of rigour (even if it may appear somewhat haphazard). And there is a pervasive sense of fluidity as well. Just because he makes an assumption or decision in one entry, doesn't mean he won't reverse it when we next encounter him.

As such, all these entries prior to 1992 can be seen as a foundation for what follows; not merely in terms of subject matter and 'Mirrors' in particular, but also in his method. And yet having said that, the 'tone' of what comes next is unquestionably different. Whether it is due to the myriad of topics subsequently considered in the notebooks or a shift in philosophy is open to interpretation. The explosion in variety which follows also raises questions about the notebooks themselves. Did he initially seem them as one thing - i.e. his 'workings out in the margins' around a single project - only to eventually regard them as something entirely different? Did their purpose change, and as a result their content and style had to change too?

Part Two - 1992 to 1993

from October 1992 (RBR)

Hills
Chills
Rills
Trills

Dead leaves in brown-water ditches

How to define cowardice?
- the decision not to try something?
- the decision to stay in the status quo?

- or is either of these courage?

A small black & white kitten in a country lane

A cottage called "Peacehaven"
- are these the 2 things we should aspire to?
- what is Peace? where is its inspiration?
- should Peace have drama and excitement?

Sand bags keep the land back...

Sitting in the 'Bell Hotel' Talgarth drinking ½ pint Murphy's and eating pork scratchings.

Never go to Talgarth. There is no bus stop. Shops boast "Home Killed Meat" and combinations of "Carpets & Flowers". There are two 'open-til-late' shops. 'Civilisation'.

What will they be doing at work now? (Monday 5th October, 11:18 am.) The fire alarm will have sounded 18 minutes ago. Someone will be going for the coffees. The alarm usually triggers that. There will have been at least one disgruntled discussion about 'the method' or 'the scope' as people, struggling with attempts at 'professionalism' endeavour to make sense of it. 5 days a week, 7 or 8 hours a day.

This - and all it encompasses: holiday, relaxation, self-discovery - is not easy. Maybe self-discovery never is.

Having people around you, to talk to and interact with, having "things" to do - both allow for the loss of self and the absorption in other things. We can forget ourselves; we have taken away the mirror. Other people are looking at us. We do not have to.

I wonder if exile is like this. It would be, I suspect, for most people.

How much, then, do we live our lives through other people; for other people even? How much do we subsume?

What then, in the face of all this confusing paraphernalia, is man's search for truth? In which sphere is he searching?

I share the bar with two solitary male drinkers. Locals. Remember it is not yet noon on Monday morning. One reads a paper. The other sits. Are they in exile? With who do they communicate? Have they managed to shut out the forces of self-discovery?

Another drinker makes a triumvirate. There is talk of the weather. A heatwave in mid-week. And now talk of the dole. The "Old King Cole"...

❂

Strange how we seem to return to places known before, and how often! How LIFE has a habit of bringing us full circle.

I sit writing this where - what? 2 years ago - we began our 'Team Walk' to Velindre.

Q> (at a time like this) What has changed?

❂

Civilisation is a road-sign.

❂

<u>Re-Reading List</u>

Essentials

Shakespeare	key (+ notes?)
	(TN, R&J, O, RII, MoV, Mc,
Milton [1674] 2	KL, JC, AYLI)
Donne [1631] 1	
Eliot [1965] 6	
Tennyson [1892] 5	
Blake [1827] 3	
Wordsworth [1850] 4	

Austen [1817] (P&P, MP)	1	
Conrad [1924] (N, V)	3	
Hardy [1928] (Tess, MoC)	4	
James [1916] (GB)	2	
Joyce [1941] (U)	6	
Lawrence [1930] (S&L)?		
Orwell [1950] (1984, AF)?		
Tolstoy [1910] (W&P)?	Woolf [1941] (TTL, MrsD)	5

What is the physical/real trigger for this ===>
|
Kick-off train of thought

Memories are the insatiable harlots of history, <u>taunting, and</u> dealing tricks with
predictable outcomes.   ?

Later - poorer and unfulfilled - ....
|
or richer
Later - for richer, for poorer - a
marriage of the unfulfilled

taunting | haunting?

❁

Poem about regrets from the past / missed opportunities

memories -   (are)

the insatiable ~~whores~~ of history
    (~~insatiated~~) (harlots)

taunting; dealing tricks (with predicted outcomes)
        poorer; unfulfilled

<u>dead leaves</u> in <u>brown water</u> ditches
     | |
     | which spring cleans…
…and regenerates

memories are the insatiable harlots of history,
dealing tricks in predictable outcomes.

and? —>

❀

1 -   Study List

                          <u>Structure?</u>
        Reading only?   Depends on MA etc.
            | ↑
        1 hour/day   (If not |, some sort of log?)

2 -   Writing Projects

        Stimulus from 1?

3 -   "Sharpeners"

        Chess?
        PC developments?
        Painting?

~~~~

What is all this, and what has motivated it?! This seems like a new voice. Or perhaps there was something inevitable about such a scatter-gun approach to the first entry after such a long time - and after those years' focus seemingly dedicated to 'Mirrors'. Are the breaks suddenly off? Yes, there are lists and loose plans for how time is spent, and for reading (which is new); and there are also snippets of poetry and the process of reworking those, mentions of work, a fragment of a travelogue, some philosophy.

But there is nothing relating to a major writing project; not even the contemplation of options. What is missing is almost as telling as what is present. And why is that? What has happened during those last two years (from Spring 1990 to Autumn 1992) to lead us here? Or is that even relevant?

~~~

<div align="right">

from Nov. 5th 1992 (RBR)

</div>

In the slick-suited city,
       grey gents - pinstriped and pot-bellied -
nurture and network, a contact here,
       a contact there;
slimily smile, fawningly frown;
       and offer boyish bonhomie to temporal chums
       chasing diamond-crusted? deals.

Gucci-shod, Cartier-timed,
       business treads and ticks -
       clip, clop; tick, tock;

"Bill, you old bugger! Banged that
       big-bosomed secretary yet?!"
"Sorry; seven seventeen from Surrey, slipped
       on leaves near Surbiton."
"Five percent, plus or minus, take it or
       leave it, back it or stack it"

Cuban cigars and priceless tie-pins,
       cellular car phones and expense accounts.

Bandaged in weather-beaten blankets,
       on cold comfort corner he watches money march past;
an unclean, outstretched palm
may plead but does not pursuade;
       where is the profit or kudos in charity?

"Penny for the Guy, Sir?
       Penny for the Guy?"[3]

✻

---

[3] This was eventually reworked in the summer of 2021.

In the Grounds of the Black Castle

Cezanne's impressionism

      * "shaped" colours
      * not an attempt to re-depict, or redraw
      * up close, simply colours

+ Literature?

one-layer medium
      each "word" has <u>meaning</u>
      each "colour" does not   (or does it?
                        Black/white -
         (text/plot)   invested meaning?)

∴ the picture must be built up using the meaning inherent in the word
- this is not a restriction that painters face.
      - they can choose not to depict, they can still paint.

Writers must struggle with words having meaning: if they are to do anything "impressionistic", they must do it <u>in addition</u> to meaning + depiction

Words have structure too. They are not freeform. Also, they are not dynamic.

Finnegan's Wake here?

What is the logical extension for writers?
      - remove meaning + structure
      ==> sound, if spoken else mental what?

Abstraction

~~~~

Surely the most interesting nugget here is the Painter-Writer parallel and the comparison between paint and words - especially the freedom a painter's medium gives them to explore abstraction. Is the sense here that he sees such interpretation as impossible for a writer, or something to which one could aspire?

~~~~

PERSPECTIVE

Turner's experiments with...

Fractional movement in any direction changes perception (<u>3D</u>)

In art, this is not so. Singular, planar vision from one point

Is there an alternative?

+ Literature - singular, planar view <u>plus</u> the investment in impression, interpretation, translation etc.

Art "achieves" some of this i.e. "mood" - perhaps <u>all</u> of it but to a different extent and in a different way.
- Less concrete.

How can a non-singular, non-planar view be taken / expressed in Lit.?

How can we move "a fraction" and get a different perspective on things?
<u>Points of view</u>?

One story, but multi-facetted.

e.g. "Look at Françoise"
- an attempt at a rounded image

<u>or</u>

make story dynamic, sense of movement and changing perspective

e.g. "My Dear Polly"
- keep the flow, the movement; never settle on a single viewpoint. Bonus from the use of Stream of Consciousness.
Unstructured - as experience & interpretation is unstructured.

Pulling-in of disparate images; not simply those seen ("real"), but also those triggered from the subconscious, the past etc.

Woolf, Joyce, James?
|
       cerebral? structured.

Interesting how he has continued to pursue consideration of the art-literature comparison here with the shift of focus from 'abstraction' to 'perspective'. Was he searching for some kind of stylistic peg on which to hang his hat, an artistic trope he could apply to writing and its output?

For reference, 'Look at Françoise' was a short story (based on Renoir's "Luncheon of the Boating Party") in which he examines the one scene from multiple perspectives, the characters Renoir inserted in his painting. To the best of my knowledge the story is lost. 'My Dear Polly' was first published in a University Arts magazine (1980 or 1981), and later reprised in his collection of short stories, Secrets & Wisdom.

~~~~

Photographs distorting the memory of events?
i.e. what one sees is not what one remembers

      Relationship between the two?

Relationship between photograph and memories
      "the harlots of history"...

✿

"He stared at the photograph. It was not how he remembered it. It had been less sunny, surely; and there appeared no trace of wind. He thought he had been wearing his green jacket - the old one with the torn inside pocket; it was the only thing he had to protect him against the cold.

"And Alison. She had not been smiling. How could she have been smiling?

"Mike - for once the showman behind the camera - had said 'say cheese' in that exaggerated fashion of his. Flamboyant, confident. The drink helped - not that he needed it. It helped all of them.

"He studied the photograph more closely. Julie, coy and sort of curled up on the edge of the photo, was wearing Mike's coat. He strained to see if there was a stain on the left shoulder. Had it been that afternoon the seagull had shat on the coat? The photograph revealed nothing.

"Later, as they had walked on - further from the cottage along the shore - Julie had asked him about Alison. Was it all over? Finally? He remembered asking her if she fancied a fuck. Julie had, for a moment, taken him seriously. Still coy and curled up, she had drifted away from him and back to Mike. He had picked up a stone and skimmed it into the sea.

"Later, much later, when Julie had grown out of her coy reserve - and after they had become lovers - she had laughed at his question. Or was it her own question which she had found amusing? Somehow he felt the photograph should offer him a clue."[4]

<u>Study</u>

Lever-arch file / dividers.

Sections:-
      Novels (by Author)
      Poetry (by Poet)
      Plays   - (by Playwright)
              - Shakespeare
      Criticism

Where to concentrate first?

* CRITICISM *

Untying the Text
Textural Strategies
Saussure?
Chomsky?
Derek's book (Routledge)
+ new readers.

*

What is this desire to write?
To describe?

Is it to make real "reality"?
To solidify our existence?

---

[4] As far as I am aware, this scene was never developed further.

To prove - to ourselves, not to others - that what we see, feel, think etc. is tangible, real, linked in some inexplainable way to "truth"?

I see a book. I want to describe what I see. Why?
- to make the book real?
- to make myself real?
- to define the relationship I have with the book?
(that space!)

Is this it? The definition of "relationships", of the gaps between things, rather than the things themselves?!

This concurs with Pierce's idea of
Object - Sign - <u>Interpretant</u>
|
the motivating force…

❈

• Civilisation is a road sign…

• Memories are the insatiable harlots of history,
dealing tricks in predictable outcomes.

• for richer, for poorer - a marriage of the unfulfilled

• In the Grounds of the Black Castle

Can the "Black Castle" be where the writer is? or is <u>not</u>, if he is in the grounds…

<u>Black</u>: - darkness - <u>the colour of ink</u>!! - <u>bruise</u> - mourning -
as thunder - smoky (unclear?) - funereal - night -
<u>hell</u> - <u>exclude</u> - evil

<u>Castle</u>:- fort - <u>stronghold</u> - <u>refuge</u> - <u>keep</u> - barrier - moat -
<u>wall</u> - rampart

Castle is <u>defensive</u> ∴ defending something…
|
∴ <u>dangerous</u> to those who would trespass

Poems about being on the outside. Mythical. Legendary. Attempting comprehension, of what might be on the inside (the unattainable) and therefore, longing...

Poems?

* "In The Grounds of the Black Castle"

* of memories
         (understanding relationship with history)

* the road to the castle

* the castle's treasures (imagined)

The castle is, of course, deserted...

         (or is it?)

The castle needs to be manifest; a physical embodiment of that for which it stands. Need, therefore, for <u>realistic</u> concrete images + responses to those images. (Role of Interpretant)

The Black Castle as an embodiment; a place from which the writer is <u>ex</u>cluded. (No Ivory Tower!)
The Black Castle becomes the predominant image, even though the key, for the writer / assailant who lays <u>siege</u> to it, is that which lies within; safe; secure.

The <u>grounds</u> must be significant too (the <u>title</u>!). What of these?
And which side of the moat?
Is there a difference?

What is there that needs to be described, understood, the relationship to defined, <u>interpreted</u>...

The Castle itself (real, temporal)
What it may contain
The grounds - real / imagined
The moat
The road to the castle
         (in reflection / flashback
         ∴ history here?)
Location with oneself (how?)

The Castle's mythical past / legend

A damsel in a tower?

In the Grounds of the Black Castle - and other poems (1993)

In the Grounds of the Black Castle

Land's End

Not Even Early Mesopotamia

❋

The Black Castle

To have reached it suggests the culmination of some kind of journey, or a trial or pilgrimage. (Does reaching the castle offer or symbolise some kind of transformation, or victory, or failure even?)

Arriving ∴   mature / weary / enlightened
                 - but not vigorous? happy?

And does it represent a looking forward or a looking back? And in either event, is the image not a fragmented / fragmentary one? (cf. Cezanne's painting)

❋

What scope for a novel here?   Yes, pos.
Mythological journey? Quest?   ?

Modern-day knight   (No)

~~~~

In these entries his focus seems to have swung almost entirely away from fiction (or at least ideas for fiction) to concentrate on the nature of writing and poetry. Indeed, the last entry we had relating to a concrete fiction project was over two years earlier in 1990. The nature of writing - having been compared with abstraction and perspective - is now explored with Cezanne's "In The Grounds of the Black Castle" as the comparative work. In this instance, going beyond that concrete parallel he seems to be suggesting a collection which, in some way, 'interprets' the painting and its style and turns it into poetry - if that isn't too fanciful a notion; something more than a simple ekphrastic work, perhaps. Yet many of the elements he includes as candidate subjects above - such as the moat, a tower, even the castle itself - are absent from Cezanne's canvas; they are only present either a) in the title or b) by implication, in that we assume a castle should have a moat and a tower. He even extends the latter image to suggest it might be home to a damsel! Was he trying to wrestle with the translation of one to the other, from the painting to the poetic? An attempt to create 'interpretants', perhaps. Is the fascination in the execution of that translation - taking life and turning it into 'Art' - or in the journey from one form of artistic impression into another? If so, it is hardly a like-for-like transaction because of what he considers 'adding' to the mix (and, presumably, 'taking away').

~~~

From "Hands of Light"; 12 areas for consideration, experience & fulfilment:-

1	Meditation
2	Physical Exercise
3	Good Food
4	Good Hygiene
5	Rest
6	Clothing
7	Home
8	Pleasure
9	Personal Challenge
10	Intimacy & Friends
11	Self-care (in accident & illness)
12	Healing for Family

9   "your deepest inner longing, that which you want to do more than anything, is precisely what you have come into this life to do. Your best assurance of health is to do it."

1   Breathe in the future & breathe out the past. They are not related.

2   Do what you enjoy doing.

6   Make sure what you wear expresses who you are.

8   Have fun.

10   Take a chance.

I am not sure that the "Hands of Light" he refers to here is the book of the same name by Barbara Brennan. Based on what we know, the idea that he would have any truck with - never mind buy and read - a book about "healing through the energy field" seems absurd. But if it is not that, then what? Perhaps something that bled into his personal life from professional management training; after all, number 12 - "Healing for Family" - would seem to offer strong circumstantial evidence of the Brennan book's influence in order to convict.

Does it matter? On one level, undoubtedly 'yes': because the framework he latched onto and what he subsequently did with it is an insight into his thinking, how he was at the back-end of 1992.

~~~~

30th January 1993 (RBR)

Having dug-out all that 'unfinished' work, I see a deal of potential.

The need is to rekindle the enthusiasm, the spirit. To light the blue touch-paper ~~~~ to give birth again to Vocal Ordinary Men.[5]

10th February 1993 (RBR)

... or is it? Now moved (M + 12 days)
a refinement (?) of the picture.

The Twelve Tenets:

1 - Meditation	Paula weekly breathing exercises mental 'rigour'
2 - Physical Exercise	Badminton (weekly)
3 - Good Food	* Action * Yet to sort out dietary regime
4 - Good Hygiene	Clean enough! Domestic?

---

[5] The title of a series of poems he produced - and read - with Tom Furniss when at Southampton University, including the two-handed 'Haiku Play'.

5 - Rest	Sufficient sleep
	TV = relaxation
	<u>READ</u>!

| 6 - Clothing | * Action * |
| | but budget-driven |

7 - Home	* Action *
	needs sorting!
	will be dependant on job location though

8 - Pleasure	Plays <u>Read</u>!
	Films
	Drinks
	Badminton

9 - Personal Challenge	* Action *
	Work / professional
	"Other"

| 10 - Intimacy & Friends | * Action * |
| | depends on "home" location |

| 11 - Self-care | OK? |

| 12 - Healing & Family | ? |

— || —

Calls on Personal Time:

| 1 - Meditation | <u>OK</u>, ad-hoc |

| 2 - Physical Exercise | currently Tuesdays 5-8 <u>OK</u> |

| 3 - Good Food | Restaurant once a month? |
| | <u>IDEA</u>   (+ £30) |

8 - Pleasure	Plays etc. "Live event"
	1 eve / fnt? (+£10)
	Films
	1 eve / week? (+£8)

Drinks

    1 eve / week?   (+£7.50)

    (+£25.50 p/wk)

9 - Personal Challenge   depends on what "other" might be

10 - Intimacy & Friends   combine with 8 -
          don't do much alone!

— || —

Pleasure budget must be £100p pcm

Food budget = £30 pw + £30 "one-off"
        (£160 pcm)

* Re-examine budget for March
* Use Cathedral analysis book
* plan 'social' ahead

(NEW JOB IS KEY)

~~~~

Although not necessarily self-evident, there are two themes here which are arguably profoundly sad. The first is contained in the two words "Now moved". Although he doesn't make a fuss of it here, in many ways they encapsulate the early part of his life (until he was around 20) when he was no stranger to such nomadic activity[6]. I call it out simply as a 'marker'; it will return as a specific theme later…

The second is the persistent return to his lists. Yes, in this case it is the disputed "Twelve Tenets", but as we have seen - and will continue to see - it appears as if he was unable to make sense of his life (even to live it!) without analysis in some form or another. Perhaps he couldn't help himself. Perhaps a list, a structure, a regime, was his default construct to justify action; and maybe even more than action, to justify himself, to make sense of the world. If he knew that a "new job" was "key", then he didn't need to write that down to know it. Similarly with some elements of the tenets. Even the predilection to arrange time and money on

---

[6] See also his 2021 collection of poetry, *The Homelessness of a Child.*

paper, to calculate how they were spent, surely points to needing authorisation to act. Was he, at heart, afraid of living?

Where the lists sometimes do bear fruit (because they seem not to when it comes to the material workaday world) is when related to his writing. As we have seen with 'Mirrors', the working and reworking, the nudging and nurdling, ultimately led him down a fruitful creative path, one with a meaningful outcome - unlike, you may argue, all the nonsense about hours and days, pounds and pence.

~~~~

<div align="right">

February - July 1993 (RBR) [7]

</div>

Mid-Winter Worthing at Dusk
Is ~~like~~ an old lady getting ready for bed.

Slippers off, she stretches ~~her~~ arthritic toes
pushing at ~~the~~ wrinkles^d stockings with ~~an~~ effort,
pushing at years of (awkward wearing) ? -
Curlers out, her wispy greying hair - <u>faded now</u>
<u>from its true colour</u> - mixes elegance
with ~~her worn-out~~ tired beauty,
fragile and vulnerable

✿

"<u>BRIGHTON</u>"

What are the issues?

                         "Mechanistic" questions

<u>JOB</u> - work
       money
       car
       environment
       location

<u>What do I want</u>?

<u>SAL</u>

---

[7] The thirteen or so shortish undated entries which follow were written at various points between the last dated entry (10th February) and the next (3rd August).

OK - now attitude to work...
|
    the important things?

    - Move
    - Establish Social Circle
           (Semi-Circle?!)

<u>Attitude</u>   -   <u>Fun</u>   -   <u>Fulfilment</u>

<u>MOVE</u> - out of Noreen's home for retarded men...

Other objectives?

    get a car?
    get a PC?

establish 'satisfactory' budget

- emphasis?   "Non-Restrictive"

           "Prudent"

establish social mechanism

    use of SAL?   Badders?
               Chess? X

    Travel - how much?
        Paris in April or <u>save</u> money?

Need a prioritised list
|
    what is important?

M.A.?   (remember that?)

Writing (ditto)
|
    make packet?!

~~~~

If you consider what is in play in this last entry, it is possible to see this time in his life (early- to mid-1993) as a truly low point. Consider all the things about which he is clearly uncertain: where he lives and works, who he works for, his finances, the absence of a social life. Then the damning labelling of his accommodation at that time: "Noreen's home for retarded men". Is that how he sees himself? Has he underlined 'attitude', 'fun' and 'fulfilment' not because he needs to define what he wants from them, but because they are missing altogether? And again that tragic "Need a prioritised list"...

What is also telling is that, although there are nods to poetry (the initial drafting of 'Worthing') there is no mention at all of any kind of writing project. What does "(ditto) - make packet" really signify? It is interesting that, at this point, the notebooks start to do double duty as a place for drafting poems. 'Worthing'[8] has always been one of my personal favourites, and it is interesting to read the draft about jigsaws - especially in the context of his previous entries.

~~~

Mid-Winter Worthing at dusk
is an old Lady getting ready for bed

Slippers off, she stretches arthritic toes
pushing at wrinkled stockings with effort,
pushing at years of ......
Curlers out, her wispy greying hair
mixes elegance with tired beauty.

(fragile & vulnerable)
                    |
          to what?

❊

Someone gave me a jigsaw.   edges
And tho' ~~but~~ the box-cover was blank,   square
and the pieces, all the same size,   no ~~right sides~~ -
were patterned on both sides.

Someone gave you a jigsaw too,
it was - ~~almost~~ the same as ~~mine,~~ -
except we ~~could~~ did not count the pieces

---

[8] Eventually published in *Collected Poems (1976-2016)*.

nor swear it ~~was~~ ^{might} be the same design.

Finding some pieces that seemed
^{happy} ~~to go~~ together, you made immediate progress -
while I, in my slow methodical way,
laid my puzzle out logically,
in row upon row, considering all sides.

Now, having got so far, you catch
yourself wondering ^{if the pieces actually fit,} if you are solving
the right picture; ~~in~~ and wondering
if the solution might actually be face
down to the table on the other side.

And I - for all my ^{neat + self-contained} rows -
wonder if I should be so correct,
^{if there can be a suitable outcome}
^{given the absence of boundaries to work within.}
~~to achieve results.~~

And ^{after a short time,} I wonder who gave me my puzzle.

Was it a present to myself -
        or a present ^{from us} to each other?

~~~~

Someone gave me a jigsaw
And tho' the box-cover was blank
the pieces -
                ~~all~~ the same size,
^{without} ~~no~~ square ~~edges~~ ^{sides} -
                ~~were patterned on both sides~~ ^{carried a double-faced pattern}.

Someone gave you a jigsaw.
It was the same as mine -
except we did not ~~count the pieces~~ ^{compare the pieces' count,}
nor swear ~~it might be~~ ^{it being of} the same design.

Finding some pieces that seemed
happy together ^(was it / this? instinct?)
you made immediate progress -
while I, in my slow methodical way,

laid my puzzle out logically,
~~in~~ row upon row, considering ~~all~~ both sides.

Now, having got so far,
you ~~catch yourself wondering~~ question
~~if the pieces naturally fit~~, the integrity of the fit
~~if you are solving the right picture~~
and if the solution you require might ~~actually~~ be hiding
face-down to the table. as you view it?   *(rhyme…)*

And I wonder if I should be so correct;
if - given the absence of boundaries to ~~work within~~ -
there cab be a ~~fitting~~ suitable outcome to match
~~despite~~ my neat and self-contained rows.

After ~~a~~ this short time, I wonder who made me this gift.
Was it a present to myself?
Or ~~a~~ presents from us to each other?

❋

Story about a man who, distraught and disillusioned, decides to commit
suicide. Before doing so he decides to translate his life, his worth, into £. He
sells everything; ditches his 'baggage'.

He makes a list of things to do (with his money) and gradually does them - all
the time approaching his nemesis.

Doubt? Second thoughts? Is there enough to dissuade him from his course?

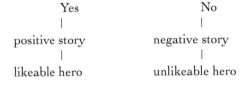

Yes	No
|	|
positive story	negative story
|	|
likeable hero	unlikeable hero

1 - Scene setting - e.g. job dismissal - to give the background to his mental
state

2 - The decision making process. How he decides what he's going to do => lists
of what he is to sell and how much he gets for it…

3 - The list e.g. visit Paris

4 => The events

(n-1) The final struggle

(n) The denouement
|
    Include both options?
    Allow him to imagine both (i.e. dual ending?)

    Is an inconclusive ending ok?

What is statement i.e. Life vs. £
|
    and the role of £ in life?

    A means to an end

And when the money runs out
    - what does this say about Life?

Balance sheet at the end of each chapter, seeing money going = seeing life ebbing away.

Importance of receipts? - become a kind of log or diary of his life...!

(Book has an appendix which is a photocopy of some of the receipts?)

~~~~

And then, at some point before August, a glimmer of light, whether he was to realise it or not; an entry starts with the word "story". Although the subject matter he has started to sketch here - suicide, the meaning of money - is arguably less than uplifting (and presumably to some degree based on his recent personal experience), it is surely significant that he has begun to think creatively again. Did this go hand-in-hand with changes in his domestic circumstance - e.g. the departure from the "home for retarded men"? Who can say?

~~~~

It's all a question of self-image, and attitude;
    of having a relaxed philosophy

"relaxed" = what the hell; nothing is <u>that</u> important...

Cannot be driven by fear.
Having the key things under control…

Key?   = £
         = work
         = relationships

＊

Open, honest
eyes of ice blue
    ~~yet without the~~ offering no threat,   5 ~~6~~
    no ~~the~~ fear, no ~~the~~ danger.   5

Open, honest;
~~with~~ an air of trust
    ~~of and~~ naivety, ~~of~~ comfort,   5 ~~7~~
    of ~~of~~ some warm certainty.   6 ~~5 6~~

Open, honest;
going forward, ~~with knowledge~~
    complete, prepared, ~~happy~~   6
    ~~happy at~~ knowing what lay ahead.   6

Open, honest;
I fear for you
    and the hurt ahead   5
    despite your countenance.   6

＊

CHILCOMPTON[9] (1)

Here (there) is the space for adventure,
for discovery;
the chance to make and mould,
to create an image of the world
as it is perceived.

From each room, doors offer escape -
to other rooms, to cupboards,

---

[9] A village south of Bristol where two friends, Gill and David, lived.

to small alcoves with their own doors,
and their own promises -
and despite their abundance, no two
seem the same.

My mind parallels the house with life:
the fun of opening a door to look
beyond; adventure, discovery.
It is excusable, perhaps, to envy
your opening of doors;
the moulding of your lives
as room by room, wall by wall,
image after image,
you fashion yourselves.
Yet I have my own 'Gainsborough'
which awaits a nervous touch;
and on bright spring mornings - today, tomorrow -
I push open other doors and look beyond them.

❋

LIVING ON THE EDGE

For the second time this week
Someone described me as ....

〜〜〜

I would argue that, in the main, the notion of someone "living on the edge" conjures up the adventurer, the risk-taker, the devil-may-care type. Based on the reality of his recent existence, surely only the interpretation he can place on the idea is an ironic one and entirely the opposite, more akin to "living on the precipice"...

In terms of the poems drafted in his notebooks, their variable quality is clearly visible. 'Worthing' made the cut, but understandably 'Chilcompton' did not, neither did the one that follows the next entry - which is, to be honest, pretty awful. In this case however, we might read it as a tangential comment on the life he was leading at the time (or the life he was not leading). In spite of his age - he would have been thirty-five at the time - perhaps these efforts are a reflection of his living through a period when he was still finding his voice, somewhere mid-transition between what was effectively advanced juvenilia and his more mature work.

~~~~

Conflict between the <u>Romantic</u> and the REALISTIC

i) idealistic notion of something to which one "must" aspire

      positive values of peace, harmony, love etc.
      negative aspects of self-effacement, bondage

ii) practical response to the everyday world in which one must "function"

      positive values of freedom, self-expression etc.
      negative aspects of selfishness, emotional impoverishment

Differences in linguistic expression; not just the choice of words, but how those words are used.

Is there - in "living terms" - a suitable balance, embracing all the +ve aspects?

❀

We should be as sponges are,
living in the pool of life,
soaking up, absorbing whatever
the waters of life may be.

And if we become saturated
- for whatever reason - and
are unable to experience more
then we owe it to ourselves
- and to life itself - to
squeeze out some more of the stagnancy,
flush it away, reject it.

This takes courage, self-confidence,
a lack of fear, and a belief
in what is really important.

❀❀ find an image for the above ❀❀
and try translation…!!

      - absorption of plankton…

❊

<u>Tate</u>

      Hornel
      Dadd
      Waterhouse
      Watts

Art galleries are as much about watching people as anything else…
… the cool of the Clore gallery
the wonder that Sir Edward Duveen had so much cash that he could afford to
build wings for both Tate & British Museum…

Mondrian's view that life is made up from the harmony created by the
juxtaposition of opposites e.g. horizontal and vertical…
- not a conflict, as one might imagine

Realism & Romanticism?…

Van Dyke's painting of Charles I.

Ridiculously small horse's head (proportionately) allows a direct parallel
between Charles & the Horse: the shape of the heads/noses; the look into the
distance; the arms of the man vs. the horse's legs; the sheen on the armour vs.
the horse's flanks…
Attempt to show Charles as strong as a horse? The painting of a metaphor?

❊

                              (BM)

"Their original purpose is uncertain"

"Provenance unknown"

〜〜〜

The only association I can give to "BM" is "British Museum" - this given the
subject matter immediately preceding it. And even if that is the case, where do
the quotes on purpose and provenance originate? I can only assume he read
them on a display during a visit there (though the focus above seems more on the
Tate and art).

In any event, the return to art as a comparator for writing is interesting, in this case the relationship between Realism and Romanticism. Did he ever explicitly follow this through in his writing, or - if present (even subconsciously) - is it more likely to exist as an undercurrent. Achieving any kind of balance between the two would surely require him to demonstrate both creative maturity and personal detachment.

There is a philosophical question here too. What effect did his internal debates about Art and its parallels in literature - Realism vs. Romanticism, Abstraction, Cezanne and The Black Castle etc. - actually have on his writing? And how can we possibly know? Would it be unreasonable to assume that here and there seeds were sown that would one day germinate and manifest themselves in something subtle, like the traits of a characters, a thread in a plot? But this could end up being another line of study altogether.

~~~

9th August 1993 (RBR)

Cisswood Hotel

Some months since the beginning of this book. More significantly, some months since the first attempt at defining some sort of "structure" - entry is dated 10/2.

(There is a subsequent entry too...)

Now - given my current 'situation' (that continually revising image of myself) - it seems a good time to review again. Another stab (in the dark?) at the 'big picture'.

Pin the tail on the donkey...

1 - Mediation:
    no Paula
    no regime
  - this does not appear to be a problem now.
  No action required.

(my 'professional' (anal?) neatness, demands of me an "Action Plan"...)

2 - Physical Exercise: Badminton

- when I can (i.e. when work allows) I am seriously thinking of getting a bike - cycling for fitness + fun and as I can't afford a car.
And learning to swim, because I feel a need to and because there seems a desire - at the moment - to enjoy and experience the 'freedom' I imagine it to offer.

* get a bike
* learn to swim

3 - Good Food: well...

- OK, I don't eat as well as I ought to (e.g. not enough fruit).
Debbi says I have lost weight. She may well be right (exercise, worry or poor diet?) I still think the restaurant idea is nice and practical. And I would like to be in a position to 'entertain' a little.

* Buy more fruit
* The odd treat eating out (but not alone)
* Entertain

(Both the latter have other dependencies)

3 4 - Good Hygiene: same comment as months ago!

5 - Rest: sleep, relax, read

-wasn't really too much of an issue - until late nights with B. Shot the whole thing to pieces (and work sometimes...) Sleep and relaxation should be OK - driven by circumstance. I should find time to read more.

* find time to read more...

6 - Clothing: "action"

- budget driven, but carried out. Comfortable that I am now in the frame of mind (and money) to be able to ad-dress(!) this issue as and when I feel the desire. Keep it up!

7 - Home: "Needs sorting!"

- Nothing changes! Sorted once - and served a very good purpose in doing so. Now comes the time when it needs sorting again. Definition of requirement will be key. And I guess independence will be the number 1 factor. Now I no longer need the company from a financial viewpoint. Emotionally? Probably need the freedom there too.

* Move to "my own place"… still 'baggage free'? (an unanswered question…)

8 - Pleasure: Plays, films, drinks

- has gone in bursts, but has been more or less satisfactory. Needs some dedication - and freedom - to schedule ahead. Will need to accept the possibility of doing some of this alone - but no too much!

* Plan 'events' in advance. Nothing too extravagant. Maybe one 'thing' a week. Possibly a little more adventurous…

9 - Personal Challenge: work, "other"

- Ah… Well, at least work is a little more satisfactory, and now resides within a suitable framework. Part of the balance is there. For the rest… a bit more later…

* To follow…

10 - Intimacy and Friends: "Action" - as ever!

- The excursion with B has proven something - possibilities and problems. Not a failure: an awakening, an opening - the 'proof' of something to be achieved. Not to be chased too hard (the 'natural'…) There is a goal of course. And a need to be clear and honest about this.

* Pursuit - but on my own terms and within an overall framework (that word again…)

* Based on any 'new' factors…

… So back to '9' and the 'other'. Re-reading the entries in this book suggests that much of what is here is expressing the sorts of thing that I actually want to say - and even the way I want to say it in places… So why not incorporate some of this - or all of it?! Why not try to satisfy myself rather than some sort of absurd notion of what someone else (an indefinable "other") might want to see.

And how about a ' theatrical' format? Something more expressive…

* Of course!

— || —

From all of this, there can be a summary list: how does it sound -

1   Get a bike
2   Learn to swim
3   Buy more fruit
4   The odd eating-out treat
5   'Entertain'
6   Read more
7   Get my own place
8   Plan 'events'
9   Intimacy pursuit
10   Action
11   The Old Chestnut...

...I forgot: the writing letters initiative. that should be somewhere...

12   Write letters

*

The next day - and all the above seems OK. 1 - and its consequence - may need a little planning. 2, certainly does...

If I go for something theatrical then I need a list of characters - and their preoccupations...

~~~~

Is there something desperate about yet another rehash of his twelve tenets? He clearly is sufficiently self-aware to appreciate - if not avoid - the trap into which he walks: "that continually revising image of myself"; "another stab in the dark?"; "my 'professional' (anal?) neatness, demands of me an Action Plan".

Some parts of this entry pique one's curiosity - especially the reference to "B" under "Intimacy and Friends"! - but apart from that, the old themes prevail; for example, more references to 'moving' and his need to "get my own place". Perhaps in all of this, the most desperate throw of the dice is the left-field suggestion he writes "something theatrical". Is that an example of 'when all else fails'?

And what about the comment "Why not try to satisfy myself rather than some sort of absurd notion of what someone else (an indefinable "other") might want to see"? I wonder how much this was a cheap throw-away line and how much of it he tried to live by...

~~~~

<LOG>

Letters to Natalia (Russia)
    Beate (Germany)

Started re-reading A.U.D.

So much for the log?!
Poetry & Short Stories maybe favourite for the new house. Lots of material for the poetry - especially if I consider the older stuff.
Short Stories - some old bits to work on (like The Man Who Grew Bonsai Trees) to fill 'The Empty Box'...

- not that the date is significant in any respect other than it offers some kind of relation to previous entries...

Before I go on, the numbers game...

1- got a car! 2- not yet 3- ✓ 4- cf. 5- cf. 6- ✓ish 7- yes!! 8- ✓ish 9- ...
10- OK 11- ==>

- not bad for six weeks really.

Inspiration from something in Gill's last letter. A comment from David about the local Vicar. A real story there. Prime material for a short study. And maybe that's how I should think of them, studies.

(On the 7am train to London, with the fog outside and Genesis inside...)

"The Empty Box" - the name, of course, now possesses a wealth of significance, for my 'Box' is truly empty.

Having now got my house - and my car - I have managed to divest myself of excuses. "What now?" is a question suddenly without many of the barriers I had been putting up - or which had been erected in my way, out of my control. Of course there is still work and all that entails, but in _my_ time I now sense the need to be busy, occupied, committed - <u>not alone</u>! (This latter is a fear, of course: in many ways a not unnatural consequence of finding myself with more than four grey walls...)

So what have I got to go into my box, and how do I get it there?

"The Man Who Grew Bonsai trees"
The Vicar story

- both stories about obsession, neither particularly positive. But "studies" rather than stories...

And discipline? Either early morning or last thing at night?

① Early Morning

- up at six (say)
- breakfast
- write (until "finished")
- get dressed
- go to work
- go to bed "early"; eleven (say)

② Late Night

- start writing at eleven (say)
- write until finished
- go to bed
- sleep; get up (no alarm clock unless necessary)
- go to work

I've tried ① - tending to be preoccupied about "the time" and the need to get to work... Shall we try ② (Buy some Guarana?)

<u>The Vicar Story</u>

Name?

Man who wants a daughter. Why? Because he grew up with all brothers/sisters and wants that familiarity/newness?

He has 4 sons.

His prayers for a daughter, at first gentle - i.e. in keeping with his professional role - become more extreme with each birth; i.e. more challenging of God. More desperate.

4th son turning point. Wife says she wants no more children ∴ his chance has gone (or has it?)

Effect on his faith is key.

Parishioners notice the change in his sermons over time.

Change in his attitude to his wife and his sons.

Second turning point? The arrive of a young female parishioner?

What does he want from a daughter? Replicate the relationship he had with his Mother? something sexual?

(Early miscarriage of 1st child - female?...)

Short story starts after 4th son; decision of wife.
Much is authorial reflection ∴ must be judgemental(?)

✤

WRITERS GROUP. Is there anyone interested in forming an intellectual, rigorous and challenging Writers' Group? Please contact...

WRITERS GROUP. Members wanted to form new group. Unashamedly intellectual, vigorous and challenging. Interested? Contact Ian...

✤

'PROGRESS'

They're building a new road
       to cut through the centre of the city.
From the security of my railway carriage,

I can see nothing but bridges;
~~this~~ discs of (a) * city backbone.   * the truant?
        Hoardings proclaim the advent of
an arterial spine "breathing life"
* (- more (a) lung than (a) spine -
to the heart of the city...   * more blood than air,
        * What physiological monster is this
that we (have) given -ing- birth too?   - are -
        and what will be its offspring?
(if one may torture a metaphor that far!)
        A fourteen-screen cinema?
A forty-alley bowling complex?
        Parking for four thousand?
Meanwhile, as construction goes on
            - made in seven months, not days -
the city limps on towards some bionic future.

        *

WRITERS GROUP. Meeting soon, new writers' group for those unafraid to talk seriously about their craft. Not for the uncommitted - or those whose idea of criticism is 'That's nice, Dear!' Unashamedly intellectual, rigorous and challenging. Interested? (Ffi. Ian 345181 (work) / 660834 (home)).

~~~~

For reference: The Writers' Group <u>was</u> advertised and did meet a few times but was essentially undersubscribed. The first meeting was in the bar at Bristol's "Watershed" and coincided with one evening the late comedian, Jeremy Hardy, performed there.

The Vicar story was never drafted.

~~~~

20ᵗʰ October 1993 (RBR)

Life should be full.

It is not something to be afraid of.

We should pack our existence with all that we can.

We should strive for variety.

We should try new things.

We should not shirk from contact with others, for there is Life fully lived.

We should be confident in ourselves, our self-esteem.

There must be love.

Another entry on the Temple Meads - Paddington train. This one simply to log the fact that I picked up the empty box again yesterday: a child looking for bricks to fill it...

And badminton last night was not terribly good: Elwyn, recently fathered; Barbara, recently widowed - and with corpse still running around! As it were.

And as the New Year approaches - really! - thoughts turn to some kind of "Life Log" (Diary) which will single-handedly fulfil the failed ™, replace it (and the other "pocket" version)... Minor fare, of course!

And for the box, the resurrection of the story about the man who translated his life into £... Still a good idea. And workable.

That, the vicar - plus the little bits I have nudging away in my portfolio.

"Michaela" aka "That Certain..." (what was it?!)

Story triggered by a photo of two people - man, woman - separated by "a large white space". The story, of course, is about the <u>space</u>, not the people!

❊

The Man whose life is Money...

The Vicar...

The space between people...

❊

Sitting on the train to London, watching the world go by - sense of independence from it

- what does it matter what I do to anything outside this train, to that field, to those cows; to anything beyond these eyes and the interpretation their vision is given? A kind of emotional sterility? Or lack of commitment? Or a blank surface awaiting imprint (plasticine on the long-jump take-off board?)...

A sense, I guess, that I might as well be here as anywhere else - which doesn't sound particularly positive!

Or maybe a sense that I should be "out there" somehow (geese in a field), "in touch"

Adjusting to free time... thoughts to Gill?

~~~~

Something existential about that last entry - or is it redolent of hopelessness and being lost?

Although strictly outside the remit I have set myself, I feel obliged to add some colour here. Gill was a writing friend of his who was soon to die of cancer. She and her husband David lived in Bristol before moving to nearby Chilcompton (about which there was a draft poem in an earlier entry).

~~~~

Notes from Trafalgar Square

* A large Jewish man, quite young - though this is more guess than fact - pulls a camera from a tired carrier bag and takes photos of the attractive young lady he is with. Young? No need to guess here; while he, black-capped and bearded (beginning to look unruly) seems a hybrid of ages and cultures.

* Man, be-denimed. Early fifties? Short, dapper. Possibly Italian, despite the silvering hair. He sits across the way, alone. He consults a guide book. Not only does he seem solitary - like me, perhaps - but somehow vacant.

* A seagull walks by, head buried in hunched shoulders like a grumpy tailor who has spent too long at his cutting table. He harries another bird bemoaning - presumably - something to do with the weather, or the food, or the fact that the galleries don't open until 2pm on a Sunday. Disturbed he flies off.

*

Home. Not so much 'where is it?', but more 'what is it?'

(Another London-bound note. The Inter-City shuttle more 'home' than not?)

And perhaps that is one of the reasons I'm enjoying all the travelling at the moment - it removes the <u>need</u> for a home, its requirement. An intercity seat, a Renault 19, a night in a hotel - all are substitutes, all (for a while at least) are where I 'live' (in the most basic of senses). I have become, somehow, nomadic. A second emotional state of rootlessness. The first is not having 'emotional' roots at the moment. The house offers a physical base (where my 'stuff' lives maybe)…

…So how much difference would Horsham make? Or is this another issue altogether? Is this a different notion of freedom? Does 'distance' give me something? Is my desire to 'move on' after five years or so no more than mythical restlessness?

What would it take to 're-settle' Bristol? Not that much maybe. The 'emotional root'; a successful writing group? All easier said than done?

(Sudden thought: have I given up fighting without realising it? Has resignation taken over? Where - excuse the phrase - has the spunk gone?)

We live our lives in a perpetual state of self-delusion.

✻

Eyes like a cat,
like an Egyptian cat
resurrected from a Pharaoh's tomb
and reborn, (transplanted)ˣ
alive again in your head,
darting, slanting, simultaneous image of
threat and promise.

Outside, a winter's mist clings
to fields dressed with two days
(of) heavy frost; cold, hard,
ready for the inevitable fall of snow…

or is the mist mysterious, romantic, inviting?…

…much as these pages
- long as my life in preparation -
await these thoughts, this pen.

✿

So the prospect of another move after Xmas. Not to Horsham or London, so still Bristol-based (though within the increased radius offered by having a car...)

And with, once again, another couple of evenings sliding unfruitfully by, the need to address some of the 'big' issues. The need to structure, perhaps; to rediscover emphasis; to balance something against work... to reduce its dominance.

Perhaps the circle[10] will help, if it happens.

And the struggle to find a woman. ("Struggle"? I'm hardly trying...)

✿

So is life a bit like chess (sitting playing chess; disgruntled by my last two defeats...)

- in that if one doesn't have a plan, a concentrated line of thought, a "modus operandi", one gets crucified? The drift from 'good move' to 'good move', when - at the bottom - none of them are really good moves because they don't work together. All are illusory, failures.

Echoes everywhere of structure, discipline etc. etc. But not to stifle the impromptu. Can that be built in? Is it not the <u>way</u> things are done rather than the doing of things themselves? Does anyone - by 'impromptu' means - get into "big situations"; or do people in "situations" do impromptu things to make them "big"? The latter I fancy - and, if so, then getting into the <u>right</u> kind of situations is key...

Does this mean Ritzy's on a Wednesday night? Where does one draw the line? Or start the line? And in what - with what - is it written?

But what I don't want is another 'New Year' attempt to discipline myself into some hide-bound routine that would appear to offer 'salvation' of some kind. (Is that what I'll end up with, I wonder?)

But pursue the chess analogy. My opening. Known so well that I take it for granted, don't study the moves, the position. Then I get to a place where I can

---

[10] A reference to his Writing Group.

win - and I miss it through lack of 'concentration'. There must be a parallel with life systems here. Discover the discipline, the structure, then abdicate all responsibility to it; "the 'plan' will see me through". Result: failure...

✽

The end-of-year-beginning-of-year questions seem to be coming quite early this time around - which is good in a way I suppose (the supposition being that they should come at all! Or need to come...)

First, the 'Group', the 'Circle'... Should we have some kind of log? Should I keep a log (private, secret)? (I'll ask Gill and see what she thinks.) Is there a need to record / celebrate its existence, its dynamism, its "life"? Big questions.

And 1994. Do I keep a diary? (Today's question...) Should I keep it - A4, A5? - by my bed and scribble every night? (I could take it away with me...)

OK, nice idea. Practical, because it's a discipline. But what's the aim? Who's it for? Does this book[11] work the oracle in a more sustainable way? It's certainly more fluid, flexible - not tied to a day, or (worse!) a page a day...

Is that my answer?

Or how about a "poetry diary"? Scribblings every night... Or a "novel diary"? An enforced 400 words a day (146,000 words in a year!)

The old notion of the 'modern' dictionary; a word a night. 365 "A"s...? Volume One; 'A'; 1994... etc. Life enforced to the year 2020, just to keep the diaries going...

How about "yes" then, to the above. "Bedside books". Poetry - 15 mins; Novel - 30 mins; the Dictionary - 15 mins. Or early morning with tea? No, probably not.

The planning can get pretty mechanistic here. e.g. Poetry A4, Novel A4, Dictionary A5... etc. (Dick Francis does it - mechanistically that is) Talk to Gill?

And apart from all this, another move early next year? To what? To where? What do I want?

---

11 i.e. his notebook(s) reproduced here.

✿

A ritualistic "sorting out" of my notebooks etc. - all that finished and unfinished work (mainly the latter, of course...)

And the Writers' Group has to provide some kind of impetus - or else, for me, it will have failed completely.

Perhaps I should consider a number of "projects" (does this sound too familiar?)

e.g. a collection of poetry or prose (or just poetry if "the Empty Box" fills)

> reworking "Seekers"...
> AUD...
> Mirrors...
> Something new (prose)...

Stimulation would appear to be the key. Sitting here - <u>not</u> writing, of course - I can "afford" to get all fired up. Sipping Brandy is a comfortable option - a means of <u>not</u> doing, while having the illusion of being constructive (but not creative...) Good / bad? balance?

I can feel a schedule coming on...

~~~~

So the end of 1993 is all about searching and asking questions - many are familiars. Is it any wonder that years later his fictional characters should to some extent be consumed by the questions that face them, that they feel the need to answer?

There are fragile shards of hope in the darkness of these entries - the reference to 'Mirrors', the first in an awfully long time. And perhaps in knowing what <u>doesn't</u> work too e.g. "planning can get pretty mechanistic", "what I don't want is another attempt to discipline myself into some hide-bound routine that would appear to offer 'salvation'" - though knowing and acting on that knowledge are, as we have already seen, two very different things. But at least the coming new year forced him start to once again to look 'out' to his writing, as well as 'in' to his existence.

~~~~

Christmas is, if not in general, then for me at any rate, a time for contemplation, judgement, planning. Maybe it's where all the seeds for New Year resolutions germinate (have been sown at odd intervals throughout the year).

And maybe this year in particular. Having discovered (recovered?) my own space, to have it violated by family. (It happens every year, but this year because it's <u>mine</u> alone, maybe the intrusion seems so much greater.) And the fact that my parents seem to forget that I'm a man of 35, and still treat me like a little boy sometimes...

Perhaps it's being concerned by 'big' things at the moment - and then to be bombarded by inane nonsense for days on end.

This time (this year's end, I mean) it feels much more like the closing of a chapter and the opening of another. The prospect of a New Year where - more or less - I have only to concern myself with me: for the first time in, what?, ten years? What I want for myself in the New Year has, thus, a little more significance.

Of course, there is the nagging doubt that - based on years of experience - 1994 will be pretty much the same as all the other years, and that plots and plans will go the way of their forefathers...

(It's the 27th - still a few days to go.)

Significantly '94 starts with a holiday - or rather a few days from work. That might be useful, if I do something with the time, that is. (I'm re-growing my beard for the occasion...) And the first question of '94 may be: 'do I have the balls to just take off in my car for a few days, without plans, a mini adventure?' We'll see...

I feel that '94 should be about regaining balance too.

A little less biased towards work.
A little more committed to my writing.
A little more committed to myself.

Of course, the big challenge for the first part of the year is to see if I can get myself into a reasonable relationship. That has to be the number one priority, as it should offer strength etc. to all the other initiatives.

I still feel as if I have a desire for independence - where independence is what I actually have, and it's just that I don't know what to do with it... Ah; feels like a sore spot I've just hit!

~~~~

It would be all to easy to underestimate the potential of the coming year feeling "much more like the closing of a chapter and the opening of another". In some senses the transition from 1993 to 1994 probably felt like the chance to wipe the slate clean and start afresh. If you consider his recent non-writing preoccupations - such as where he lived and where he worked - he has made progress, particularly in the former where the "home for retarded men" is now a thing of the past (though his relationship with 'work' will never truly be resolved).

'Independence' is something new thrown into the mix here of course; the realisation that he is freer than he has even been "in, what?, ten years?". Did this feel as daunting as it was liberating? And what was that to mean for his writing? 1993 had been an essentially barren year starting with an obsession on the 'twelve tenets' and subsequently focusing on how he was living rather than what he was doing with his life. It was a year when writing took the back seat. Yes, there were moments when he talked about starting something, the odd poem here and there, but these were essentially damp squibs. He lit the blue touch-paper only to watch it fizzle out. Would 1994 be any different?

Part Three - 1994

3rd & 4th January 1994 (RBR)

Southampton

Is visiting Jason an exorcism, a laying of old ghosts? The echoes of my time here seem so far away, without any immediacy and almost devoid of that romantic longing for re-enactment.

What is reinforced (through his photos of those "last days") is the need to belong, for there to be a group, friends, identification outside oneself - as if I hadn't come to that conclusion anyway…

I had intended to write so much, but maybe tomorrow…

…Tomorrow indeed.

And it occurs to me that where I am now (35) is the same "distance" from 50 as from 20 - which was when I started at Southampton. Significant? Not really, I guess, but a 'point to ponder'.

Looking through Jason's photographs last night at a few faces from the past; recollection was pleasant, but insight was better.

I don't want - for example - to be part of that crowd again, to renew, to continue. (Who does? It's not realistic anyway.) Perhaps guilt over contact with Barbara - and regret over contact with Tom (where it really is too late - which Jason didn't deny…[12]) - but that's about it.

There's a line that needs to be drawn under the time, the image, the memory.

SOUTHAMPTON UNIVERSITY

Something like that; to close it off, the chapter. Maybe wandering round there today (for the last time?) will do the trick. Do others need to do this, immediately? Or do they manage from a distance and let it fade away?

---

[12] Twenty-five years later this theory was to be disproved.

The other insight was that, quite simply, I don't have anything in place in my life now which compares to it. No social network, none of that <u>vital</u> stuff which - all those years ago - materialised in weekends at Boltons, trips to Wales, parties and intellectual intimacies. The mistake would be, of course, trying to recreate that same environment again. The <u>spirit</u> is different now ('spirit' - Jason's "mot juste"). We aren't in Neverland - thank God! - and at 35 the spirit has changed. Like it or not, we actually want different things - we only kid ourselves that they're the same. We work within a completely different set of parameters, under a whole new (and <u>vast</u>!) set of constraints.

And in a pause (for sip of coffee) the fundamental point that I know I need to take responsibility for my own life. Maybe I didn't realise it, but there has been too much abdication, the sense that I will be affected by external things working on me rather than the other way round. Life really is too short for that.

All this imposes a degree of pressure, and will require a tremendous amount of effort on my part. Concentration too, on what is important.

The new PC is good because it has made me take a look at my writing again. A little a day has to be the immediate medicine. The daunting prospect is, of course, the social.

Jason has lots of acquaintances; friends seem to go back to 1981 - which is ok, but only as a supplement. He seems to meet people who are transitory: they are moving through Southampton while he stays still. I don't think he looks as 'vital' as he did the last time I saw him. Maybe finishing with Janet (a long, drawn out mess, by the sounds of things) took too much out of him, I don't know. Anyway, looking at Jason is a bit like looking into a mirror, and there are things there I see and I don't think I like very much.

Last year I made that list about having people round for meals... I still think that was a good idea; a kick-start if you like. Maybe it never really got going because of the people in the list; there was, essentially, no-one "new" there.

Formulas on their own aren't good enough.

(From a crappy old TV movie yesterday, the truism that people eulogise about the past <u>not</u> because the past was so great <u>but</u> because the present is so shitty. Difficult to counteract that as an argument - at least in my present frame of mind...)

… And still later that same day (me now tucked up in bed (early) tired from lack of sleep last night…)

The walk round the University was interesting. A kind of anonymous experience really. Wandering through the English Common Room only to feel vague echoes of the past; not to be grabbed by something… Perhaps that was the best reaction to have, to bury vague, impossible notions.

Or maybe the chance meeting of Bella and John who, 12 years on, are still doing the same things as they were way back (more or less) was even more effective. Their envy of my job, or Jason's tenuous life as a "freelance" - while we envied them their Ivory Tower academia…

In a way, I guess it suggested that work in itself is not the problem. The stuff I wrap around it is the key (more anon…)

But the social thing - to digress and record the point. I get back to Bristol to find a card from Alison, and on my return here, a phone message from Sarah and an invitation to 'supper' on Thursday. (Turning out to be a _very_ social holiday!)

(Prayers for level-headedness should now be mumbled…)

One last university thing. Jason typing in 'GOUGE' on the library's computerised catalogue system, and coming up with 2 copies of 'Play for Three Hands' (Reference only, Special Collection…). Some kind of mark made…

And talking of which, leads me on to the fact that I need a project to work on. Something to feed an enthusiasm. Not ' The Empty Box', because - although fine as a concept - I feel the need for a single goal just at present. Something to carry me forward for a few months.

Time for contemplation…

~~~

This entry is massively powerful, not simply from the perspective of his own life and the holding up of a mirror the visit to his Alma Mater offered him, but in its tenor and preoccupations, a lead-in (if you like) to perhaps the major concern of many of his later fictional characters i.e. their relationship with the past. Of course the entry is concerned with the present and the future too (that throwaway about the supper invitation from Sarah!), but it is all predicated on the past and *his experience of it. He uses what happened, how he felt and who he knew, as the yardstick for what should come next; he doesn't want to replicate what he once had, but it does serve as an illustration of what was missing from his current life. In that sense, you could argue that what he experienced during that visit to Southampton was less an "exorcism" (the removal of something 'bad') than the waking after a long sleep only to be confronted with the stark realisation of what was missing. There is clearly a difference.*

It is also a realisation which tells him what he does and does not need: he doesn't need a formula and sees that 'The Empty Box' (was an initiative ever so well/ poorly named?!) is no immediate solution; he recognises that he needs a project and that he must "concentrate" and apply himself.

I wonder how much of an impact finding his name on the University Library catalogue actually had on him - "some kind of mark made" - and what difference the whole experience made to what was to come next.

~~~

<div align="right">

11ᵗʰ January 1994 (RBR)

</div>

Well here we go again!

(London-bound. 8am 11/1/94 - but at least I've waited until after Swindon this time!)

But the comment refers not to the journey nor this entry, but the apparently certain embarkation on a new relationship.

Sarah feels more 'positive' than Barbara; less forced, more relaxed. And I should try to avoid the pitfalls from last summer - especially my initial feeling is that something of reasonable duration is called for...

✿

And after last night's Philosophy Circle[13] -

    Am I an existentialist?

           (discuss...)

✿

---

[13] Primarily, a group of UWE students, lecturers and other academics who would meet once a month in a room of The Colston Arms in Bristol. It was where he met Sarah.

<u>Nev. - chapter 3.</u>

Phone call to Broker who advises selling all shares (he sounds a bit 'different')

Calls back with net gain…

face-to-face interaction with "real" people not possible until he has resolved his inner conflict.

Need for a thread to run thru what is essentially an episodic piece. Idea: woman, met continuously in different guises. Ultimately the object of desire. She is symbol of what he is aiming for: - almost religious enlightenment?

Based on 2½k words per chapter, we're looking at 40 chapters - or, if 1 and 2 are logically '1', then 20.

Need to build a list to cover these; also to identify 'lessons' to be learned. (Role of Bus Driver as 'guide'?)

Final chapter must be set in Malvern.

Chapters 1 & 2 should expand by about 40% = 4k chapters (25 tot)

3 = Car Park and final money list
4 = 'to do' list
~~~~
25 = Malvern II
24 = some kind of denouement.

∴ 20 things 'to do' / 'to see' / to learn.

(concepts of time & travel? Animated Travel Clock?)

Some sort of gift from Samuel to Nev?
A "temporal guide"?
Or a calculator carrying his o/s balance?

| | | Chaps? |
|---|---|---|
| Visit Paris | | 5k \| 2 ≥ |
| Eat in a posh restaurant | | 1k \| 1 |
| Go on a cruise | | 10k \| 2 ≥ |
| Fall in love again | £? | \| |
| Play football for England? | | \| |

Fly a plane                                    2k | 1
Save a life                        £?

~~~~

Just a week later he is taking his first steps in a new relationship - and is already working on the draft of a novel that would eventually become 'The Big Frog Theory'.

Where - you might ask - did that come from?! Was it the "single goal", "something to carry me forward for a few months"?

The idea of a man translating his life into money, and then spending it, is one we have already seen from him[14]; what seems to have happened is that he has found a peg - a framework - to hang it on. Not only that, but the 'magic realism' style in which he has begun to write (admittedly not referenced here) has seemingly come from nowhere, almost as if, in order to draw a line under the past - in the same way as he physically drew a line under the words 'Southampton University' - he needed something 'new' in order to free himself. The style is an escape in itself.

It is surely no mere coincidence that this sudden writing should begin after both his visit to Southampton and - more importantly - the commencement of a new romantic relationship. If you consider his recurrent preoccupations in entry after entry, it is almost as if he had been able to address two of his most fundamental ones in the space of, what, fourteen days.

~~~~

15th March 1994 (RBR)

Chaps.   10 - Failure
         11 - Eiffel
         12 - With Samuel - "Here endeth the first lesson"

Need to consider the 'domestic'?
In London, perhaps, for the puchase of a Tuxedo.

Last   = Malvern
-1   = Buying the Camera
-2   = Denouement with "Mirelle"

---

[14] In his 1993 entries.

Towards the back;   University Challenge
                              The Bookshop
- kind of intellectual confrontation?

Where does he meet his final "Mirelle"?

∴ What is left to fit?
                - the cruise?
                - the meal?
                - flying the plane?
                - the Pyramids?

✧

6th April 1994 (RBR)

(Returning from Keswick)

Dennis Potter is dying. I have just read a cut from his interviews with Melvyn Bragg and regret I missed the TV programme. He has some form of stomach cancer, perhaps with only weeks to live.

I sense that, when my time comes, this will be what gets me too.

Potter is now a driven man. So much to say and so little time... In a way I envy him his drive, but not (of course) his situation.

It does put a slant on things though, the knowledge that the man of *Blue Remembered Hills* etc. is about to bow out for good. 'The Final Interview' indeed.

How much time do any of us have!

~~~~

In a slight departure from process, and because now is the right time for a preview...

The next set of entries - begun four months later - are the only ones made throughout the remainder of 1994. And they are extraordinary for three reasons.

The first is that, although we now know that his relationship with Sarah was to blossom during the first part of the year (and to continue for many subsequent years after), there is not a single mention of her.

Secondly, there is also no word on 'Nev' / 'The Big Frog Theory' - even though he managed to complete his initial draft of the novel during the first half of the year.

And thirdly - and most significantly? - these entries (which accumulate to some twelve pages in this digest!) are solely and entirely about 'Mirrors'. Apart from a throwaway reference to the project at the end of the previous year, not only does he make his first serious attempt to address the work in four years, from August onwards (presumably over the subsequent few months) he maps out almost the entire book. The entries begin with a review of his thoughts from prior years and then simply explode with detail: Beatrice and Simon are reinstated; not only is Mark's father (Charles) now front-and-centre and pivotal to Mark's story, but he was worked out the entirely of Charles' canon and history - and in some detail too! Characters are rounded-out for the first time, even the minor ones, and the relationships between them are sketched in a way we have never seen before, including candidate events to be considered and/or included in the book. There are dates, specifics; even chapter-level synopses. It is, in its 'wholeness', a quite remarkable landmark.

If you consider the dark places he had been inhabiting during 1993 - "Noreen's home for retarded men", writing little of note, profoundly unhappy - the following twelve months stand out as an incredible step forward and represent a remarkable transformation. Not only is he in a stable relationship, but he has managed to draft a complete novel - 'The Big Frog Theory' - in around four to five months (whilst working full-time!) and was able to resurrect a notion he'd had some eleven or twelve years earlier and transform that into a sophisticated and cohesive whole. What must it have been like to have lived with that idea for so long? Had it been gestating all the while? Had the notebook entries across all those years done their job to perfection, allowing him to shape and refine it along the way? Consciously - and undoubtedly subconsciously - he must have been whittling away at the idea of 'Mirrors' for all that time, readying it for the moment when, emotionally perhaps, the stars were aligned.

If so, 1994 was that year.

~~~~

- Question of how one sees oneself & others. The importance of perspectives & viewpoint.
- Mirror as a means of perfect reflection. This 'accuracy' is its disquieting feature; the notion of some form of 'true representation' is the disquieting factor. Breaking of the mirror is the breaking of this spell, but also symbolic of destroying a view on the real (i.e. escapism).
- Where is the mirror image in the novel?
- A reflection suggests an opposite, of course…
- A relationship offers a means of "seeing" oneself through another; how someone else responds gives a clue.
- Use of photographs as an image/mirror on the past. Destruction of the photos = a break with the past too.
- Importance of Mark's book as an artefact of research into the past:
  - another's & therefore a reflection on that person
  - his own…
- There must be something in Mark's past which he wishes to avoid. The book/photos acting as a "mirror" on that time, much as the mirror does with regard to the present.
- "Mirrors" implies a multiplicity of mirrors. Therefore:
  - the Mirror
  - the book
  - the photos
  - other people
- Is there a place for a past relationship (i.e. sexual) or should it be something else?
- Mark needs to be responsible for something from the past (i.e. the book). It is his own responsibility from which he is running. (Is the fact that he is constructing the book relevant here? Re-making history…?)
- How far is Mark prepared to take the physical destruction of things in his purge? How many of the mirrors will he try to remove (i.e. other people?)
- Idea of Mark's history attempting to lose its fixity, the place he has secured for it in his mind, and become free, loose… a hazard because he has to live it again.
- 'How much history is left?'

- How much past/history can be shared with others? And what about 'shared' history? i.e. the familial with Beatrice? Whose version of events is, in any sense, "correct"?

- Notion of disclosure. Mark, as historian, has this as his "job". But as a tortured individual it is something he fights... because there are repercussions in disclosure.

- Question of power as well as responsibility. Mark, in his role as historian (creator of myth) he is in a position to define 'reality' in an historical sense. Difficulty as this intrudes on his youthful reverence for history as the study of reality - not its recreation...

- History is mutable; subject to the vagaries of individual memory. It can therefore be destroyed if represented by artefacts... And something one can free oneself from.

- What is the role of the narrator here?
  - we see everything from Mark's viewpoint (i.e. anonymous)
  - the narrator invades; is aware of the machinations of Mark's mind; the place of history - including the book's relationship to it.
    - Mark as guinea pig; the animal in the experiment. The real protagonist is the reader & the reader's relationship with their own 'version' of history.

- And the structure of the book too? Some fragmented testimonials? The power of language in memory & history: because of the book, history is language.

- Historical precedent suggests a doomed future for Mark? Destiny; history defined in advance...

- Book is about Mark but contains textual insertions of the biography he is writing about his father and samples of his father's writings. (critiques of these writings?)
  - biography is Mark's attempt @ understanding his father (as the novel is our attempt @ understanding Mark)
  - also, his father's writings Mark sees as a reflection on himself, and tries to understand in that context.
- Novel.
  - Mark's history
  - Mark's book
  - his father's writings
- Mark has multiple attempts at certain portions of his father's life ∴ the rewriting of history.

✿

OUTLINE OF PLOT STRANDS

MARK   1 - Present   2 - Past

CHARLES   1 - the book (the history)
    (sub-plots here? - i.e.   the literary life
                       the personal life)

Mark's relationship with the book + his father's history must pervade the novel. And grow as we go through the novel.
Does he begin to think about the biography so much that the delineation between the two begins to blur?

Mark + Julia   Charles + Mary

1   Claire   George Walker
      Beatrice / Simon   Max Smedley
      Publisher   Arnold Harriman
                      the "Women"

2   Lesley

Charles' canon:			aet	
	Pieces of Eight	1957	25	SS
	✿ Scenes from a Life	1988	56/30	Auto
	Sixteen Sonnets	1961	29/3	poems
The Novels:	Dawn	1963	31/5	n.
what inspires	Under the Olive Tree	1965	33/7	n.
him to write	No Easy Fight	1969	37/11	n.
these?	If Time Was A Book	1973	41/15	n.
	A Suburban Bandit	1975	43/17	play
	Uncertain Genesis	1978	46/20	n.
	Beggars and Choosers	1985	52/27	n.
	✿ =>			
	unfinished / death	1989	57/31	n.
	A Small Enough Impulse			

(Mary's death 1970?)

✿

<u>Mark & Julia</u>

Julia concerned about the change she sees in Mark. In his eyes, this appears as a change in Julia. She becomes burdensome to him, especially after his remembrance of Lesley. (Embodied in the mirror). This increases the attraction in Claire.

Events? (not so easy with Julia a victim of so much…)
- Shopping
- Visit to Art Gallery (mirrors his father's visit) Tate
- Meeting Laura & Tim (their wedding ~ the mirror ~ hangs like a threat over Mark)
- Climactic event? (in addition to the fire?)

Mark & Claire

Mark's interest in Claire grows as he perceives a change in Julia. This is also suggested by a sense that he should 'move on'. His father's lifestyle plays a part; as do the characters in his books (who Mark sees as images of himself).

Events?
- Social (but references only - to keep Claire in the frame)
- *The advance + rejection (one of the climactic moments)

*(Does there need to be something before the end?)

Mark & Beatrice/Simon

Beatrice becomes more important to Mark as an independent witness once <u>he</u> is involved in his father's history. He should want to talk to her more often. Simon becomes something of an encumbrance therefore, and Mark begins to major on his Uncle's weaknesses / flaws.

Events?
- A dinner party
- More conversations*
- A literary function (with Simon)

(* one of these should be suitably 'big' for Mark, with Beatrice unloading a few truths about his father)

Mark & Publisher (Bruce Congreave)

External pressure on Mark to produce more accounts of history. Emphasis on accuracy & correctness; the 'truth'.

Events?
Various meetings to discuss work. (the publisher becoming more concerned). (Does he need to withdraw Mark's work?)
- 3 meetings? initial (slight concern); middle (more specific concern); final

<u>Mark</u> (general)

He needs to build a sense that he is being betrayed: by Julia, Claire (her rejection), his publisher, his Aunt, and (even) his father. Perhaps the greatest betrayal of all is by history.

Mark, as his sense of betrayal grows, feels the need to take root in something he can rely on. Hence the obsession with historical fact.

Other betrayals. His father's betrayal of both Mary + Mark and…

<u>Mark & Lesley</u>

A relationship, brief and temporary - though not to Lesley. Mark, unable to handle the reality of the situation, can find no clean way out - so he hurts and betrays her (Happens to character in father's book - 1985?). Thinking about Lesley, reopens his memory & his guilt. He has no other reference for this (e.g. Beatrice or the books) so must regenerate his own history.

<u>Events</u>?

• Their meeting (photograph - triggered)
• The high point - the deterioration
• The betrayal (Claire in present is another enactment)
• The denouement (what happens to Lesley?)

<u>Charles</u>

The '63 novel is a natural progression. A return to prose.

Meets woman _____ in literary circle. Affair.

'65 novel partly inspired by that brief affair.

Some 'political' wranglings in '66 (partly of Charles' making)

The '69 novel is a 'serious' response to this. Earns him praise, fame + a decent living.

Another affair. Mary becomes ill + against a backdrop of Charles' success etc. dies.

Charles - briefly celibate - eulogises Mary in '73 novel.

Another success. Paid to write only play in '75. Establishes him.

'78 novel written as sequel to '73 work. Not a happy period for Charles (memories of Mary; guilt)

Turns to alcohol & general self-abuse. No stable relationship.

'82 meets <u>Simone</u>. Begins the book published in '85.

She leaves him a year later.

Charles vows to write his "one real book".

Unfinished @ his death in '89.

Charles and	Mark		Critics=>Frank Wilson
	Mary		P.J.Cole
	George Walker	|	Derek Shutts
	Max Smedley ©	| minors?	

Arnold Harriman |
Stella '64
Pru '69/70
Simone '82

in '70s: Hellen
Heather
Stephanie

Charles and his literary speeches?...

✻

Dawn (1963)
Novel about a man coming to self-knowledge. Struggle. Loosely based around
Charles' experiences working in the factory. (Demonstrates perception; an
insight into others; a command of language). A 'domestic' novel.
Hero: George Maxwell (debt to George Walker). Put-upon, confused
individual. An unsatisfactory life. Decides to fight, to find himself. Backdrop of
Union / Management struggle.
(Charles goes part-time at the factory)

Under the Olive Tree (1965)
Inspired by Stella + a visit to Greece (with G.W.) in 1964. Story of an artist
who leaves England for Greek island (Hydra?) to paint. Again theme of
freeing oneself + discovery.
Hero: Anthony Shipley. Meets local Greek girl; Constantina. Their
relationship. This struggle with his art; acceptance etc. Tragedy. The optimistic
return to England.
(Charles gives up work)

No Easy Fight (1969)
Born from a dispute with Harriman's old company re rights to "Pieces of
Eight" now that Charles is more well-known. Charles fights in court and wins.
Story of a man taking on "Authority". Semi-tragedy in that victory is achieved
at a price. Context?
Hero: Arnold Smith. (Anonymous). (Arnold: guilt regarding Harriman)

If Time Was A Book (1973)
"Tribute" to Mary. The family moves in late '69. 4 months later, Mary dies.
Charles (with support from Beatrice) brings Mark up alone. Guilt regarding
the way he has treated Mary.
Idea that time is a book; one journeys through it a page at a time, chapter by
chapter; but the book can only be read once. If it were a book, one could re-
read, re-understand.

Heroine: Elizabeth. Discovers she has a terminal disease. The book is the story of her last three months of life (13 chapters) (An "if it happened to me" exploration)

(Interview in The Sunday Times, 1973)

A Suburban Bandit (1974) (Play)
Story of a middle-class social animal, a "climber". Without scruples, morals; full of ambition and greed. A financial entrepreneur who knows what he wants and doesn't care how he gets it. (10 years later this would have been a condemnation of Thatcher's Britain ∴ later described as visionary). Charles' first anti-hero: Alexander le Moins (Name changed to some French ancestor's). Alex's rise almost irresistible. (Comparisons with Brecht's Ui & Hitler). Alex destined to be crushed by the system he espouses. Dog eat dog.

Uncertain Genesis (1978)
Sequel to ITWAB. Some of the characters taken from the '73 work. Specifically requested by publisher. Large fee - Charles' first thoughts about his 'prostitution'.
Hero: William Wilding. A minor character from '73. Reaches early manhood to discover that he is a foster child and, obsessed, sets off in search of his true parents. A kind of detective work; Charles not comfortable, nor at his best. Despite his searching + discoveries, Wilding never actually succeeds with no-one willing to accept responsibility for his presence in the world. Parallel with Charles' sense of being "lost" - esp. in terms of his writing.

(Interview in Stand, 1982)
(Interview with David Frost, 1984)

Beggars and Choosers (1985)
Inspired by Simone. Parallel to Mark/Lesley relationship, though with stronger heroine à la Simone? A story of three couples, each individual illustrating the nature of being either a "beggar" or a "chooser"; with or without power - and how people confuse the two and misplace their position on the scale of things.
Characters: Michael; unpleasant and manipulative person (Charles' self-image here). Peter; weak and lacking moral courage (Mark sees this as a criticism of himself). Susan is a strong, individualistic person (Simone). Leandra completely docile and vulnerable (Mark thinks this is Lesley). The book wins Charles the Booker Prize nomination, and a return from something of a wilderness.

Scenes from a Life (1988)

Slim autobiographical volume. Not a "life", as such; more a series of thoughts and jottings on the past, Charles' works, and the future. Written after Simone has left him: a kind of "summing up"/"taking stock". He feels the need to put the record straight, and has begun to talk about 'posterity'. He has seen some friends die, and is concerned that his health may not be at its peak. Question as to how genuine / truthful some of the book is.

A Small Enough Impulse (1989...)

❁

Charles and Mary
Marriage is followed by a good year, then P of 8. Decline. Birth of Mark, '58. Next few years OK; sees Sonnets then Dawn. Charles becomes less devoted husband and father. Suspects Mary of an affair (with George W.). Leaves her briefly for Stella in '64. Returns. After UTOT ('65) faithful. Heavily into his work and earning a reputation as best he can. Begins to drink. Some dark moments (history cloudy). Mary short spell in hospital in '68. NoEF ('69), more success. Charles pledges himself to Mary. They move. He begins affair with Pru. All cut short by Mary's death in '70.

Charles & Mark
Mark aware of mother's unhappiness and Charles' role in it. An uneasy truce in '70 on Mary's death; they lean on each other. Charles a different kind of father from then. Mark sees the women & the drink, but misses any closeness. They move in '76 after the success of ASB + and on the advances for UG. Charles has "arrived". Mark grows up resenting his father and that which takes him from him. He also beings to harbour an unhealthy philosophy towards women partly from jealousy, and partly because he knows how his father treats them. (Lesley is first enactment of this). Despite all of this, Mark is in awe of Charles and develops a kind of hero-worship - because everyone tells him how 'lucky' he is.

Charles & George
Friend from early Warwick days (woodworking?). Charles' confidant - except for a brief period in '64 when he suspects George of having an affair with Mary. George is a teacher; Charles often uses him as a sounding board for his work. Debt to George in '63 as model for George Maxwell. George dies in '87 as Charles is writing SFAL. Eulogy.

Charles & The Critics

Frank Wilson (from Stand). Very pro Charles (interviews). Question as to Frank's honesty; a little sycophantic. Not sure about ASB - but never says anything. Charles tolerates Frank, but doesn't respect him.

P.J.Cole. Harsh critic; always asking serious questions of Charles' work. Not a bandwagon man. Praises B&C, and Charles regards this as the greatest accolade.

Derek Shutts. Reviewer & the man directly responsible for Charles being paid to write ASB and UG. Charles finds Derek's greed repulsive (because he sees elements of himself there).

Charles & Stella

After Dawn, Charles (with Mary's prompting) joins a literary circle where he meets Stella. Stella is impressed by the fact that Charles is published, and attracted to him physically. Charles imagines that such an "opportunity" is the result of his success. He does not love Stella, but starts the affair through ego, lust etc. This notion of a relationship born of art, partly inspires UTOT. End affair with Stella as soon as it begins to stale; Stella is untalented, not inspiring (really) and too sycophantic.

Charles & Pru

Pru is a Labour Party activist. Finds NEF inspiring, and reads socialist messages into it. Contacts Charles to see if he has any unfulfilled political ambitions. Charles finds Pru more stimulating than Stella ever was (she believes in things). They begin an affair which begins to get very involved and complex. Mary's death forces Charles to break with Pru. (Did he want to? Would he have given up Mary? Does he ever forgive himself?)

Peter Healey @ MacMillan

Charles & Simone

After a number of brief, unsuccessful and unfulfilling relationships in the '70s, Charles meets Simone (a mature French student of lit, in '82). Their affair helps Charles get back onto an even keel, and he begins to work on B&C. He tries to persuade Simone to give up her degree and remain in England with him. She refuses, and when she leaves at the end of the summer of '83, their relationship is over.

It leaves Charles more positive about the future however, and he begins to work hard. Interviews and pre-publication publicity bring him back into the public eye, and B&C is published to unprecedented acclaim.

❉

Mark should make a conscious decision to lie about his father's past at some point.
This represents the mutability of history; Mark's 'changed' relationship to it; the fact that "history is language".

"It didn't matter what he wrote; he knew that now. They were just words on a page, and irrespective of his choice or their order, nothing could either change - or reproduce - exactly what had happened…"

❊

Chapter 14
Buying books. Foyles. The labyrinthine nature of the shop.
Difference between the way Mark & Julia shop for books. Their attitudes to them - and the books they look for.
Mark's interpretation of the difference between fiction and historical fact.
What sorts of book does Julia look for? Trashy fiction? Domestic trivia?
After Foyles? Julia wants to go home - Mark wants to go for a coffee / drink in Soho maybe…

❊

Ch 21/22
What does Beatrice know about Constantina?
Does her version of events (her source?) vary from that depicted by Mark?
Mark's attitude to Simon? Is he nervous of Simon remembering about the diner and Mark remaining with Maxine?
Does Julia take the opportunity to "probe" a little given the "cover" & security of Beatrice and Simon's presence?
Does Beatrice believe that there was further contact with Constantina?
Knowing something Mark doesn't? Something in UTOT perhaps? And discussion of Constantina over dinner - further blurring the distinction between reality and history / fiction.

❊

Lesley is Constantina's daughter. (Or is she? is the possibility enough for Mark, or must it be historical fact?)

❊

Ch. 25
Mark recalls his meeting with Lesley. (Does this have a different style? e.g. "I"
and present tense?)
Roused from this by Maxine's voice calling him.
Where is the place for his "it was a lottery" kind of philosophical reflection
here? Inserted in the memory?
How does his father react to Mark's relationship? (how do the chronologies
overlap? i.e. with Mark's book?)

＊

Ch 33   1974-75
Charles between ASB & UG ('78)
Mark aet 16/17   Puberty. First experience of girls.
↳ reflections on relationship with Lesley
        signs it is failing ('81) - to be later paralleled in B&C
        ‖
        v
        echoes of relationship with Julia
        ↳ Mark has sense of mirrors in his own life
            ‖   for the first time
            v
            what does this mean for Maxine?
                Catalyst or Casualty?

Part Four - 1995 to 2004

Three years ago or so (when I started writing in this book) I discover that I wrote "Never go to Talgarth"... Now I am sitting in the garden of a B&B farmhouse about 1½ miles outside Talgarth. Sarah is upstairs sleeping off her night shift. Dinner is in less than an hour.

I have been reading Alan Bennett. Apparently Somerset Maugham set himself to write 2000 words a day (my old preoccupation). Well, I think, he could afford to, couldn't he?

This morning, before setting out for our long weekend in Wales, I looked again at the map of the Peak District (a flat representation of something far from that) and wondered "How am I going to get there?".

It occurred to me that perhaps I should produce a project plan (I would if it were a job) - or maybe I should consider trying something different. Making my name as an intelligent Sports journalist springs to mind - and starting my illustrious career with a "Leave Linford Alone" piece. Also, to try and spread it around a bit. Concentrate on some of the unsung heroes. Ever read a piece on Mika Salo? Who? This might give me a chance to prove something - but then the entrée could be as unrealistic (if not more so) than writing novels.

(Andy Leslie manages a little journalism with work, so why not?)

- Around the farmhouse (more a cottage) a German guest goes about taking photos of everything. It is obviously his last day -

✿

I like hotels because there one can remain anonymous. In B&Bs one is forced into community; trapped into inane conversation with Ron and Audrey; or left to feel ashamed of being English because we force Belgian guests to eat our shite food.

If I were famous, I think I would prefer to stay in B&Bs. Having given up anonymity, it is probably better to only have to share oneself with three or four other people - and there's always the chance that they might not know who you are...

Oh yes. And never go to Aberystwyth.

So the Linford thing. Why do journalists do it?
Because of envy? Build LC up into a hero figure - there to be knocked down.
Like playing God?
Difficult for LC. There is a limit, a peak. Does he want not to go past it? Nigel
Mansell can go past, then blame the Team etc. and fade quietly away. LC can't.
One day he won't be able to cut it. What then? And the preoccupation with
money? If he's got one good season left (when it pays) why shouldn't he make
the most of it? And maybe he does want to fade away, but the press won't let
him. Footballers can - because they're one of a team. Golfers are OK too - they
can go on the Seniors' tour, where you're paid to be past it. Who wants a guy
who, aged 39, can do the 100m in 11.4 and used to be good?
So it's a power thing for the press. Swarm like flies round the heroes they
made, waiting for decay. Laying maggots maybe…
What should they do? Clean reportage. They should ask Linford what he
thinks and wants, and report that. But they can't: a) they're not inclined to and
b) even if they were, LC isn't going to trust them anyway.

29th August 1995 (RBR)

(Train to London)

Someone has stuck up a small (A4) note on the wall proclaiming:

> "Service" on this line is diabolical.
> Time for a Passengers Action Group.

I wonder how the "Group" would "Act". What could they do - boycott the
service? No-one would care; except perhaps their bosses.

The man who put the note up looks like the kind of guy who loves meetings.
Probably belongs to several User Groups of various flavours, and surfs the
internet as an amateur enthusiast. (I may be being unfair, but who gives a
fuck?)

Travelling to London (on the move again @ Slough) and towards the large
unknown question that hangs over Devolution (not that I'm expecting
anything to be sorted today). The threat of being asked to move to London
looms fairly large, and - to be honest - I'm uncertain as to the way I'd be
inclined to jump. "Not" gains some ground. Both options (if I am unable to

steer a middle course) are not entirely comfortable. I wonder if I can put off the evil hour for a couple of years, by which time other things may have begun to crystallise.

Having said that, what things? The only extended influence is Sarah's degree and job. And the house... How much difference do 2 years make? And doesn't a move to the Peaks raise similar issues?

More masturbation.

~~~~

*How telling is it that, after the flood gates were opened in the previous year, these two somewhat inane entires - almost entirely unrelated to his writing - should be the **total** output for 1995? Does it not beg the question as to what happened during the twelve months leading up to August 1995, and to surface once again the knowing that there are answers to be had outside of the notebooks?*

And most relevant of all in the context of our study, what happened to 'Mirrors' after the launchpad of 1994?

Though superficial, perhaps it is sufficient to suggest that 'Life got in the way' and leave it at that. Previewing again (merely to set expectations), there are no entries at all for 1996, and only two bookending 1997. Indeed, the next few years are not only sparse in terms of commentary on his writing (superseded to a degree by his focus on the practicalities of living), but where observations are made, they could be interpreted - on one level at least - as regressive. You might also be forgiven for feeling a sense of disappointment given the relative high of 1994, as if you had been conned into believing something wonderful was about to happen, the blooming of a rare flower. I wonder how this period must have been for him. Had he felt as if he had finally made a meaningful and comprehensive breakthrough - and if so, how desperate did he feel about what immediately followed?

Of course the up-coming years were not barren, so it might just be that they were inadequately documented. Perhaps that is the best way to reflect upon them.

~~~~

9th January 1997 (RBR)

Sixteen months since the last entry - and just over sixteen days until I start my new job at DePuy.

It would be inaccurate to describe this as a difficult time. It almost feels as if it is though. Perhaps it's the bundle of uncertainty - leaving date, starting date, home - that is the cause. Hopefully within the next few days the last of these (a Leeds address) will be known and then I can really begin to look forwards. Thus far I've only been peeping really, attempting a glimpse rather than a long hard stare. It's a bit like not wanting to look in a mirror; not so much because I don't want to see myself, but because of what might be behind me.

The move to Leeds represents a massive personal investment. It's not the changing of jobs or the physical displacement that's the real issue (though they are, of course, challenges). The key aspect of the entire project is the opportunity it offers me for a radical "redefinition" of who I am and what I do. The very real chance to get "closer" to how and what I want to be. Failure here: that is where the real fear lies...

(later)

[Perhaps it is symbolic that on this, my last day in London for Sun Alliance, the trains should fuck up. Cancellations and late running in both directions!]

There may be another aspect aligned with the notion of "failure" above. Of course I was considering the situation with respect to my persona as "writer". The new job will demand that I also fulfil the very public role of IT professional. Obvious potential for failure here too. And on two fronts: can't do and won't do. I don't believe the former to be true; hopefully I have too much experience for that. As far as the latter is concerned, success will be dependent on me accepting for myself that I am an IT professional, and that there's no shame in that. Maybe its critical to success all round that I embrace my new professional (paid) challenges as I will be expected to, and not treat them as an encumbrance for an as yet unfulfilled dream.

~~~~

Would it be fanciful to suggest that his discomfort with his chosen - or 'public' - profession has been an issue lurking in the background from the very beginning, and that he - 'the writer' - and the required 'persona' - as 'IT professional' - were never truly comfortable bedfellows, especially when all he had ever wanted to do (since he was five, remember) was write?

Is that dichotomy at the heart of his comment about "redefinition"?

~~~~

Tempted by the desire to retrace my steps and reread from previous passages
(and certainly the one immediately before this!) I decline, aiming to look
forward. It has been a year worth chronicling - but not here.

So where are we? (This facing another week's Christmas holiday - that strange
luxury! - and a New Year and 40th birthday on the horizon...)

Work is good. Very. I am in control; I can command, direct; I know what I
have to do and the parameters within which I need to work. It has been a solid
investment.

But the unresolved issues are the same old issues. The Achilles' heel of
unfulfilled creativity. Of direction. Of drive. (The latter particularly difficult
considering where I am with work and how much of me that takes. A
comfortable theory to make a nice excuse?!)

I want to build things. At work. At home (the house; my relationships).
Perhaps I am in the business of relaying foundations.

If so, some are now there. But the finer details?

I could create goals for myself. How about "write another novel by my
birthday"? Seems like a laudable aim. But is it one of the "unfinished" ones or
something new? Is it something I could throw myself into whole-heartedly?
(With work going as well as it is, I even find myself questioning this "creative
premise", even though I know it to be undeniable.)

and I wonder about my ability / inability to finish things off. Nev, perhaps. Or
that "collection" of poems. Things gathering dust, not quite in the attic.

(I've just checked. This book represents seven years of musings...)

So much to do, so little time... etc.

So what to do?

Easy ones: continue / restart trying to peddle Nev.
               try to peddle Walking Thru Fire.
Shouldn't be difficult; all that entails is sending off letter after letter and
ducking when the rejections come.

OK, shall we do that then? I'll need a stack of envelops and then it's only money... Hoorah!

But the more tricky stuff. The stuff that takes time. The stuff that requires a real commitment, real ideas; that isn't just mechanistic. (Was Nev inspired and everything else not...?)

(And if it isn't writing, but painting say...)

Jan 1 -> May 21 = 141 days
      - just for reference.

So think...

Two lists - Nev & WTF - and a plan to cover 141 days...

~~~~

And so he has arrived at 1997 and three years on from those golden moments. At least he gives us some clues in this end-of-year reflection: "write another novel" is surely a desire to following up on the unpublished 'The Big Frog Theory' which he speaks of trying to "peddle". Thus far, Agents had not been kind. 'Walking Thru Fire' - something else he saw as 'sellable' - was a collection of poems, and although this is the first we have heard of it, the fact that he had managed to pull together a volume he must have regarded as vaguely cohesive suggests a modicum of progress, does it not?

But the bad old habits are back: the questions about what to write next, the desire for structure or a plan (this time based around the artificial end-date of his birthday)... You could be forgiven for thinking that - in the writing sense at least - 1994 never happened.

~~~~

8th March 1998 (RBR)

On a train (of course!) to Bristol.

Idea for Travel book: Yorkshire by Train. Day trips armed with a notepad & camera; boundaries of Yorks; all on foot. "Various" places...

Over 2 hours later   and no inspiration.

❄

- The Adventures of a Duck called Drake

story of migration of duck with broken wing

e.g. "Drake sets sail"

'Drake considered himself something of a philosopher.'

~~~~

Clutching at straws perhaps - even if the children's story about a duck sounds like a good idea!

The following entry (two months later, just after his birthday) is long and reflective. Unsurprisingly, it largely follows the tropes of so many of his earlier internal debates. But there are elements in his somewhat comprehensive navel-gazing - all 2,000+ words of it - which would benefit from either context or observation.

I offer such an insertion here (even though it is informed by knowledge beyond the notebooks and, as such, is clearly contrary to our initial ground rules).

The "personal vision" to which he refers next relates to an exercise he undertook on a work-sponsored management training course. Starting with a considerable list of attributes, delegates were guided through a process to reduce this down to the five that were the most important to them as individuals. The choices he made not only gives him the basis for the analysis you are about to read, but might also be useful as context for all he has said thus far. How many of these five topics recur again and again, if not in plain sight then semi-disguised in what is, thus far, over fifteen years of self-analysis?

~~~~

23rd May 1998 (RBR)

Forty.

Half-way?

Key to success will be biting off those things on my personal vision. 5 things if I can remember them (the evidence is at work...)

1   Inner harmony
2   Creativity

3	?? was this achievement...?
4	Personal recognition (?)
5	Financial Security

OK, I can't remember them all - but probably enough to philosophise...

| 1 | Inner Harmony - presumably delivered as a result of fulfilling all the others. (it's a theory anyway...) |

| 5 | Financial Security - taken out of order but being achieved thanks to DePuy - so I shouldn't knock it should I? Let's leave that one as a "green" for now... |

| 3 & 4 | Achievement (sic) and Personal Recognition - both driven by 2, which is the key it would seem. |

2 - Creativity

Face facts; I'm the kind of person who needs to express themselves through something creative: writing, painting. Perhaps the quality of the output is less important than the output itself.[15] (Maybe that's why I was so prolific when I was younger and "free" to be so...)

When I'm not being creative, when I don't have a 'project' on the go, everything else suffers... Is it that much of a fulcrum? Yes, it is.

Stop denying it!

OK, but there's nothing new there. I mean, it's what I've always known -

- and consistently failed to live up to...

Why? What stops it happening?

Much of the Achievement & Personal recognition is self-esteem rather than (or above?) the recognition of others. Where, for example, do I get the biggest buzz? Finishing things that I think are OK: Nev, the poems, the Thackley article, the Derain paintings...

Why don't I finish more things then?

---

[15] This may be the first time he has made the distinction between output and the quality of that output.

Because I do the wrong things?
Because I blame time?
Because I make up excuses?

- knowing all these things are spurious and actually doing more harm than good.

Perhaps I pursue 5 because I am forced to i.e. I have to work, there's no excuse. And because I can use it as a means of justifying why I don't do 2...

Perhaps I have too low a view of my own efforts. Maybe I should be more confident - arrogant even - about the things I produce. This might encourage being prolific.

I not only need to believe in this, but I also need to believe in the vision. I need to see it as realistic, achievable, somehow ideal. Others have done it.

Cowardice?

Remember, 5 is OK. In the short-term nothing should be done to jeopardise this as everything would collapse. So I need to accept it as good, ok, normal, essential and all that kind of stuff.

Balance has to be key.

Environment - getting to the stage where I can finish 50 "things" a year - must be the goal. There must be positive pursuit, not negative retreat.

We're talking about arriving at a situation where things (in the broadest sense of "Life Experience") are actually viewed as profoundly OK.

Perhaps I have forgotten how to be positive...

Hanging on the result of a few plastic balls dropping at 8pm on a weekly basis[16] - with the consequent disappointment - is not an acceptable way to continue. It offers nothing. The dream becomes more important than living and aspiring to the vision. The vision is lost, takes on the status of dream[17]; becomes one and the same thing, and therefore - through continual disappointment - shifts from something that is realistic and attainable to

---

[16] The National Lottery

[17] Approximate definitions for his use of these terms: 'Vision', something articulated that is achievable; 'Dream', something vague, unachievable, and out of his control.

something that is ever-further out of reach and impossible to conceive. It moves to something out of my sphere, over which I have no control, and therefore an element of frustration. The frustration leads to excuse-making, and thus the downward spiral. Fulfilment becomes something over which I abdicate control - not something I have within my power to grasp. This is essentially a false and paradoxical position because 5, while it places significant demands on my time, is more an enabler than anything else. The centre of my "world", my "vision", becomes therefore a void: something black and un-wholly / unholy, a thing to be defied, not embraced. There is a profound "lack" at the centre of all things - which denies 2, prevents 3 & 4 in <u>any</u> sense, and makes 1 impossible. 5 remains all there is, and is therefore to be resented as it is seen as something that has supplanted <u>all</u> the things that are more important.

Take a bow, Mr. Freud!

*

Six hours on and the above still makes sense. In fact, the duration has seen the next logical question beginning to nag.

What is the next step?

There have been attempts in the past to move forwards; to create an environment or regime (if nothing else!) in which something can be achieved. I have pursued framework above all else, trying to tackle the partially defined problem as analytically as I might anything at work. It seemed that there had to be a plan...

Which in one sense is absolutely correct - but it needed to be a plan which freed and enabled, rather than constrained and restricted. A plan made up entirely of rules by which one attempts to bind oneself is, after all, just another means of abdication. It is not an example of the exercise of control, but rather further relinquishing of control. It removes the need to think, to be flexible, to be constructive - to be imaginative and creative in a "living" sense, and surely this is a prerequisite to any attempt at creation? (Perhaps the Thackley[18] piece was partially satisfying because it represented something more dynamic; an unplanned event which yielded a result - a result achieved through a more genuine creative impulse than "it's 8pm on Monday and therefore time to write a poem"...)

---

[18] Refers to the Thackley Locks on the Leeds & Liverpool canal about which he wrote a small impromptu piece ('travel' or 'colour').

Again, nothing earth-shattering, novel or unknown here is there? But it still doesn't help in terms of finding a way from the bottom of the vortex. Where is the impulse that begins, drives, continues progress up the spiral? If I assume that these notes alone will not work the miracle (and experience helps this analysis) then I need to find some other aid, structure or whatever, to provide that momentum.

Should it be both internal and external? Think back to the influence of the writing Group in Bristol[19]... Is something akin to that an option? And for other than writing?

But one step at a time. There are still some fundamental questions which need at least reconfirmation, if not re-visiting and re-answering.

In no particular order:
a, in what "form" do I choose to express myself?[20]
b, if "Art", what sub-form should I choose?
c, and what subject?
d, if "Writing", what sub-form should I choose?
e, and what subject?
f, and are there any other "forms" that I should be considering?

g, and then again; how do I make the next step? (which is where I've just come from...)

So, more answers...

a, Easy: writing and drawing/painting.
b, Also Easy: oils, watercolour, ink, pencil.
c, ah...
d, East too: prose, poetry, speech, non-fiction
e, ahhh...
f, Probably - like toying with the idea of sculpture...

But before g, just how obvious are the answers above? When, for example, did I produce my last piece of play-work? How many pieces of non-fiction have there been? Who am I kidding?

---

[19] At this point he has been living in Leeds for three years.

[20] Isn't it astonishing that, after all this time, he is still asking himself the same questions? It seems as if there remains - and perhaps there always has been - a fear to commit to the one true answer; the one he has known since he was a boy.

(As an aside, I am beginning to wonder if my great liberator - the PC - hasn't actually conspired to entrap me. It does, after all, force a creative location, demand a certain environment - all of which is an example of my abdication of control perhaps...?)

So perhaps b, and d, should be "anything". That should be the more correct answer. 'Whatever seems right' is better; 'whatever I <u>feel</u> like' perhaps better still. After all, I thought Nev was going to be a poem...

When I was young, I filled notebook after notebook with freehand... And why not a sketchbook too? And why shouldn't they go wherever I am?

OK, redefine the answers to b and d... Which only leaves c, e and g.

Only. !

Encore.

What do I want to write about?
What do I want to create visually?
Where do I start?

I guess my traditional view has been that the novel is the prose form I should aspire to, and that which I should pursue. Similarly, I might have reasonably parallel considerations about painting, oil and/or watercolour.

These assumptions / inspirations may be incorrect. Just saying, OK? One could make a case against them from the viewpoint of how long they take to 'complete' - certainly as far as the novel goes. And remember, denying the novel (for now) does not deny prose. Obviously.

But I could muddy the waters too much here by searching for some kind of "global" argument which purports to give me an answer to everything - which is impossible.

I also do not want to force myself to choose; in choosing there is a process where something is rejected and in rejecting one builds the cage of limitation again.

Is it reasonable (or workable) then to say that everything is included, everything valid? And if so, how does one begin to answer the third question - or g, - about making a start? What role structure?

Maybe a return to the dream / vision[21] debate would be useful. Perhaps I need to generate a realistic and achievable version and work towards that. Example? Dream - the forever elusive - a published, best-selling novel. Vision - the realistic goal - a completed, but unpublished collection of poems. (I could create similar images for the Art-side.)

Rejecting dream in favour of vision does not negate the former or say that it will never happen. It perhaps puts it into perspective; allows one to regain control over the vision - which then becomes the first in a series of steps towards the dream (which, by the way, may never be fulfilled - but a succession of visions achieved is probably more than enough by way of compensation!)

Following on from this, creation of a series of "vision things" is the first step towards answering the "what next?" question.

Easier said than done? Let's try...

<u>Vision things</u>

Are they - or should they be -
     Concrete?
     Realistic?   Yes   Yes
     Tightly definable?
     Measurable?
     Qualitative?   Yes
     Quantitative?
     Focussed?   Yes
     Time-bound?
     Scheduled?   ^   ^
                    | |
   Writing answers here — | |
      - and Arty answers over here — — |

Examples?
- a collection of poems
- a sketchbook

We could end up with a list of vague 'nice to haves' which maybe won't actually allow much progress. But I can't stop now. This maybe the best

---

[21] For me his whole 'Dream vs. Vision' proposition is in danger of becoming cloudy and muddled-thinking: are they the wrong way round? Is one actually the other? But rather than try and edit it to make it more coherent, I have decided to leave it as drafted.

narrated analysis of my frustration, so it deserves the chance to get worked out doesn't it?

Writing first - because it's probably easier to debate, and I have a ready example:

A collection of poems

Concrete?	Vaguely
Realistic?	Yes
Tightly definable?	No
Measurable?	Only by a sense of progress and completeness - which is OK.
Qualitative?	Yes
Quantitative?	No; why should 60 be better than 16?
Focussed?	Possibly - though not in terms of subject matter I suspect
Time-bound?	Only if I want to fail (and failure should be built out of the equation)
Scheduled?	See answer above!

Which gives us a vague and poorly defined objective - but that might just be ok... In fact, I'm sure I can live with it in this case; but where does the stimulus come from? What is the driver? What makes me pick up my pen?

I sense an impasse that needs time to breathe...

✿

Of course, I did have those ideas about creating a magazine of some kind (based on Lottery money and "young" writers) as well as publishing a volume of my poetry myself. Neither of these seemed (at the time) to be particularly wild ideas - and I have to say that, some months on, they still appear reasonable. Vision rather than dream.

Of course, these being fundamentally 'practical' goals, they require a different sort of commitment - not only time, but money too. Still, no reason to give up just because of that (DePuy - money - an "enabler", remember...). A plan (in the strictest sense) would obviously be called for here: maybe I could do worse things with my time than rough something out...

✿

And then there was the idea of making train journeys. Possibly not weekly, but after the Thackley experience perhaps a series of "travelling" pieces might be a good / refreshing experience.

A spin-off (non-literary) of the travelling pieces would be to take the sketchbook too. Killing two birds...

So, some poems and a few 'travel' pieces will make up a 'casual' collection - almost as some kind of background programme. No hard and fast targets, but lots of opportunities to finish things.

If I added in the more "editorial" possibilities there would be a lot of work there. Time for anything else?

27th September 1998 (RBR)

Not even tempted to re-read that last lot until I've got this down. (but just let me make a note of these: Inner Harmony; Creativity; Privacy; Economic Security; Time Freedom. The real 5 - the last ones were close, but not close enough. And maybe I'd question Privacy now...)

Anyway, let's get on.

In 5 days time (or thereabouts) I start my "new career" as a freelance IT consultant; a move away from permanent employment and into a slightly less certain environment. Risk? I guess. But at least I've got a "safe" start.

Enough of the boring practical facts of the matter - Let's analyse!

The most critical element of this whole process - this "breaking free" - is the very real notion of selling my most precious commodity, my time, on my basis, and to the degree which I choose. My rules. I can't possibly define the sense of "rightness" of the move; all I know is that I've the chance now, and if I don't take it...

Especially as it's a step along my timeline to the future I think I want. One tick in the box. One of the things I know I needed to change in order to make very real progress. Now I just have to make it work...

So let's have a little look at the impact on the "big 5", just to make sure that the general direction is right - practically logical as well as emotionally sound.

Or emotionally life-saving.

Time Freedom. Big ✓ here. Probably cutting down my average working week from 5 to 3 days or thereabouts. And not only that, as much "holiday" as I can afford to take. The move does, quite literally, "free time".

Economic Security. The risk is here. There would have to be a **X** for the general principal. But if it works well, I can get a big ✓ (though too big, and I'm in danger of jeopardising the time thing). Mustn't lose sight of why I'm doing all this. Shall we say **?** then - until proven.

Privacy. May need to come back to that one.

Creativity. Ok, so there's more time. It can only be up to me to make the most of that time. The answer has to be a big ✓ or else I'm failing myself. Making the most of the new "free" time will be critical - but it will be less like the old dilemma because it won't be an all-or-nothing thing. It should be more relaxed, more manageable.

Inner Harmony? With 2½ / 3 above then the signs have to be good, surely. This could be a pretty major step in a very right direction. No bull.

And I think I may have to can 'Privacy'...! I'd probably have to give it a **X** - in the sense that I'll need to sell myself to ensure that there's a flow of work. On the other hand, I could take the view that being an "outsider" offers me insurance against getting involved on a 'permanent' day-to-day level with people. I have to be responsible for - or responsible to. I don't know. Another **?**.

Even so, that's 4 / 5 if it goes ok.

So not a bad move then...?

—

And now I've read back, 3 things strike me.

1 - the power of the dream / vision analysis
2+3 - the ideas of the collections; poetry + travel - which time conspires to aid in delivery...

~~~

Although there are clearly echoes of the "twelve tenets" in the above, the five priorities on which he alighted were surely more appropriate, meaningful, 'personal'. You might argue that it was just another example of the same self-delusion, the belief that there was a formula somewhere that would work for him to de-mist - and demystify - what he was constantly staring into, the conundrum he was trying to solve. But wouldn't it be more charitable to regard these efforts as attempts to crystallise what was profoundly internal and nebulous, as if he were trying to find a way to approach 'the problem' from the other way round?

That's all well and good, of course, and any framework might have suited his purpose; but whichever one he chose, success would depend on the decisions he subsequently made and those being followed through to some kind of conclusion.[22] Does it matter that his articulation of dream vs. vision may have been inadequate or muddled; wasn't it more important that he had come up with something? Perhaps seeing something through and turning theory into output had always been his biggest issue, encapsulated in the fact that 1994 appeared to be - indeed, should have been - the launchpad.

But then he was just about to try again...

~~~~

<div align="right">

16th & 17th October 1998 (RBR)

</div>

My first "day off" under the new regime (after a whole week, and another 4 days of work). Little difference really - except that the occasion is marked by coming out of Leeds for a short weekend with Sarah in Derbyshire.

Next week begins the critical time in a sense. Tuesday. A mid-week day off, away from work; my time. Here will begin the measure of making the most of what I'm buying into.

The day will probably contain a run and at least one game of chess[23] - two things I'm targeting to help re-establish an all-round sense of well-being: fitness both physical and mental. Somehow I don't have any real concerns about these two... The measure will be avoiding spending the bulk of the day in mindless pursuit - particularly redundant game-playing. (My vice, I know.)

The age-old question of making time spent worthwhile re-surfaces in a somewhat different guise. Almost certainly I'll need to spend part of these days

---

[22] Though he was kidding himself to think that he had any meaningful talent in 'art'.

[23] Played against his computer.

in "professional" mode: doing accounts, reading journals, even trying to write pieces myself - published and selling, the establishing of "guru" status. (A kind of investment in its own right.)

I've thought of entering into a contract with myself, financially based where I reward myself for "output". Novel idea! Say I get a flat rate for my consultancy work - maybe £2k pcm. To earn more over and above that I need to produce things and "get paid" accordingly. So we could be looking at a certain amount per poem, painting or 1000 words... A matrix. Words per month; payment per 1000 words:

	5,000	10,000	15,000	20,000
£10	£50	£100	£150	£200
£25	£125	£250	£375	£500
£50	£250	£500	£750	£1000
£100	£500	£1000	£1500	£2000
£200	£1000	£2000	£3000	£4000

If I needed £200 pcm extra as a minimum then I'd have to shoot low - £10-£25 per 1000 (£10 per 1,000 is 1p per word...)

Is this too fanciful; too rigid? Is it too much like the forced formula I was trying to get away from? Should simply having the time be driver enough?

Probably.

Is this eye off the ball? A retreat into the mechanistic - which has failed all too often in the past?

On Tuesday 20th, I'm gifting myself around 9 hours (8 'til 5) that I didn't have before. It's a present. I've managed to put myself in a position where I can do this. I can take a bus, a train; stay in bed, write all day; walk in the park - whatever. So why be prescriptive in advance?

It would however, be nice to start this period with a new project. Like the running, or playing chess. Something embryonic.

Maybe that's what I spend the next 3 days trying to decipher...

❂

Idea in the Biddulph Grange tea room.

"Man sitting in café looking out of window at leaves tugging the trees. Autumnal. Memories of a previous visit and a woman. Café fills. Another man comes and sits at the table. Starts conversation. Angel? Need to establish relationship between the two quickly. Sense of dependence, one upon the other (2nd & 1st) when in reality the dependence is the other way round. needs to be something charming about the 2nd man; perhaps a childish helplessness that attracts the first (non-sexual)."

What is this? Echoes of James Stewart and Clarence? Danger of being coy, so must resist the obvious. Need to be mysterious and a little obtuse. Things must be "cloudy" and opaque.

It may be a short story; seems too fragile to offer more than that. Of course there are two major elements outstanding - a middle and an end! A premise shouldn't be too difficult (based around the woman) but given that it might be a sort piece - and therefore need to be "taut" - I'll need to be aware of all elements before I begin.

❋

The tree is a bay tree, and the café based on the café in Bosham. The man is reflecting on the woman he met there once (name? Katherine perhaps) and the opportunities he had to get to know her later but did not take. The second man - Matt(hew) Angel? - acts as a kind of confessor.

After they leave the café, Matt asks about an old church nearby, and the first man shows him the old Norman church. Matt seems a little too familiar with it (the way he touches the Knight Templars' cross etched on the lintel, for example).

As they walk round a woman's voice calls out. It is Katherine. It appears that she too has met Matt before, and now he acts as the catalyst that brings the two of them back together.

The three walk round the church, but at some point Matt disappears, leaving the two of them together (and thus fulfilling the first man's dream). Katherine suggests tea, and they return to the café where they first saw each other. It is here that they play out - or replay - their brief history apart.

The story is about regret and missed opportunity. It is also about the damage that "what might have been" can do. Matt gives both the man and Katherine a chance to exorcise their past and cleanse themselves of the negativity such emotion brings with it.

The question remains over the conclusion: how do they leave the café? What has happened in their separate pasts that now drives / restricts their futures? Is it

a) a positive ending, in that they are free to begin the relationship they both had wanted?

b) a positive ending, in that they both realise that they have "good enough" lives anyway and that their time together might have been fatally flawed (this exorcises the regret and completes the circle).

c) a negative ending, in that they are both still restrained / trapped by circumstance (rather than failure of personality) and are unable to consummate the relationship that they still feel they desire - the lack and regret remains.

d) or a combination of b) and c) in that they decide to embark on some kind of illicit relationship which might compromise their individual "presents" in order to give them a chance to fulfil their "pasts".

Of course, the ending could be one-sided - but hey! this isn't reality!

~~~~

He wrote the story. Titled "The Bay Tree", it appeared in his collection of short stories 'Secrets & Wisdom' which he was to go on and publish in 2017. So that first week of his new regime did succeed in delivering something - but, like 1994, it was to prove another 'false dawn', and 1999 offered just two further entries in the notebooks.

~~~~

17th April 1999 (RBR)

Six and a half years since the opening of this journal...

And only a few months since the last entry - much changed however.

The new regime is fine - given that I haven't changed "employer", am working less, and getting paid so much more... "Fine" is a bit of an understatement!

But then this isn't about domestic arrangements, this book. It's been about being creatively productive - and there have been movements too...

An experiment, which could be seen as a combination of the kinds of ideas I had been playing with, visiting racecourses and writing about them: some history, fiction, fly-on-the-wall reportage. And OK because I like racing and find it interesting.

However, after Southwell, Wetherby and Newcastle, my trip to Market Rasen (now some two or three weeks ago) remains undrafted. The question I have to ask myself is "why?"

My concern is that I may have been defeated by the "sameness" of the three chapters thus far. That there is only so much that can be said about a day's racing. That mixing 'business' with 'pleasure' isn't working. That the days have begun to be associated with failure (in a betting sense[24]) and hence the lack of desire to keep repeating the experience.

And, more telling, the possibility that the lack of creative opportunities is the most frustrating of all. If that is the case, then completing the exercise - another 17 chapters! - is unlikely to be on.

Again there is a need to do something as the frustration of not being productive is beginning to tell...

Balance, equilibrium - words that keep recurring. Knowing when work is there, taking advantage of it is critical perhaps. Ensuring that I take advantage of the non-working days is also critical. So, balance and equilibrium...

Do I need to go through the same old debate and process of elimination?

A couple of ideas that popped in early this morning (before I was out of bed, almost) 1 - a book on Systems' Management (that "Guru feeling..."); 2 - Big Frog Books, funded by the day job. I suspect 1 may be more realistic / rewarding than 2. It might be easier to get published too!

OK, so getting the output is probably not going to be too much of an issue. Execution of a plan, after all. (And given advice from that crap book I read not long ago, planning is all.)

Nev wasn't planned - what does that say? Once it got going it had a life of its own. Should I be looking for something like that again?

~~~~

I suspect "lack of creative opportunities" is shifting the blame somewhat. Was the real issue during this fallow period more to do with a lack of ideas? That and the considerable personal pressures he had been under (see the next entry).[25]

---

[24] Though in truth, he never lost very much money on these days.

[25] On a happier note, he and Sarah married in June 1999.

It occurs to me - this seated on a train (where else?) to Birmingham to see Ed in the kids' hospital there[26] - that this log (which might well turn into a book of it's own - <u>how</u> ironic!) is filled with questions begging answers, but where none of the answers amount to very much.

Of course for a transitory period - the end of the experiment, the end of the journey, the end of the entry(!) - they must have some kind of validity, but...

For the sake of an update, both the racing book and the systems' management book - which got as far as a plan and some draft words - are at publishers doing their own interpretation of begging. Mind you, after 7 weeks or so, I suspect they're actually lying in a doorway begging coppers rather than on their way to returning home flushed with success! (If they did come home victorious, wouldn't <u>that</u> put the proverbial cat where it wasn't wanted!)

Assuming the realistic route then the questions that beg at my door are the usual ones. Mind you, there is an added pungency this time. With my contract at DePuy having finished I am - in Actors' parlance - "resting". Such an ability to "rest" was something I'd always argued for on the basis that I'd use the spare time to address my bigger issue i.e. it would remove the greatest block on my not writing.

As I had perhaps suspected all along, this may well have been no more than bluff. Look at Nev...

It is interesting how he returns to The Big Frog Theory, holding it up as an example of not only what could be done, but <u>how</u> it could be done i.e. the organic spontaneity of it rather than slogging his way through a detailed but sterile plan.

And there are glimmers of hope here too. Evidently he got far enough with his ideas for both the horse racing travelogue (the free time to do so funded by his new working regime, remember) and the IT management book for the propositions to be submitted to publishers.

On reflection, in spite of the apparent paucity in terms of forward movement, 1999 shouldn't be regarded as a complete disaster. The next entry comes thirteen

---

[26] His son from his first marriage (only infrequently and tangentially referred to in these notes) who was then undergoing life-saving surgery, aged 7.

months later, and you can decide for yourself how much progress you feel he has made - not just over the prior year, but all the way back to 1993.

~~~~

<div align="right">

10th October 2000 (RBR)

</div>

And now, 7 years on, still struggling with the same questions - and still trying to find a fountain pen I can be happy with (and how much is this a symbol of the larger search? a failed talisman)

So the "rest" has come and gone, and with it the descent - once again - into professional hell. Needing money; taking the first job; the poisoned chalice.

Still, I have never been as "wealthy" as I am right now with £12k sitting in savings accounts - even if £7k of that is needed to pay off the car. But Paris for the weekend? "No problem Sir!"

What does remain a problem, of course, is the eternal question of creative satisfaction despite various half-arsed attempts to "get the ball rolling".

I can point to some success - though even this is being tarnished with the passage of time. My IT Strategy and Management book 'bought' by a publisher (contract and all!) but where there has been an ominous silence since the heady days of late summer! Time to rattle a cage - and to discover my plumed messenger dead on its perch. Not even asleep I suspect. Phythonesque.

So, preoccupations with work and the tracking down of something akin to professional satisfaction. A demanding and all-consuming effort, at least from an emotional perspective; leaving little time for consideration of how else I can satisfy myself (even knowing that a head buried in computerised football management games is masturbation).

The theory (I am sure expounded in other pages here) is one of a downward vortex (more powerful than a spiral!) which sees the cancer of dissatisfaction with work eating at healthy things until all that is left <u>is</u> the cancer. This has happened before: Sun Alliance, DePuy. So no surprises.

But, in order to attempt salvation (once again!) perhaps to argue that I allow it to happen; embrace it as an excuse for collapse - rather than adopt the alternative position. Namely that creativity generates a positive, upward vortex that allows work to be carried in this direction rather than the other... Thus the call is to break in... And like phantoms from another life (all too

<div align="center">117</div>

repetitive) the words regime, structure, pattern, plan come back to haunt me, and I feel the urge to chart - and con myself in the process! - rise inexorably.

But one should take the positive view. To do nothing is, well, to do nothing.

And it's not just about work or writing or creativity. It's about being fit, healthy, ready to give the next 30 years a shot. (Aside: seeing a book advertised for 'Great Sex for the 40-50s'. Was I supposed to have stopped enjoying it already? I certainly don't feel inclined to pack it in. Indeed, after 7 years (was I really already 35 then?) "packing it in" embraces a greater degree of finality. One day when things are 'packed in' that is undoubtedly the way they will remain. And that day draws physically (in all senses) ever-closer.)

So, status quo then.

But not quite. Perhaps not if we try a different spin. Shovel in a few different words like 'enthusiasm', 'motivation', 'hobby' - almost anything to take the mystique away.

And some different motivations too. The idea, perhaps, of doing something positive every day; something of which one can be proud, or which makes a contribution (like this entry). Remembering the idea of self-esteem - and recognising the need to go searching for it in the dustbin once again. Where did I leave it...?

So much is down to laziness. That I just can't be arsed to make the effort, and on that basis will just let things slip on by. "Where did September go?" is a question that actually works on at least two levels.

Markers. Some sticks in the ground. This is my position. This my goal. I have a compass and a ready smile (remember those days!), the tools to engineer some kind of resurrection.

(And that nagging voice again that wants to see a list, a chart, a plan; that demands to know, to foresee - and forestall! - the future...)

So. (Having made coffee and partially lost the flow.) The notion of doing something positive every day. Take tomorrow. How about going to work and defining my new role i.e. what I want to do and contribute (at least until the next professional challenge comes alone...)

And, racing ahead, something simple for Saturday like sorting out an Autumnal garden and "arranging" the greenhouse. (Maybe the question is a very simple one after all: "What can I do that will make me feel 'better' once I have done it?" - and on this basis, consider the cumulative impact of steps of betterness...)

This is a relatively simple notion - and goes nowhere near the difficult taboo subjects of creativity and creative satisfaction. Perhaps that makes things easier.

(Absurd notion? Each week becomes a heptathlon, with 7 events/days, points earned based on achievements that week. Records would tumble...)

On this basis a list might well be viable, lining up potential "events" for the week, thus:
                Running * Exercising * Squash
                Gardening * Decorating * Theatre
                Work * Photography * Cinema
                Writing * Drawing * Painting

This is a different kind of list, with a different kind of balance. And there could be others too: eating fruit (!) +ve; drinking alcohol (-ve)

A kind of "life diet"...

And why not? Where is the harm? Who else is going to work on this but me?

The alternative - as we have said so many times before - is remarkably unpalatable. More than that, it is by definition inactivity, and as such is negative, debilitating and wasteful - in the most profound of senses.

My heptathlon scoring chart could of course be biased towards the creative; more for writing than eating fruit... But to set a daily target, a weekly target. To have the evidence to back-up the fact that you <u>know</u> you have had a good day... Made tangible... Proof.

Something diaries were made for?!

Running - 50 Breaking record +1 pt/% time
Exercising - 20 Increasing reps by 10%, +5 pts
Squash - 30 pts (or more); fruit + 5 pts
Gardening - 10 pts per hour; booze -25 pts
Theatre - 100 pts; Cinema 75 pts
Photography - 100 pts per session (min photos?)
Work - 25 pts per positive action / contribution

Writing - 10 pts per 100 words...?
Drawing/Painting - 100 pts per hour

Needs refinement, but a minimum of 100 pts/day...? Target 200?

Also: Reading 1pt / page
           Making love 50 pts
           Computer games -1 pt / minute

Time out...

All fine. And even the act of putting this (something!) down gets me a little closer with tiny imaginative ferrets running towards the notion of a collection of something: short stories, poems... The ability to put pen to paper - literally or via the monstrous chip?

Tomorrow? or Now? Saturday? When does the week start? When will the deflection begin?

...trawling through the PC to identify the scale of unfinished things...

Gisella	- Italy, travel & letters	July '00
Book One	- the A-Z thriller	Nov '99
The Test	- Futuristic & all planned out	Oct '99

...and older...

Mita's shopping	- Nev's sequel	Mar '97
Mirrors	- !!!	Nov '96
Hit & Run	- another thriller	Dec '97
141 days	- the last year diary	Jan '98

...plus other bits and pieces

Where the fuck did time go?

And isn't there enough here, <u>really</u>?!

~~~~

Well, isn't this just more of the same ague? Hasn't he just rewound ten or twenty years? On one level, undoubtedly yes, recognising he is "still struggling with the same questions". But in this entry there is a harder edge, a sharpness, a greater dissatisfaction not just with his 'position' but with himself. There is more of the Realist in this self-berating.

However, I wonder how much of what he is saying here was born from the 'need' to say something, and hence the repetition: 'I have a notebook and I'm going to write in it'... If you were to filter out all the noise (for there is undoubtedly noise) what would you be left with? It depends on your perspective and what you wanted to see in the first place. It is always thus. As ever, the proof of these individual little puddings are in the eating - or, more precisely, what comes after the eating. I am tempted to suggest that the harshness of this self-analysis sets a new tone and is a good thing. I would also not want to skim over the success with his professional book - in spite of it being dismissed in a tone which anticipates last-minute betrayal and disappointment. [A short update follows in the next entry...]

And most notably of all, at the end of the entry his list of "unfinished things": 'Mirrors', dated to 1996 even though we know it has been unfinished far longer than that; the idea for a follow-up to 'Nev' (therefore, I would suggest, validating for him its presence in his canon and his achievement in getting it there); and 'Gisella' which - thanks to the corruption of foreknowledge - I know is something to which he will return.

The rest? Essentially false starts; projects which never got off the ground in spite of significant planning (in the case of 'The Test') and some initial - but minimal - drafting in one or two others.

~~~~

15ᵗʰ October 2000 (RBR)

"The scale of unfinished things…"

But my book is going to be published; there's even a dedicated page on the Publisher's website.

And I have an interview for the IT Director job at Sheffield Hallam University.

And I started on my life diet programme yesterday, and actually went for a run… 3 hours gardening this morning…

The power of words…

But now, sitting at the PC (switched on) and attempting to resist the lure of one form of football or another over...everything...

So, for the moment, I've shut it down.

This period is always the most difficult. The two-hour window, open to be filled however I choose - inevitably to choose the easy option: something that requires minimal movement, effort, creative thought. (Often accompanied by a lame excuse about being "tired" from work - as if!)

But I might run again later. Another 50 points as I chase yesterday's total of 90 (sic).

I know I need to write, of course. The prospect of SHU[27] brings mixed emotions: excitement at the potential; fear at the expectation - theirs, not mine. Published! Worth a few points I would imagine. But beyond that. To work again in an environment which demands mental discipline and rigour; knowing that it will be harder to "get away" with things... Best not to contemplate it too much...

So, I need to reconcile how I'm going to earn my 10 pts / 100 words. It was one hell of an unfinished list...!

Maybe after '7th Day' there will be a clamour to follow this up. Perhaps the definitive 60k words on 'Horizon Planning'... Who knows? In the interim something other...

Something old, something new, etc. etc.

3rd December 2000 (RBR)

The points-thing worked for a short while then went by the wayside. It did help a little in terms of focus though - and if nothing else, helped to provide a value framework around my running.

So, having now joined a gym (via E²) I have a goal to work towards. The Great North Run 2001. To this end I've a running schedule (3 days a week) and efforts at the gym are bearing fruit in terms of stamina, fitness, weight loss.

If I can keep this up - and keep to my planned schedule - then I have one box with a very big tick in it.

---

[27] He didn't get the job at SHU, so carried on working for the Internet service provider (Energis²) that had been employing him since early 2000, hence the reference in the next entry.

Other boxes?

Well, after 4 years, I have finally got around to finishing Chapter 31 of "Mirrors". Now @ 130k words - after effectively 20 years! It would be good to finish…

The block (as ever) is the degree of uncertainty over my role at E^2. Having said that, my new position (starting in earnest in January) offers me the chance to re-start my E^2 "career" and remove the need to look for a new job, upheaval etc. No doubt that engineering something @ E^2 to keep me occupied and positive is the most sensible thing I could do. It would remove a number of concerns, promote stability, and ensure that I was financially OK.

(Evidence of the latter is the trip to Kenya in March/April and France in July/ August. The former also excites me in terms of taking some watercolours with me…!)

So, the next 3 weeks will see a degree of focus on my work - and the preoccupation with engineering something that will keep me busy / happy. I am reasonably confident that this will come - but we're still at 70/30 or 60/40 and these numbers need to change over the next few days.

If we can get to the 22nd Dec with this resolved - i.e. I have something to look forward to in January from a work perspective - then that will be 2 boxes with ticks in!

Key to all of this - i.e. my Sanity! - may be the change of attitude. I'm trying casual at work (because I can) and suits only when I need to. The environment allows this, and a more relaxed physical attitude is a good thing (I hope!).

✱

Self-esteem is a major thing. Not sure I realised how major. Perhaps when young, youthful arrogance is invested with - or born from - so much self-esteem that there isn't really a problem.

Maybe 3 years ago I began to realise its criticality. Maybe more recently than that, I've seen how much has leaked away over the years.

So the running is about self-esteem (as well as health & fitness). Work would be about self-esteem too - and there's no doubt that I've taken a kicking here since leaving DePuy. Maybe even while I was at DePuy.

Going to Kenya - being able to <u>afford</u> to go - is about s-e. Having £14k savings is about s-e. (even if half of it goes to paying off the car...)

Following the tack, writing becomes another element of s-e. Finishing "Mirrors", for example, earns big s-e bucks - and coming back to where I started this entry, my points log, is about s-e bucks too...

~~~~

Is there a sense here that 2000 could be a turning point? How significant is it that, after all this time(!), he is able to say that he has actually finished another chapter of 'Mirrors'? "It would be good to finish" feels as if the project had been elevated in importance.

Obviously this thread revolves around his recognising the criticality of self-esteem; and, taking that as a lens, some of his earlier entries - especially the one of 10th October - could, I suggest, be re-read in a new light. If you consider what is giving him hope at this point, then you have to recognise - as he does - how his self-esteem is tangibly boosted by his running and the upcoming visit to Africa. Would it be fanciful to argue that the challenge with writing is that it offers far less tangible results when it comes to the improvement of self-perception? Perhaps in this context, the mere existence of 'The Big Frog Theory' is even more important: proof, in the form of real words on (at this stage) virtual sheets of paper, of what he is actually able to achieve. All the rest of it - the ideas, the notions, the plans - are nebulous ephemera until they are turned into something concrete. As he said a little while ago, "to do nothing is, well, to do nothing". If that is the case, has his struggle - across all these years - been with things he cannot actually grasp, that are not, in a profound sense, 'real'? And if so, is that why he has been simultaneously preoccupied with - if not blown off-course by - work and money and relationships, because those are real and affecting and impactful?

~~~~

17th December 2000 (RBR)

Only 2 weeks on - but far enough to be able to add a couple of items of confirmation.

1 - Running is working! I am about to apply for entry for my first ever "competitive" run: 10k in February, aiming for a time of around 50 mins. Today, after nearly 4 weeks in the gym, I re-ran an outdoor route and took 3 mins off a 29 min time for 4 miles. Works wonders for confidence!

2 - It appears that I do now have a fresh role at work which will do for me. More flesh on the bones next week, but I'm reasonably certain that it will result in something contributive and stimulating enough to take uncertainty away.

So - as hoped - ticks in 2 boxes!

Of course, in the search for another "tick" - the creative one - I need to recognise that 1 & 2 will consume much of my time. Consuming that and physical / mental effort leaves a limited resource. This has been proven in that my aim to finish "Mirrors" collapsed very quickly, the end of Chapter 31 seeing the end of the effort.

So if it's not "Mirrors"...?

Looking at my running, I'd say it's working because a) it's enjoyable, b) it's regular - but not too demanding, c) I can work to a programme, and d) I can measure achievement. (Nearly said 'improvement', but that would be too restricting a word...)

I think the challenge has to be to find a creative outlet which allows me to work in an a, b, c, d environment.

(Maybe I've been down this road before - but never with a working example!)

I also wonder if it should definitely not be PC associated. (Another Old Chestnut, I know, but maybe still valid.)

So: a - Enjoy
       b - Regular
       c - Programmed
       d - Measured achievement

Given such criteria, how does writing fit?

Like many things, I guess it could be shoe-horned into such a framework. "c" is possibly not so easy - unless there's a clearly defined outline of what needs to be produced and when (akin to distances, times etc.). "d" equates to output. Is this enough though - even though it will be tangible?

(break).

And in the break I applied for 2 races...

Another false start for 'Mirrors'. At this point, did he ever think he was going to finish it, I wonder? Did he believe it was always going to be there in the background, like an itch he couldn't scratch?

In the above, only the commitment to running is really new ...

~~~~

There is something inevitable about disappointment which, while it can be either debilitating or enervating (if not both!), is unfortunately undeniable.

Which is one reason why this diary is begun on the 2nd of the New Year rather than the first. And why there are no more New Year's resolutions.

Because their failure is inevitable. Because any commitment to a daily record is surely doomed - so why not get the disappointment out of the way as early as possible i.e. miss the first deadline to get it over with.

Christmas is, of course, a time of general disappointment. (Sweeping statement which, I recognise, may only hold true for a proportion of the population; but nevertheless, a proportion to which I belong. Something which is looked forward to with increasing anticipation as the years go by - possibly paradoxically - and which fails to hit the mark with an ever-increasing degree of inaccuracy.)

Oddly tangible things - like the reaction to presents, given and received - to more significant instances; more solid and defining incidents. Things which help to clarify and solidify so much about oneself; about how you really want to be.

In many respects, of course, none of this actually mattered. It was merely what it stood for - encapsulated or signified - which was significant.

~~~~

For the first time I have taken a hatchet to one of his entries... This one majored on the domestic lows surrounding Christmas, and in particular disappointments relating to - and driven by - his parents. There was nothing in the seven or eight paragraphs I deleted which had any connection to writing.

~~~~

A couple of things worthy of note - or at least passing recognition…

MB2000 yesterday confirmed that the editing of "On the Seventh Day"[28] is progressing and that I should have the proofs (and another cheque) by the 14th or thereabouts. They say publication on or about the 26th, which is going some. Providing there's no wool-pulling going on - and providing the editor finds my draft acceptable - I could be officially published sometime in February.

Which will be a strange phenomenon. Something I've aspired to for so long and which will have come about not through a work of fiction but as a result of my professional exploits.

Whatever, I'm expecting the event (in addition to requiring Champagne!) to force something of a review in terms of "what next". Indeed, last night as I struggled with sleep again, the prospect of finding an agent prepared to take on "The Big Frog Theory" came back to haunt me. Has to be an option worth considering. As does another Management book of some kind. If I could turn out bollocks once a year, who knows where it might lead! A world-renowned Management theorist!

The second thing - perhaps more symbolic - is a pair of lycra leggings bought today in Harrogate complete with 'go faster stripe' for running in. With my first race now only 4 weeks away, I do find it slightly amazing that I am embarked on this particular sport.

There is no reservation about it, don't get me wrong, but it does somehow seem extraordinary that after all this time - i.e. at my age - I am actually taking something like running seriously. Not to be comparatively good of course, but serious enough to purchase lycra tights! The whole thing has succeeded in offering a focus external to anything else (particularly work) which is, at present at least, very positive. The contribution it is making - in terms of self-esteem, goal achievement etc. - is quite remarkable, if not therapeutic.

Will publication lead to something similar? A question worth asking…

12th January 2001 (PBS)

Allegedly - or at least if the Editor of MB2000 is as good as his word - a package will arrive tomorrow containing my first set of proofs and a requirement on me to give my words (now slightly tightened, no doubt) the final 'once over'.

---

[28] The IT Management book to which he referred in entries of the previous year.

Quite something.

And then - he said - I can expect to receive books "smelling of print". No other smell quite like it.

Helps to map out the time between now and mid-February. Enough work to keep me busy; two 10k races; a murder/mystery evening (enter Colonel Ben West); Sarah's birthday; her final piece in the exam jigsaw; and a meal to celebrate much of this!

I'm sure we could still fit in a win on the lottery somewhere!

In any event, post "7th Day" the search for an agent for other matters must be resurrected, at least for a short while. Begging letters to a degree of course, but at least there will be <u>some</u> substance…

And I'm sure the temptation to put a proposal together for MB2000 will be a strong one - particularly after the smell of the print! Perhaps they might even have an idea of their own - who knows…

The 8-mile run of last week (hopefully to be repeated on Sunday) qualifies me in my own mind as a little more bona fide than before. I am expecting a ton of nerves before Dewsbury[29] - but also anticipate a strengthening of this sense of achievement and self-labelling.

I can see my training schedule expanding to allow me to achieve say 10m by the middle of May and the taking on of a 10m race or two in the Summer in preparation for Newcastle.

When you think of it, quite a positive start to the new decade (if you measure it - conveniently - from 1/1/1…!)

~~~~

You may well challenge me and ask why I took out the Christmas material relating to his parents, yet left in all this stuff about running. Surely neither are writing-related?

My argument is a simple one. The running is about him being able to do something on his own terms: his goals, his plans, his execution. It is influenced by no outside force. I would argue that it offers a distinct parallel to the 'process'

---

[29] In West Yorkshire, the location of his first 10k race.

of writing - in terms of goals, plans and execution. He is running, but he isn't really writing. Surely the disciplines for the first could apply to the second... If you accept that as a premise - however flimsy - then there is a relevance, a link between the two, at least on the process level.

And emotionally the connection has already been made, namely as they relate to self-esteem.

~~~~

20th January 2001 (PBS)

So, the correction of the edited proofs of "The 7th Day" is now complete, and the wedge will be on its way back to Gloucestershire tomorrow. The ultimate transaction (if you exclude the financial) will be the arrival of a package containing 6 books with my name on the cover. Real books!

Hopefully they will arrive by 19th Feb, which will allow our meal at Rascasse to celebrate these along with Sarah's birthday and the completion of her degree course.

I'm reasonably confident that my work is going to be OK for a while i.e. I am going to be kept productively busy. And the money will keep flowing in... Two months today we'll be at a beach hotel in Kenya looking forward to our safari on the morrow and beginning the process of unwinding.

I think that I want to return from Kenya with a degree of clarity in my mind in terms of future goals. There will, of course be a number of significant ticks in my boxes by then - work, the book, the 10k races - and it will be a question, in some instances, of kicking on to the next stage. In others, starting something afresh.

Only 42 I know, but my running (amongst other things) promotes a <u>new</u> sense of mortality, of time, of the need to get things done and moving...

So more mapping out and planning is inevitable. Void-filling or life planning depending on your view. The need for something akin to a 'strategic' plan.

Perhaps I should read my own book to get a few tips!

Probably none of it particularly difficult; or at least not as difficult as I sometimes choose to make it. Maybe at bottom it's about organising time, or choosing how one goes about moving amongst it.

Running   (as at 1/4/01, let's say)

Dewsbury   10k ✓
Pennypot   10k ✓ (hopefully)
Best distance   10 miles or 16k ✓
                (next weekend?)

futures: Great North Run   16.9.01
                    13+ miles
                Maybe some 10m races in the summer
                The Great South Run in October?

This one is relatively easy. It's time-bound and measurable. It sits neatly on a plan in terms of a programme which is definable, achievable, realistic - I hope!

It has characteristics which may - or may not - be easily transferable to other spheres.

Dangerous I know, but let us take work for granted. Let us assume that E^2 continues to utilise my services and that I'm happy with the variety, stimulation and wage. Let us assume that I am happy not to lust after greater glory and responsibility and that I can resist the urge to volunteer for a role that might demand 10+ hours a day. And let us also assume that I refrain from wanting a European (sic) move for a little while longer...

Holidays   (as at 1/4/1)

Kenya   ✓ (well, it will actually be our last day...)
France (in July) - Planned and paid for more from duty...
Will want a weekend away in early autumn with Sarah. Perhaps away at Xmas too.

And then to start thinking about holidays in 2002. The Caribbean? Alaska? America? Australia? Hey! A trip through the alphabet! Might be fun to at least draw up a list...

(Pause for lunch and other 'domestics'...)

Back - with little more than the inevitable conclusion that something has to follow "7th Day". It would be plainly daft not to try and capitalise on this success (not yet in terms of sales!). Something has to follow it. I need to be generating some kind of momentum from this - and from the fact that I have actually been paid for my efforts... (Sudden thought to negotiate a reduction in hours with E² to allow me more time... or perhaps unpaid holiday...? Later...)

Of course the next step might well be career-defining, at least in writing terms. Perhaps if MB2000 come back at some point with a proposition - if they work that way. Maybe the question needs to be answered in terms of what kind of writer I want to be (I can legitimately ask that with a book on the streets). Or parallel questions about future; about reliance on writing for income; about balance between this and "paid work".

There are differing strands, make no mistake; perhaps I should use the time in Kenya (in part) to see if I can resolve this particular equation. Management books or novels? Sports or travel books perhaps? What else?

Maybe use the experience in Kenya. Write a piece on it and try to sell it...

Advice - in any scenario - has to be of some value. Perhaps the agent need again...

In any event, it would be good to return with a goal - not unlike the GNR. Something I can map out achievement against.

The questions are, of course, the same as they have always been. As I sit here today, however, the landscape in which they are asked has changed - and finally for the better.

~~~

All self-explanatory. Just one thing of note (and I may as well cover it here). As remarkable as it might seem, there were no immediate entries following the trip to Kenya (not that I could discover, anyway) - which is somewhat astonishing given the nature and scale of the holiday. Perhaps a forgotten notebook will turn up in the fullness of time.

Indeed, there were only four more entries across the remaining eleven months of 2001...

~~~

And on a train to Edinburgh - which makes a change!

Berwick-upon-Tweed looks like a nice place on the edge of the North Sea and with sheep perilously close to the edge. (We've just been past a sign that said 'Edinburgh 50 miles'). On the whole, a journey much more pleasant than going to London, if longer.

I now realise how important Sunday's race is becoming for me. I hope it goes well. I can see myself training up for marathons and punctuating my years ahead with weekends in Prague or Vienna, all to flog my guts out. It is, I have to say, a prospect which is quite delightful!

Odd, in a way, that it will all depend on a cold Sunday morning in Dewsbury[30]...!

5ᵗʰ & 8ᵗʰ February 2001 (PBS)

Sunday proved to be something of a triumph - apart from picking up a (temporary) injury. The time, five minutes faster than I'd managed on my own, was something of a vindication of racing - despite the blizzard! Sufficient for three applications to be awaiting stamps, including an entry for the Leeds ½ marathon in May.

So, some structure and ambition guaranteed.

❀

That last entry did scant justice to the sense of achievement gained from the Dewsbury run. Of course the complications which followed - an injury which is nearly ready to take training again, followed by a day-cold which keeps me pretty much to my bed today - seem to be conspiring against my appearance in race number two on Sunday in Harrogate. This and the threat of blizzards again!

Whatever the immediate outcome, the experience was sufficiently energising for me to enter another race before Kenya (9m near Doncaster), a Rothwell 10k after, and the Leeds ½ marathon the day before my birthday. (I said I wanted to run a marathon by the time I was 40; maybe 44 - next year - is an acceptable alternative[31].)

---

[30] That first 10k road race. This would would be followed with dozens of road races over the next nine years.

[31] He was, in fact, fifty-one when he ran the London Marathon - his one-and-only to-date.

In addition to the race, the week promises the arrival of 6 pristine copies of my book. (Perhaps the door will be knocked as I lie in bed?) The MB2000 website now actively promotes the book as 'published', so it can only be a matter of time.

Also a matter of time must be the follow-up; whatever that will be. I had intended that Kenya be an opportunity to mull that particular issue over, but I sense that it might actually be a good time to rough something out, the notion having gestated in the 6 weeks or so prior to departure.

If I'm going to hit that kind of deadline then I need to be turning the grey cells over PDQ. Let's hope the new books will be the catalyst.

13th February 2001 (PBS)

…dawns as something approaching a catalyst, even though that is far from being the correct word.

My cold - which attacked last Wednesday night (predicated - who knows? - by running in a blizzard) worsened enough for me to go and see the Doctor yesterday (Sarah's birthday). Either it or I was sufficiently impressive for him to sign me off for the rest of the week. Today, somewhat revived by a decent night's sleep (the first for nearly a week) sees me facing the free time I have discovered with one eye on the future. In this sense, having the time to plan / reflect is catalystic.

More so is the fact that yesterday morning a box arrived with six pristine copies of "On the 7th Day" inside. Bright yellow, 'limp' covered, with my name writ reasonably large on the front, and very bold on the side! Sitting on a shelf in the bookstore, the spine will be 'grabbing'…

I'm not sure what I wanted to feel when the books arrived. Moreover, I'm not entirely sure what I did feel; which is more to the point… There they were, the words "Ian Gouge" standing out - and from which I felt strangely disembodied. After all this time - these years - for those to be the ultimate evidence that I had wanted to see… I felt strangely ambivalent. Perhaps that is the best word, and ambivalence the best description of my feeling.

I tried out a few words yesterday to see how they felt: "amazing" was one; "remarkable" another. And while these held a modicum of truth, they were only part-way there - and at the end of it all, felt little more than words. A philosophical conundrum which may warrant further investigation elsewhere…

It feels as if my mental benchmark - for achievement, progress, self-esteem, whatever - is my running. In itself this is in many ways an odd or obscure notion. On a fundamental, practical level it's easy to see why (as I've probably already said): easy to measure, plan, track, log etc. Easy to identify goals. Easy to establish the rewards of gratification, self or otherwise. (The inability to run in the Pennypot 10k was a real blow…) But not only is the running this kind of benchmark for achievement, it also sets a datum for importance in terms of how much things matter to me.

Example. No question I will be well enough to return to work before the end of the week. My immediate response? "Great; I can start running again!" (I've even thought that working away from home wouldn't be so bad as it would give me the chance to train 3 / 4 evenings a week)

Some of this is positively dangerous I know; but take the bundle of the last 24 hours together (as a crystallisation if you will) and add to it the prospect of 3½ days of 'freedom' - well, you can see where the idea of catalyst comes from.

In all of this there is nothing new. "What can I but enumerate old themes?" WBYeats or thereabouts. Enumeration or elucidation is all very well, but action is required and in a format that delivers (à la running diary).

Of the book, Sarah said that it was a shame that it didn't say "The Big Frog Theory" on the front - and as I sit here perhaps the penny drops that this is real success that would remove any sense of ambivalence.

OK, so I can do it, write a book. I've always believed that I could. This is tangible proof (for me and the rest of the world). But as such it's only half the battle. It's a book about something for which I care little and which has limited importance to me. Almost as if I were writing an extended essay or a report for work. It's formulaic more than anything else, and maybe proves that I can follow a plan; can construct logically; can put two words together, one in front of the other. Maybe it's like learning to jog, the putting of one foot in front of the other at slightly greater than walking pace. If so, then I want to run: that would remove the ambivalence.

One interesting thing. The notion dawning that "The Big Frog Theory" has to be the next book in my stable. That, if I am going to accelerate from jog to run, then this has to be the way to do it. That if I am to avoid a second dose of vague ambivalence (which might result in me throwing the towel in altogether) then it might be the only possible solution.

Something to think on, if there's a plan to be formulated…

~~~~

If you were to argue that his 'professional' writing - those bright yellow, limp-covered books - were an irrelevance, an offshoot, a cul-de-sac, on one level I'm sure he would be inclined to agree with you. What is clear from this entry, however, is the importance not of the books themselves but the impact of being published. Whilst it was proof of ability of some kind, it was also exposure of a 'gap', what the book cover <u>didn't</u> say, what <u>wasn't</u> contained within it.

He talks, clumsily, about a 'catalyst' when what he is surely saying is that the 13th February 2001 should be a pivot point, the launchpad which has seemed within touching distance on more than one occasion. The Dewsbury run (that parallel between running and writing holding up once more!) certainly seems to have worked in that way, providing the mental stimulation for physical action. But did 'On the Seventh Day' have the same effect?

~~~~

18th February 2002 (PBS)

Amazing that today - 18th Feb - is just over a year since the last significant entry here. Amazing too how much has, or hasn't, changed since then. It was interesting to re-read the pre-occupation with running, especially as the year saw me enter and run in a number of events including 13.2 and 10 miles… and 2002 sees a belated start to my season with a 10 mile race on Sunday (bad back permitting).

Interesting too what has happened in terms of book-writing - this with me 32,000 words through book 2, publisher 2; a second tome related to IT management theory. OK, so it isn't 'The Big Frog Theory' - but is there any real surprise in that given my track record to-date? Having said that, there are some potential saving graces - such as the purchase (at considerable cost) of screenplay-writing software, and a gleam in the eye (in the light of 'Harry Potter') of Neville as a motion picture. (Driven by ££, I know, but there it is!)

The most significant thing is that the dream is still alive; possibly as healthy as it has ever been in many ways. If 'The 7th Day' did anything, maybe it was that proof / catalyst that perhaps took a little while to sink in and take effect. Another driver - and one born in 2001 - is the dream of living in France; a dream to be funded by being fundamentally successful at putting one word in front of another. Much pipe in this dream, of course, but there is a plan (which has much of the retirement about it given the timescale) the keystone of which will not be the current book, but whatever follows. The prerequisite is that whatever follows has to make money…

No talk of work? Roles come and go, but I find myself working for a company which is going down the toilet - at the same time as it is recognising my "potential" and may be about to offer me a major-ish role... How is this particular circle squared? In the same way that it always has been I suppose...

~~~~

Was the second management book undertaken to prove the first wasn't a fluke? Or because he could? Or because he thought it might lead to an income? Or because it meant he didn't have to try and write anything more 'inventive'? To some extent, probably all of those.

And how much of his thinking here is pragmatic, rather than 'pipe dream'? And how long did it last?

~~~~

from 3rd April 2002 (PBS)

"Challenge & Growth"

<u>A LIST</u>

Travel more
Live abroad F 32
Move (anyway)
Child(ren) F?
Animals
Hobbies (new)
education
Writing F?
Sport
Career
Career Change F
[Constraints (financial & others) F]

✤

3.62   30:24   3.8   31:10 33

---

32 There is no indication as to what the 'F' may refer.

33 These are running times: miles and minutes.

136

en France:

19/5	4.7m	38:56
24/5	7.6m	61:09

Dorset:

9/5	27:33	3m?

✻

IDEA

Story about a man who wakes up feeling a failure (because of missed opportunities, career etc.)

Use of conscience as a character?

Story of George Best in the hotel room - "what went wrong George?"

Ability to travel back through time and attempt to replay situations (through imagination).

Ability to put oneself in a situation and play it out (again through imagination).

Book attempting to examine what it is to be a man.

Components: current relationship (assumed)
                career
                previous relationships, career etc. all of which carry some
                stigma of failure

Book is both an attempt to regress / redress the past, as well as an attempt to make sense of the future.

Trigger? Perhaps last day as a 39-year-old. Dawning of the "Big 40". Also far enough along the track to act as a barrier for radical change.

The mid-life crisis.

Start with
> "It hit him / came to him / dawned on him…that he was a failure."
> - remainder of the book is an exposition of the notion of "it"…?!

Man must be "normal": job, wife, children, friends in the pub, mild interest in external activities (e.g. football) plus some kind of "hidden" passion - creative maybe - which acts as part fuel for his adventure…

There needs to be a present-day issue which is taxing him i.e. about which he needs to make a decision and upon which his reflections of the past have a significant bearing.
- pos. the decision as to whether or not to have an extra-marital affair…
…or around a career move / accepting promotion etc.

Present associations will be:
> Wife. Children. Friends. Colleagues / Boss. Potential mistress (sic.)
> Other family (parents)

Past associations will be:
> Women (lovers & examples of failure and missed opportunity)
> Friends (past… but why?)
> Colleagues (if working plays a major role)

So multiple strands:
> present dilemma
> past + its re-examination
> the passage of present time i.e. the transition from 39 to 40

Requirement for humour - perhaps in one of his friends whom he regards as a role model / success in the sense that he has no truck with the notion of failure: "not in my fucking dictionary!"

Or (non-humorous, very) a colleague who is very serious about his career - weighs things up; there can ∴ be no failure (logic-driven).

Two extremes through which he must navigate (Scylla and Charybdis?)

Time line?

①	②	③
Morning (39+365)	39 => 40	40+1
	(midnight)	
Beginning	Middle	End
Sat. a.m.	Sat night / Sun a.m.	Monday

138

(The particular warmth of a hand on the arm…)

He starts playing with the numbers to see what he can do with them: e.g. Ali Baba and the 40 thieves - positive notion of manliness and bravado; danger etc.
40 days in the wilderness - Jesus, Moses, John?
Life begins at… (repeats - but what does this mean?)
St Swithin's Day / Noah?   Jonah?
Roaring forties
Waist size?
Longitude & Latitude?
39 is devoid of significance.

Anticipation of 'the moment' at midnight where he age clicks over - but is distracted and misses it. Sense of anti-climax.

The timeline offers up the structure of the book with a catalogue of events within each offering mini (but informal) chapters.

	"what happens"		"imaginings"
Sat. a.m.	waking up	"FAILURE"!	wrestling with the dilemma / notion…
mid / p.m.	shopping? DIY/ gardening? gym?	‖ ‖	
eve	the 'party' (does the party need to come 2/3 into the book?)	‖ ‖ ‖	Yes, probably ∴ on Sunday night? NO
Sun. a.m.	Party aftermath. Waking up	‖ ‖ ‖	but must come as clock 'ticks over' - and book must start on the morning of that day
mid / p.m.	Out with the children?	‖ ‖	This implies ∴ that Part One must be longer…
eve.	Birthday meal with the family	‖ ‖	maybe half the book minimum. This is where all the analysis happens…
Mon. a.m.	Back to work	‖ ‖	
mid / p.m.	Resolution with Y.	‖ V	
eve	Conclusion	FAILURE OR NOT?	

Past female failures:

"Liz" - schoolboy fumblings in the park (how far back does one go?)
"J" - university redhead
"x" - tea shop and supermarket encounter
"B" - incompetence"
"E" - passivity
"L" - lack of forcefulness / ambition
"Grace"/"Lisa" - same question re start   x

needs to be a sense of missed opportunity; perhaps of a moment when things hung in the balance - or (more accurately) - were just waiting to be tipped.

And in replaying these, how much further does one go? a) to tip the scale in the opposite direction? b) to imagine life having moved on i.e. then and now? If the latter, this could provide the framework for parts 1 & 2 of the book...

Taking this approach allows him to foresee the critical moment with "A", and roll forward the future (because he's become practiced at it) and therefore makes his decision on that basis. If so, does this move him away from the original consideration as himself as failure? ("E" as echo / preparation for "A"?)

Sequence of recollection in reverse order? i.e. "E", "X", "B", "L", "J", "Lz"...

so - (are the sequences in ① correct - probably E=>L2 or L2=>E?)
① wake up - E - action - X - action - B - action - L - action - J - action - Lz - the Party.
② the party - wake up - Lz - action - J - action - L - action - B - action - X -action - E - the meal
③ wake up - action - A* - A* - action - A* - action - conclusion (going to sleep)

35 'bits' @ 4k avg = 140k => 280 days (assume 500/day)
         @ 3k avg = 115k => 230 days

* sequence: imagined future - tipping the scales - the real action?

Does there need to be a sense of a pseudo-happy ending in that:
a - his acceptance is not convincing (e.g. resignation)?
b - that he may not have really learned his lesson?
c - that he made the wrong choice w.r.t. "A"?

d - that "E" (or someone else) is at the heart of his problem and cannot be argued away?

~~~~

Given all we know to this point in relation to the underlying themes for 'Mirrors' and many of his other ideas, it is noteworthy that he should once again focus on a man's relationship with his history. The notions of regret and replaying the past become - as well shall see - perhaps the most important themes in all of his fiction; his 'heroes' are people trying to 'work things out', to understand themselves in the context of their history, how their past has impacted on their present, and how the whole shooting-match influences their future.

The specifics outlined above are, of course, taken from his own life. (Much later he was to write a warm and generous poem called "For Liz" relating to his 'schoolboy fumblings'.) Completely unveiled here, one can only assume that he would have taken the trouble to disguise each of these relationships had the idea made it onto the page - after all, he wasn't planning an autobiography.

Inevitably, of course, all of this prompts consideration of the age-old question as to what one should write about. "Write what you know about" is the oft quoted mantra, and what do you know most about if not your own experiences? Was that his starting point here? To use his life as the core ingredients to cook up something else, and in doing so to satisfy his two fundamental needs: to write something, and to exorcise the past? Not only that, might the choices he outlines at the end of the entry - a, b, c, or d - in effect be him asking those questions of himself and his own life? Would a book with such a theme allow him to undertake exactly the same journey as his lead character, fusing him with the fiction? Would that have been irresistible?

~~~~

4th June 2002 (PBS)

So - the previous 9 pages of ideas may not be that great after all... Having scribbled 6 or 7 hundred words, the enterprise seems somewhat fraught with danger. (At least in its present form.) Getting the balance right between fiction and auto-b could be pretty difficult; undoubtedly there would be a tendency to drift toward the latter.

One possibility is to weave this into a different story i.e. a thriller. The construct remains pretty much as is, although tighter, shorter and with an anonymous protagonist. The second 'half' of the book is detective fiction i.e. the protagonist turns serial killer and the detective must find the link...

Might work. There would need to be some kind of 'time-lapse' writing involved e.g. it opens at the beginning with the guy being tipped over the edge by both his age and sense of failure; his preoccupation becomes one of not wanting anyone else to realise he is a failure.

First slice of the detective portion comes with the discovery of a body (and not necessarily the first). This whole thing would have significant planning implications; better allow a month for that i.e. to define and then weave in the second part with all the necessary detail...

10th June 2002 (PBS)

Distracted by the pursuit of a new job, my writing - as ever! - suffers. Even if the recently hatched (and recently discarded!) idea is a good one, I certainly won't realise it for a while.

If CRC[34] comes off (for example), taking into account holiday, moving, operation etc. I doubt if I'll be in any position to start focussing on anything new until, when?, the back-end of August... If CRC doesn't come off, then the impact could be even greater...

More reason for an external focus of course, and a month with two (if not three) races should help. That and staying dry and trying to get back to 13 st.... Benefits from the gym work undoubtedly paying off, though I'd be lying if I didn't express some concern over the nervous "twinges"...

As far as big picture things are concerned, I do genuinely feel more enthusiastic about another child; a second chance to become a family, if you will. The reservations haven't gone away of course, it's just that there's now more to balance against them.

An interesting thought yesterday (and here I recognise I'm rambling) is that I may be just an adjective or two short of being truly able to write something worthy from a fictional perspective. Perhaps this might be an 'opting out' thought, so I'm going to fight it. However, the notion did lead to the proposition for another book (for Springer?). No idea what this might be yet - or if they would be interested - but perhaps I should give it some thought. If it did come off, it might provide some structure in this area between September and year-end...

---

[34] There is no explanation as to what 'CRC' refers...

Sitting at work with my role here crumbling - partly because of the difficulty of execution (geography), partly because of the state of the business, but largely because I don't actually give a fuck any more. I guess mentally I have invested greatly in the CRC option, even though it may prove to be a difficult undertaking / challenge etc.

Perhaps I'm only 2 or 3 days away from hearing something definite - and then the process of either negotiation or grieving... I'm not sure what form the latter will take. The sensible option would be to attempt to re-throw myself into the current role (at least until we know what's happening with the company...). I haven't really identified any other alternatives - apart from going away for a couple of days to see if I can get my shit together. A weekend on my own in foreign climes perhaps...

I have primed Springer for another book, and wait to hear if they would entertain such a thought; and what strings they might wish to attach to the prospect... Other than that I can't conceive how I can get my head around anything specific / concrete until I know what I'm doing. I could go through the internal debate discussing options, but to be frank there just doesn't seem to be any point...

✼

Update: last candidate goes in to CRC tomorrow - which means I might hear anytime form Thursday onwards...

Questions to be answered: CRC, E², Springer...

- CRC. Came 2nd. Haven't actually thought much about it since. Was told that I was too much like an IT Director - which was what (they realised) they weren't quite ready for. So it was grief, but I think relatively short-lived...

- E². A rescued business and (another) new role. But it's treading water at best, drowning in a sea of de-skilling more likely. Alternatives have been desperately absent; but then I am setting my sights professionally high - which is where I figure I need to be to be satisfied. Is that really true? It's something I haven't substantially challenged.

- Springer. They took the bait! Contract's in the post and I need to start writing this evening (when I get back from London (yes, a train again...)). e-

Mgmt[35] is now published (both here and in the US) so it will be interesting to see what happens to it. Maybe that lecture tour isn't far away...! Three books published in four years will be something, with copies in various countries too: the Erasmus University Library, Rotterdam! I don't know where this is heading, but it serves as a diversion rather than (at present) a career. (PS. tried to get an NUJ card on the back of 7th and e-M but failed because E² are paying my way... There's a plunge to be taken there of course, but I would need to be 15 years younger... or would I? 64,000$ question...)

As ever I kid myself that time's the key when (undoubtedly) it is not. Rather time's the excuse / villain with which I pretend to wrestle as if, in over-coming it, I will gain some kind of ultimate victory. Nonsense. If anything, our Italian painting holiday (by relating time to a bit-part role) proved that; it was quite comprehensively over-turned by action / activity / desire / ambition (or whatever the 'right' word might be). Springer, for example, isn't about time; it's about a specific goal - time is "just" a factor that needs to be taken into consideration, worked with, or overcome.

The marathon would be something similar although time does have something of a more immediate role to play here...

Perhaps I should see myself as some kind of covert secret agent (an old theme!) with plots and subterfuges that are hidden from the rest of humanity only to be sprung upon them when their effect can be maximised. "Oh yes, I've written 3 books..."; "I ran the Berlin marathon last year too!"... and so on.

But this is just a minor fantasy. Perhaps the need to close eyes and reaffirm that ideal mental image - of what "B" looks like - is the first step in (again) trying to map out the route from "A".

Has "B" changed? Probably not: but now I think that i) it is closer and ii) I know more about it...

~~~

It is interesting, isn't it, that he managed to contract for, write, and then have published a second 'proper' professional book without a single mention of it in his notebook entries until now, just when he is contemplating his third. What does that say about his relationship to these works, his attachment and commitment to

---

[35] *e-Management* was his second professional book, this time published by a brand within the Bertelsmann stable.

them? Were they, in effect, no more than a linguistic extension of 'the day job', little more than a logical next step or a minor diversion? Surely that is the case; there was never a fourth.

But again, was their true contribution more significant when viewed in the round? Had writing them - and having the physical 'proof' in his hands - actually edged him a little further forward towards his ultimate goal? If so, then surely they must have provided him with a chink of light, encapsulated in that last throwaway comment about what "B" looks like and how close it may be.

~~~~

Helsinki, June 2004 (PBS)

18 months later...

- New job (on a plane to Scandinavia)
- New Baby
- 3 books written (and one idea awaiting feedback)

One book just read - "Who moved the Cheese?"

A simple enough parable, but one that begs the question about:
'what is my current cheese?'
'how healthy is it?'
'is it changing / mouldy / dwindling?'
'is it about to move?'
'do I need to go out into the maze?'

This Scandinavian week could be a significant one in answering some of these questions. A 'high flyer' marked out for Stardom...but what kind of New Cheese might be on offer? Is it the kind of New Cheese I'd want? It's also about me, my role, who I am, the way I behave etc.

There's no doubt that I continually need New Cheese in some areas - and am happy with Old Cheese in others. A kind of amalgam of all 4 characters from the book. Recognition of these traits - and the cheeses that they need / have / seek could be a powerful little tool...

	Old Cheese		New Cheese?
Hem			
Haw			
Scurry			
Sniff			

- could lead to identifying where action is needed and what that action actually is...

(Another Scandinavian plane...)

(Well, we can ignore that stardom shit from the previous entry. Too much doubt about the longer-term with the business fighting implosion - though I don't think it realises it...)

There are, of course, always revelations. It's a kind of cycle - one that a consultant might draw as follows:

But this is neither circle nor spiral (up or down, it doesn't matter). More like a succession of cul-de-sacs: revelation after revelation followed not by action but reassessment from the same position (and with different conclusions?)

Some guys can make a fortune out of this stuff... which is partly the issue (or the latest revelation, if you will).

Retirement. That's a big word. And needing a suitable income post-65 is the challenge. Only 20 years @ Outokumpu would be likely to fit the bill, and therefore there is a debate about options...

Revelation: I need to ensure a greater degree of income as I get older. Options (the stage before "decisions"...)

① - status quo, and hope to luck
② - strive to climb the corporate ladder
③ - do something else (new / additional) to increase income
④ - ?

Clearly ① is the obvious least risk / greatest risk route: an unclear outcome perhaps? reliance on others? how much does this place in jeopardy those who might be reliant on me?

② is allied with ① of course, but demands something more proactive, a need to care, to be overtly ambitious, to compromise in the short-term (and medium-term) for the longer goal. And what might that compromise mean e.g. geographically or domestically?

The 'something else', ③, is - as ever - attractive. But the hard question is what do I have to sell? I know I can write, but where is the component / idea / theme / method that turns that ability into black gold? And where is the time to come from? (but then I know the answer to that one as currently my days effectively finish @ 8p.m. or thereabouts) Always searching for the 'big idea' - but how hard, really?

~~~~

So 2004 ends, not with meaningful progress in relation to new writing projects (just the opposite, in fact!), but with uncertainty over his professional future. This preoccupation, imposed on him by 'life' and the need to earn a living, has never been far from the surface of all the notebooks. In and out of jobs, in-between jobs; how much did this lack of stability compromise him - or should we see it all as grist to the writing mill?

But 2003-2004 was momentous in it's own, non-writing way: new job, new baby. Perhaps that - subsequently followed by a move to another city, a second new baby in 2005, yet another job, another move - all conspired to what happened next. Which was essentially nothing.

There would be no entry for another <u>seven and a half years</u> - not even to mention his run in the 2010 London Marathon.

Part Five - 2012 to 2014

May-August 2012 (PBB)

This[36] is about?
>   → projection of the future
>   ↳ time travelling through language
>   ↳ projection forwards
>
>   → about giving up the present for something else
>   ↳ which may not come about or is not guaranteed
>   ↳ like placing a bet

But it is also a fallacy, because 'this time' can only be 'this time' (i.e. now) and tomorrow is, in a way, an impossible construct (i.e. when it comes, tomorrow is still in the future). It's also boundless in the sense that the only limit comes from what follows 'time': tomorrow, next year etc. - and the greater the distance in time, the greater the wager that is being placed - especially if there is some reliance or expectation being placed on the actual occurrence @ that point in time.

The opposite then is 'this time now' which places no bets and deals only in certainty (carpe diem etc.) - or is that the past?

Q1> how can language be used (e.g. tense) to project the nature of the time being experienced? - see Q4

Q2> how can the characters embody these temporal ambitions and reflect their attitudes to time (sic. life) - see Q3

And what about reflections on the past? - 'this time yesterday'? This is dealing more in absolute certainty.

Yesterday → past → certainty → safety → no wagering → risk free

Today → now → ability to change → controlled risk → some gamble / risk (on outcomes)

---

[36] Notes for the potential novel 'This Time Tomorrow' were spread across various entries (collected together here) and most likely made during the period May to August 2012. The next entry in the same notebook is dated February 2013.

Tomorrow → future → uncertainty → risk (but abdication?!)
$\hookrightarrow$ a gamble (no control)

Q3> one character for each scenario? e.g. Yesterday is a historian?

Q4> what joins threads and characters together? Reflections on a single event from the past, present & future. The today character becomes central to the action (not necessarily story). Interweaving these perspectives can tie in the language aspects too.

So, if event = E…

- Yesterday character is reflecting back on the event (historian) see Q2

- Today character lives up to - and through - the event

- Tomorrow character anticipates the event
$\hookrightarrow$ but is disappointed?
$\hookrightarrow$ never gets there?
$\hookrightarrow$ gets the wrong outcome?

Depends on the event and the motivation / message of the story.

In order for the story-telling to work, we need to focus on an event just before "E", in order not to give away the facts of "E" which should be climactic.

Need to be careful that the same story isn't just told over and over. So the events need to be different but linked and parallel in time? How?

$$x \to x \to x \to x$$
$$\searrow$$
$$y \to y \to y \to y \to E^{-1} \to E$$
$$\nearrow$$
$$z \to z \to z \to z$$

Q5> could the reflective, historical narrative actually be looking back to E - so the story is told backwards perhaps?

$$x \leftarrow x \leftarrow x \leftarrow x$$
$$\swarrow$$
$$y \to y \to y \to y \to E^{-1} \to E$$
$$\nearrow$$
$$z \to z \to z \to z$$

Q6> could the x and y characters be one and the same maybe (not obvious until E happens at the end of the book...!) The E event changes profoundly 'this time tomorrow' characters: the gamble has failed to pay off; rejection; seeks safety in the certainty of the past.

Q7> would it be possible for the x character to actually be retelling the same story as the z from the diametrically opposite standpoint? And the telling / narrative disguises that they are laying out one and the same thing?

$$x4 \leftarrow x3 \leftarrow x2 \leftarrow x1$$

$$y1 \rightarrow y2 \rightarrow y3 \rightarrow y4 \rightarrow E^{-1} \rightarrow E$$

$$z1 \rightarrow z2 \rightarrow z3 \rightarrow z4 \qquad \text{where } x1 = z1 \text{ etc.}$$

Interesting! But difficult...

So, getting the right E is critical in being able to map out coherent, credible and inter-related story lines.

Q8> WHAT IS "E"??

٭

Giving up the present for something else is defeatist, cowardly...

There is an element of perspective from one stream on the other (one person on another) based on where they start / where they are looking).

E? - logic suggests that this is the 'this time tomorrow' event that doesn't turn out as planned + causes cathartic change.
e.g. E = marriage that doesn't happen... Or, E is the unforeseen event after E^{-1} doesn't happen...

Does E need to be a non-factual event in order to make it credible? i.e. everyday, a "reasonable bet". Something unlikely (winning the lottery) would not work; people would not believe in the premise from the outset.

Other Es?   - a death (stops E happening) ٭
                - a journey
                - a missed appointment ٭

٭ opposite to the expected

Some kind of interruption or derailing (caused by character y?) e.g. in marriage scenario, y could be prospective groom, bride, best man... Needs to be in a position to influence if the catalyst for change.

E^{-1} and E have to be linked therefore.

E would both be unforeseen (because E^{-1} is assumed) and tragic (sic).

Is there also a dependency between y and z? So z is making assumptions about both y and the future, and E^{-1} not occurring - failure of the future? - leads to E - which is a 'failure' of y... This way, and in ignorance, z is making two bets about the future but doesn't realise it. (contrast x's certainty because they deal in the past).

I don't think x and z being the same characters will probably work... if not, does x's subplot have a parallel with the main action? Are they a 'voyeur' on the y & z thing?

historical x:	→ → → |	parallel	| → →
today y:	→ → → |	event	| ?
future z:	→ → → |	$E^{-1} → E$?	

It would be the post-event x that can be used to reflect on y/z in advance of E... which in its own way becomes a foretelling of events (but with more certainty?!)

Q9> how passive is z in E^{-1}/E? how 'active' is y? i.e. do either of them 'cause' E^{-1}/E, or is how they react the story?

Q10> how important is control i.e. control over E^{-1} and E for characters?

For example, if z thinks they are in control to make E^{-1} happen but it does not, one thing: if they never were in control - because it depends on y (or something else) - then that is entirely another...

Q11> RADICAL. The work is not the story, but it is this - the fictional analysis of a fictional story!! Allows all sorts of approaches and language - like quotes, fictitious references. And actually, this is supremely novel - in both senses!

I like it!

(could mean double planning...)

Is x the author?
Does it start with a quote (the story)?

Position of the author is then very critical as the author / critic actually
becomes part of the story.

❋

- It would still need to read enough like a narrative to work (but then I did this
in 'Mirrors' ok)

- the 'Author' is very much a character (and I as author am further removed)

- the 'Author' ('A') therefore needs their own sub-plot in the 'real world' which
drives their work.
    ↳ and <u>me</u> as author??!

- 'A' becomes an "I" narrator?

- If 'A' is the "I" narrator, then they become a surrogate for me.

Plot lines

1.   Mine, as the Author
2.   'A', as fictitious author
      a) outside the book
      b) motivation for book
      c) but also providing the analysis for the story
3.   x, as historical context
      a) certainty of what they are researching
      b) the parallel stream/events to the E^{-1}/E story
      (could be the same)
4.   y, the 'in the moment' character
5.   z, the 'this time tomorrow' character

4+5 are linked plot lines and dependant / same. Divergence comes @ E^{-1}, E
and thereafter. Climax of novel (story).

What about the possibility of x's plot line also being fictitious e.g. a
Shakespearean play. We know what happens in advance. Choose a tragedy…

Hmm. Maybe a step too far?

How commercial does it need to be? How long does it need to be?

Let's say, not too long - in order to keep it taut. 80k?

4 months. From Sept-Dec?

❄

Q12> Does some of the tension come from knowing that the 'looking back' character (x) has the 'answer' that the reader seeks?

Q13> What is the hook?
     ↳ it has to be from x?

Story becomes one about relationships between the protagonists - both real and fictitious. Also about the author (me) and my creations.

This could open up a whole new set of opportunities...

Adds to the tension.
Allows 'insights' into the characters
     ↳ which could provide some kind of counterpoint.
     "They may have said this, but..."

And then there's the question of honesty. Who is actually telling the truth through the story(ies) - or the most truth?

How does truth 'count' when things are fictitious anyway? Can there be any truth under such circumstances, as isn't it all a lie?

Characters are then puppets, playthings of the author(s) both.

Who do you trust? Cases for trusting a number of the players. If one underlying theme is the breaking of trust, the divergence of truth from what appears to be reality, then could E/E^{-1} be a mirror/symbol of that?

e.g. separation / divorce

Something that is not a joining together, but a breaking asunder...

❄

There could be one character who explicitly says that they tell the truth and are trustworthy. Or maybe one of the authors.

Does the author's own reality 'bleed' in to become part of the story?

Need to identify the individual plot strands and then map them out, picking out the interdependencies and intersections:

mine - my author's - the characters

The whole could (?) be thought of as some kind of WBS - which would help map out the construction of the whole.

"If only he/she had/hand't... then ..." A possible hook
↳ the 'then' needs to be 'big' enough

✼

Is 'Secrets & Wisdom' a valid title? How does this fit in with the notion of lies & truth?

Secrets = knowing what is or is not a lie?
Wisdom = knowing the difference?

Author has both?

By definition the reader is beset with secrets they cannot possibly know.

Could there be a character who represents the reader? i.e. is invested with the ignorance & innocence that the reader must have?
✓ good

The character - not x, y or z - would need to be an 'observer' to the action. Naming this character is important. Must be right.

Now getting to a place where a character list can be drawn up? need that to flesh out the plot.

✼

Me   - needs related characters?
The Author (A) - needs related characters?

```
x           |
y           | - all related
z           |
The Observer |
```

Parallels are important (between the three plot strands) as they will reflect on each other.

Approach is key. e.g. Murakami's alternating chapters for two plot lines that come to a common conclusion (somehow).

This only works if a) the magnitude of the three strands are the same, and b) the length of the 'chapters' can vary considerably. Of the two, 'b' seems most acceptable.

So, define the journeys. Start point and end point; then flesh out the stops along the way. This is critical next step.

❉

So, is the title 'This Time Tomorrow' or 'Secrets & Wisdom'?

It can be similar to 'Mirrors' but must be different.

Mechanics?
- a series of coloured index cards one colour for each stream; allows for their sequencing in a dynamic way
- use something on the PC? Is there a plotting tool?

Ideas for the (failed) premise:
- a wedding
- winning a competition (maybe a chess comp.)
- an anniversary
- a journey
- a missed appointment

Need not to lose sight of the sacrificed present for the 'tomorrow' premise.

Could there be multiple failures i.e. the 'Author' has one too?

If so, is x (the looking back character) immune too?

At the moment of climax (or just after) the true nature of all the participants - real and imagined - are revealed...? Does this allow greater tension? Makes for a more 'portmanteau' approach.

Need to be clear about who the characters are to ensure their journey is realistic / relevant.

~~~~

I have deliberately not commented on these particular musings until now, wanting to allow you to get a solid view of the process, how his mind was working in relation to this single idea. The entries prompt multiple questions and observations, of course.

Why this - and in this detail - after seven years? <u>Seven years!</u> What had been going on in the interim (in terms of writing) that was to bring him to this place?

In terms of posing questions to himself, there are clearly resonances with that great 'Mirrors' entry of August 1994; primarily that there is a 'feel' here of something well-formed and well-worked through. Did he eventually get through these musings (more follow below) and believe that he was on to something?

There is also a degree of the philosophical about what might be termed the 'intellectual rigour' he seemed to be trying to apply. And of course there are the old preoccupations; not so much about creating a plan and setting goals for words, time-to-write etcetera, but in the fascination with his characters' passage backwards and forwards through time (a reverberation with more than just 'Mirrors').

Possibly one of the most interesting notions he plays with is that of inserting another 'author' between himself and the narrative, creating not only an extra distance between himself and the end product, but perhaps allowing the exploration of what it is to be an 'author'. If, in some way, he expected to be drawing on his own life for material, his own philosophies in which to cocoon the work, would such a device have given him the latitude to do so?

~~~~

Once he had said the word it was like setting in motion an irreversible chain of events. Like throwing a switch that sent a train away from the mainline.

Here there was no option for complex manoeuvres involving signals, points, engineers, signalmen. There was no sequence of events that could return him to exactly the same point in time, travelling in the same direction. If he could get 'back on track' then it could only be somewhere else, where things had moved on, where perspectives were different, much like the view from a moving train.

"I didn't mean it!"

"But you threw the switch."

"But I didn't mean it!"

"You still threw the switch."

~~~~

We do not know if the extract drafted above was intended as a part of 'This Time Tomorrow'. Perhaps he considered it a potential opening; perhaps it was something that came to him that he simply needed to get down on paper.

To the best of my knowledge he never used it.

~~~~

"Anne, the Curator".   Thinks in terms of 'exhibits'.

Candidate for x? Or the witness?

Is it valid to create characters + scenarios for them without knowing where they are going to fit longer term?

"Considering her age and her profession, Anne X was many things she had no right to be: older than she looked; slimmer than she should have been. Given her passions - for facts, history, the absoluteness of things - she should not have been spiky, charming (and charm-able!), warm, smiling, personable and engaging. She dealt in the black-and-whiteness of 'exhibits', and all the while with the temperament of the artist rather than that of the museum curator. Which is what she was."

~~~~

On the other hand, the short paragraph above - obviously intended for the 'Anne' character in 'This Time Tomorrow' - was used later. A museum curator, Anne has a story dedicated to her in his 2017 short story collection 'Secrets & Wisdom' (a title initially referred to above as a potential alternative to 'This Time

Tomorrow'). He is creating a character within the germ of an idea in 2012, then using that person - and that book's putative title - for something entirely different some five years later.

But I'm rushing ahead...!

~~~

Forget about the narrative in a sense, but focus on the individual streams i.e. what happens. Draw the threads together later; intertwine later.

So - Anne, the observer. What's her line?

Intro - build character

Exhibits are commentaries on the events unfolding (∴ various)

Sub-plot?
↪ can there be a relationship with one of the characters?
↪ she would be drawn to x as 'historian'
↪ she would be drawn to y as a 'free spirit' to charm her

✱

Is there a common structure in that there needs to be an 'intro' piece of some kind for all the characters, including the Author figure?

Something about meetings, introductions, coming togethers?

Still need the premise / plot...

Characters all need some kind of weakness or defect too.

Work out from Anne, maybe...
↪ of what is she the curator?
↪ how is this relevant to the other characters?

e.g. some kind of estate that is open to the public.
      Provides musical events.
      Meets x + y through the planning of that event.
      One is conductor; one performer.
      In relationship.
      One (z) assumes they will marry.

y has affair (?) / betrays (maybe leaves the orchestra?)
↳ z would be the conductor

Who is x here? Someone from the orchestra y moves to?

Alternatives to orchestra?
↳ Artists?
↳ Actors?
　　　"the play's the thing…"

Open-air Shakespeare…

Would have to choose the right play. Would need to resonate.

If z were director, would need to be female if y was to be the actor who went off and charmed Anne?

x would need to be male too.

Kind of 2 couples. Midsummer Night's Dream, but without the happy ending?

The Author is a kind of 'failure' figure, playing with the characters?

Should the structure of MSND help with this structure (in terms of lateral plot lines)?

The premise for z is that life is like MSND and there will a happy ever after ending for her and y.

So that's sex. What else?
Age; name;
　　　　　(- or -)
x:　　　m. (m/f.)　　　　　　　　　60??
y:　　　m. (f.)　　　　　　　　　　38?
z:　　　f. (m.)　　　　　　　　　　40?
a:　　　f.　　　Anne Greenaway　　52?

x could be American - the destination for y. Has been a fan of y for some time. Comes to watch rehearsals for MSND whilst on holiday. Makes the offer of a job during rehearsals.

Base some of the names on those from Shakespeare's life e.g. Anne Hathaway.
↳ Oxford? - the Author's name!
↳ the Actors!

Troupe called the 'King's Company'?

z & y will need to have been working together for some time.

Alternatives to MSND? It is just one couple after all. 12th N?

OK, OK - BUT...
premise was about giving something up for jam tomorrow. What does z give up because she thinks she and y will get together? What is her dream?
↳ to start their own company / dynasty (sees them as kind of Olivier / Leigh figures?)
↳ to start a family?
↳ etc.

Is there something in y's past that suggests he is not a safe bet? Is z charmed (but more deeply) in the way that Anne is charmed?

❀

What is 'the word' said by y - to which x refers - that sets the derailment in motion?[37]

Probably something simple like yes/no in answer to a question from z?

There could be multiple such decision points in the story that sets the track for the plot i.e. does Anne agree to sleep with y?

If Anne is a more involved character now (intrinsic?!) then how do the 'exhibits' play out?

❀

Names?

Ed? Alleyn	John? Fletcher
? Beaumont	Sam? Ireland
Will Booth	? Kemp
? Burbage	? Lyon

---

[37] Referring to the excerpt drafted five pages, above.

John? Marston
Ed Oxford
John? Webster

❋

or

x: m. (US) 60	m. (US) 60
y: m. 38	f. 40
z: f. 40	m. 38
w: Anne 52	Anne 52

MSND
w. Lysander
z. Demetrius   both in love with Hermia

y. Hermia   in love with Lysander
x? Helena   in love with Demetrius

x? Oberon/Titania/Puck

12th N
z. Olivia   - not sure this works
y. Viola
? Duke Orsino

x? Malvolio

Is there another character for x? i.e. it isn't the American than causes the denouement, but someone else.

If z is female, the jam tomorrow with y could be marriage, children etc. Fits in terms of age. Also with M being younger (more flighty?), fits with the decision to go off to the US.

❋

How about a structure where there is one 'part' for each of the main protagonists (x4?) who tell the same story through their own perspective?

How to handle the common denouement under these circumstances?

Allow for variation of style e.g. 'exhibits' for Anne.

Would need to work out the common, high-level timeline first - but this should be easy.

What about the Author's voice in this structure? Acts as a kind of 'Chorus' perhaps, between the parts...

Company arrives @ house
    ↳ Rehearsals
        ↳ x arrives at house
            ↳ job offer
                ↳ denouement
                    ↳ play

(the latter probably isn't covered in the story)

Sub-plot intricacies (e.g. y meeting w) need to be mapped into this structure. Will be linear, but story may not be told this way.

These intricacies and interactions are primarily meetings & conversations. The plot is actually very simple.

Q. Do any of the rehearsal interactions actually show the cast rehearsing?

Also, what about the sub-plot of the Author? Why are they writing this? What do they think about it? What is their motivation?

✽

24.15
Some good ideas here, but the basic plot (the play) is too prosaic.

~~~~

And then, after all this effort, all this working through, he seems to abandon the idea...

~~~~

5th February 2013 (PBB)

"The Man Who Made Plans"

This is a story about a man who, perhaps not totally consciously, spends his life making plans.

Professionally, that's his job, to attempt to depict what is going to happen when (or should happen). So he's a PM, or a 'strategist' of some kind. Perhaps he works in Finance.

These professional plans are not about him, they are in no way personal. He can be detached about them; his investment in them is purely theoretical, cerebral, intellectual. He has special criteria here for "a good plan". (not based on outcome??)

His personal life is filled with a myriad of plans - from the grand and significant to the daily mundane.

Does he see these as plans? Does he recognise them as such?

The key cornerstones of the book are:
• the failure of plans
• their distance from the reality they try to depict / control
• their inherent weaknesses (e.g. subject to forces outside of his control)
• their substitution for something else (they are an excuse for living?)

The plot needs to revolve around:
• the failure of a plan(s)
• the success of a plan?!
• success (or failure) without planning

- And the repercussions thereof.

A plan needs to have a defined end-point / goal. Does he have a defined goal for his personal plans, or is this one of his key issues?

And who is he?
? middle-aged (nearly 60?)
↳ does this make his plans more or less relevant
↳ 'Jack'. not his real name but one he adopted (and are there implications here?)

What about his past? Should there be reflections on past plans failed? Do we create a theme of disappointment and regret* alongside one which is about positivity looking forward?

Who are the other people in the story? What part do they play?

Are there two stories: the present Jack and the past 'pre-Jack' - told as independent, but actually about the same person.

* these could relate back to failed attempts in the past i.e. plans (real or imagined) that failed.

Is 'The Man Who Made Plans' part of the Wednesday idea?

Series of short stories based upon a 'constrained' and diverse group e.g. at an airport, on a plane etc.?

~~~~

Given his predilection for making plans and scheduling his writing, should we be surprised to find this idea surfacing? It is, of course, a condemnation of the activity of planning - and therefore undermining one of his own obsessions. The undertone from his notes suggests planning offers little beyond failure; the possibility of that not being the inevitable outcome is met with the incredulous "the success of a plan?!" - clearly not a prospect in which he wholeheartedly believes. All of this is surely premise based on painful experience. Write what you know about indeed...

Having said that, there is also fusion here with some of his other preoccupations, such as our relationship with time and, in the two versions of 'Jack' - one in the present and one from the past - the opportunity to examine characters possessing a kind of 'duality' based on where they exist temporally.

"The Wednesday idea", not referenced as yet in the notebooks (though he must have be thinking of it already), probably relates to 'The Man Who Waited for Wednesday', an idea we will come across later and which is best seen as the next incarnation of 'The Man Who Made Plans'.

~~~~

24th June 2013 [38] *(PBB)*

"More ideas"

What about a kind of 'God' story? Comes to earth to inspect, review - to make a decision about the future.

---

[38] Although this entry is dated for the 24th June, based on the variety of pens used, it was obviously completed across multiple dates (none of which are recorded).

Allows for both detached and attached views of what he finds.

Q> Is it just a "he"? Could it be multiple persons allowing different approaches, persona, scenes etc.?

On a train
On a plane
In a supermarket

❉

'The Rites of the Dead'

"What did you say your name was?"

The rhythmic beeping like some kind of monitor. Not quite perfect.

"Have you ever thought about how...?"

A kind of intermediate step or state that allows perfect reflection. Maybe what happens when someone is in a coma but their brain is still alive?

A construct that allows them to make the decision about dying or living. As if it is actually a choice.

Structure allows for vignettes. Parts of various length and form.

And is there any intrusion of reality into this - and if so, is it well concealed?

❉

"Overheard"
 ↳ just half of stories
        ↳ the one side of mobile phone conversations

❉

'Find the time...' that's an interesting expression, as if there is some pot of golden time hidden at the end of something, waiting to be found, and to bestow on its finder the fantastic reward of... more time.

But time cannot be constructed, saved, given as a reward.

'is it always 2 o'clock…?'

~~~~

As if exercising a bizarre demonstration of his relationship with time and his history, he makes no further entry for another twelve months, at which point - unsurprisingly - we find another review of 'possibilities': half-formed ideas, part-drafted work. Many we are familiar with already, some less so. Were there intermediate scribblings about the latter elsewhere I wonder, not recorded in the 'formal' notebooks?

~~~~

September 2014 (BBG)

Things to work on:

- Who was she?
- How does it start?
- So Martin married Ruth
- Writing to Gisella
- x
- Mirrors (?)
- Something new (?)

[novellas, not novels. A flexible form - including play-type dialogues?]
Whatever!

- This time tomorrow
- The man who made plans

??   - God story
           - Rites of the dead
           - 'Overheard'
           - 'find the time'
           - "1000 weeks" blog?

- Riding the Escalators
- 7:16 (thriller)?
- David Plume thriller

Who was she?

What is this about? A man's search for a 'mystery' woman?

Does he find her - Yes or No
↳ and if No, does he 'find' anything?
↳ and if Yes, then what is the story there / that develops?

Characters:
> The Man
> Pete - his friend
> The Woman

In theory it will be easy to find the woman. He knows company, her name etc. - so finding her is not the issue. What is? Does she avoid him? Is there conflict? Or rejection? And how does he handle this?

Format:
> short story. maybe 5-10k

How does it start?

[need to re-read what's been written thus far to determine value, plot etc.]

Characters:
> The Artist, Oscar
> The Patient, Oscar's Uncle (or Oscar + someone else's uncle?)
> Simon, Oscar's friend
> The model, Rachel

Partly reflection, looking back.

Threads:

Oscar + Rachel	- must be
Oscar + his 'art'	- must be
Oscar + his uncle	I Oscar as the uncle + ANO

Does the uncle have some sort of secret or wisdom to impact to Oscar? Is there something he can learn from him?

Format:
> Novella. Maybe 20-50k

So Martin married Ruth

Reflective piece. Assume the narrator is the main focus of the story.
What is the central plot of the story, the key incident / message etc.?

What is the relevance of the Martin-Ruth relationship - or are they just catalysts for the remembrance?

Story about looking back.

Characters:

Narrator	I are each of these relationships
Martin	I explored in detail?
Ruth	I are they all failures - and if so,
Ruth's sister	I does narrator recognise it?

Is there some kind of parallel between the Narrator and Martin? Is he passing comment on himself by judging Martin? And do Ruth / her sister act as some kind of 'bridge' between the two?

Format:
    Short story. Maybe 5-15k

Writing to Gisella

Plot all worked out. Need to establish the value of completing.

Characters:
    Rick
    Gisella
    Jackson, Rick's friend
    Mita

Could be shortened to a form of novella; keeps the plot simple - there's enough in the multi-relationships.

Format:
    Novella. Maybe 25-40k

X

[need to re-read what's there already to see if there is any merit in it. Possibly parts of another story(s)?]

Mirrors

Hmmm...

<u>This time tomorrow / The man who made plans</u>

Similar, but need to settle on a plot line (original for TTT is too thin?). And then assessment of 'worth'...

<u>Riding the Escalators</u>

Only the girl accompanies Mitch on his quest. She provides the imagination; is his 'muse'. The older man is the intermittent 'sage' who provides answers / wisdom.
What is the 'quest'?
What is the relationship between Mitch and the girl (eventually)?
Mitch and Man meet girl / each other when admiring her work as she puts together another display. She and Mitch have coffee. He tells her about his challenge.

How many adventures? Do the shops somehow change / contain the adventure for Mitch & the girl? If so, choosing the shops is important e.g. music, books etc.

Characters:
>   Mitch
>   Chek, Mitch's friend
>   The Security Man
>   Suzi
>   Jasmine, Suzi's manager
>   Derek, shop assistant
>   Mr Lee
>   Catherine, ex-Mrs Lee

Format:
>   Novella 25-50k

<u>7:16</u>

Characters:
>   Mac Martin
>   Sally
>   Adam, the guy on the phone
>   Charlie, Sally's new boyfriend

<u>Thriller</u>

Characters:
David Plume
Ward
Cross
Mary O'Reilly, nurse
Morrison, doctor
Woman at house

Update:

'Who was she?'	5-10k	1 month?
'How does it start?'	20-50k	3-4 mth
Martin & Ruth	5-15k	1 mth
Writing to Gisella	25-40k	3 mth
Riding the Escalators	25-50k	3-4 mth

(80-165k)

Assume avg.	500 w/d => 5½ - 11 months
	300 w/d => 9 - 18 months

21ˢᵗ September 2014 (BBG)

Sequence?
Short first to get something finished?

Need a sense of how my time is going to pan out.

Estimates above seem quite long...

~~~~

Although there are some new ideas in this summary, you could be forgiven for thinking it was just another rehash, an empty exercise. Was that how he saw it on completion of these notes? He must surely have been cognisant that here he was, back as the hamster in his own private literary wheel, trying to run furiously but getting nowhere. Even 'Mirrors' makes its traditional reappearance - along with the qualification ("Hmmm") reaffirming that he still really doesn't know what he is going to do with it, if anything.

But we should not be too dismissive; there are hints here of progress, that he has actually been working at things even if acknowledgement of them did not make it to the notebooks. Indeed, there is a new question brewing, one which asks whether his attitude to the notebooks - what they were for, what contribution they are making - is beginning to change... But back to new progress:

'How does it start?' is clearly something he has been working on: "need to re-read what's been written thus far to determine value, plot etc.". It's another "looking back" story (like the Martin and Ruth idea); and note the reference to "secrets or wisdom"...

The plot of 'Writing to Gisella' is, we learn, "all worked out".

'Riding the Escalators' is clearly an idea to which he has given some thought, even though we have its first appearance here.

Some of the others - 'X', '7:16', 'Thriller' - are very old ideas.

By the end of the entry (the small section titled "Update") he has taken these candidate projects and whittled them down to five. Note that, once again, 'Mirrors' does not appear as a priority. One can only assume that at this stage - and remember he has already written 130,000 words of it! - it was something in which he still did not believe or was too old, too daunting. Considering those he has chosen to focus on, should we still assume that it will result in nothing concrete? Is it just the 'same old, same old', his writing needle stuck in one continuous groove?

We would have the answer in little over a year...

Part Six - 2015 to 2016

July 2015 (PBB)

With a very short December 2015 update.

"The Year of Funerals"

First person.   (or not..)

Twelve chapters, one per month.

Starts with funeral of relative in January. At funeral, the 'I' character realises how many of his relatives are either old or ill (essentially dying).

At the January funeral, he meets Eleanor, an old 'flame' with whom he was in love once but never declared himself.

The funeral causes him to reflect on this / mortality.

Eleanor is one of the major threads during the story.

* Decision: conclusion +ve or -ve?

So, who dies in January?
     who is going to die?

Where / when is this set?
What's the profile of the 'I' character? esp. age?

Character list + relationships is primary.

(A) Draw family tree!   ✔

January: Uncle Thomas
                Father or Mother
                Aunt or Uncle?
                Cousin
                Brother?

For each person who dies, there needs to be a relationship with the I character, a story to unfold. <u>Not all</u> will be family.

"I"
= male, single (divorced) → wife needs to appear
= age? early 50s
= children?
      1 or 2 (who would need to appear)
= profession?

Question over own fallibility i.e. a suggestion that December is his month? Or Eleanor's??

Start of a new decade (2nd) in new millennium. Excuse in intro for looking back over 1st 10 years: kids to Uni, leaving home, divorce, leaving home (!) etc.

'Not a great start to the decade for Uncle Thomas'...

Phone call to Ex. Was she coming? The kids? "Everyone's coming." Of course it was Uncle Thomas... etc.

Each chapter / death needs a thread; that is what needs to be planned out. (Prep for following deaths...)

Month	Death	Thread
January	Uncle Thomas	Realisation re Eleanor
February	Ceri	
March	Audrey (whisky)	
April	Trigger	
May	Theresa (Tipsy)	
June	George	
July	Tommy	
August		
September	Ginny	
October	Enid	
November	Stuart	
December	Eleanor	

❉

24th December 2015

Feels too contrived / morbid.

Not viable?

~~~~

Although there is something harsh about rejection, when it comes as it does here in the self-propelled dismissal of an idea, then it surely can be viewed as more progressive - especially when a significant amount of effort has already been invested (he had drawn up the relevant family tree, and drafted 'January'). Under such circumstances, could you not argue that there is a degree of maturity in being able to walk away from something? Does his rejection of 'The Year of Funerals' indicate that he had finally arrived at a standard in terms of an acceptable 'quality' for his writing, for the integrity of his ideas and the engagement and sophistication of his topic? If so, then to dismiss 'The Year of Funerals' for what it was (or what it was likely to turn out to be) should be applauded.

His decision was taken at some point up to five months after the project was originally proposed and the initial drafting completed, and only made formal in his December 'update'. What are we to make of it? Was it just another futile plan, another barren idea? And if so, did it presage another year of failure in spite of the review and prioritisation of September 2014?

~~~~

August 2015 (PBB)

With a very short December 2015 update.

"Losing Moby Dick"

Need to decide
a) how many times Jack goes into the room.
b) if he takes the girl with him - and what happens if he does
c) what is the conclusion?

How strong should the religious parallel be? e.g. Twerton

What is Jack's journey?
What does it represent?
Is it some kind of pilgrimage?

Also the question of how the real / 'now' Jack relates to his re-experiencing / re-imaging of his past.
a) does he re-live it differently? (maybe more so as he progresses)
b) by reflecting on it subsequently (though this could get boring…)

If a) do we see his past changing - does <u>he</u> see his past changing as he re-lives episodes from it?

He's not that old, so need to map out his timeline before we can plan out the chapters…

If it is a 'learning' journey, then should Jack take one lesson into the next. He 'tweaks' his past as he "re-lives" it…?

Friendship - Maggie
↳ moving house with brother
          ‖
          v
    shows appreciation
      - what's the lesson here?

Other big tickets items?
        Love
        Bravery   Virtues?

All lead to a final trip into the room with Jen → some kind of
(resurrection)   enlightenment

Prudence - Justice - Temperance - Courage - Faith - Hope - Charity

Chastity - Temperance - Charity - Diligence - Patience - Kindness - Humility

Theme - Actor - Lesson
1   T = Friendship appreciation
        A = Maggie
        L = Don't take friends for granted

2   T = Generosity & Charity
        A = Brother
        L = Be prepared to give to others

3   T = Patience
        A =
        Z =

4   T = Truthfulness
        A =
        Z =

5   T = Greatness of Soul & Love
        A = Jen / Self
        Z = Self-sacrifice

✿

24th December 2015
      WRITTEN   PUBLISHED

— — FIN — —

~~~~

As you read through this entry - outlining an idea that didn't even figure in his plans the previous September - you could easily be forgiven for jumping to a conclusion supported by your experience of him to date; namely, lots of ideas, much pontificating, but very little output. To use the vernacular, "all mouth and no trousers". But if this constant inability to turn ideas into something tangible is frustrating for you as an onlooker, a voyeur, then imagine how it must have been for him, years of stop-start (or start-stop), false dawn after false dawn.

And then you read the December update and you are stopped in your tracks. "WRITTEN" - something finished! But not only that, "PUBLISHED"!

The missing ingredient, not referred to at all in his notes thus far - and for which I must provide the context given it was such a pivotal moment on his journey - was the discovery of Kindle Direct Publishing, Amazon's self-publishing software. As if a magic lamp had been rubbed, he had found a mechanism which allowed him to 'go public' on Amazon for virtually zero cost. All you needed was some material and a degree of technological nouse.

So "PUBLISHED" meant exactly that - even if it was not through the 'traditional' Agent / Publisher route. His work - in this case a novella - was listed on Amazon and available in both paperback and e-book format.

The follow-on question to ask is how much of a breakthrough the self-publication of a single story actually represented?

~~~~

<div align="right">

16th November 2015 (BBG)

</div>

With a very short December 2015 update.

<u>Who was she?</u>
        short story - pending

<u>How does it start?</u>
        short story
        WRITTEN. PUBLISHED ✔

<u>So Martin married Ruth</u>
        short story - pending

<u>Writing to Gisella</u>
        novella - <u>prospect</u>
        WRITTEN. PUBLISHED *(24/12/15)* ✔

X
        Novel - unlikely

<u>Mirrors</u>
        WRITTEN ✔ not yet published

<u>This Time Tomorrow</u>
<u>The Man Who Made Plans</u>
        short stories? pending

<u>Riding the Escalators</u>
        Novella
        WRITTEN. PUBLISHED ✔

<u>7:16</u>
        Novel - unlikely

<u>Thriller</u>
        Novel - unlikely

<u>Losing Moby Dick</u>
>Novel - pending
>WRITTEN. PUBLISHED *(24/12/15)* ✓

<u>The Year of Funerals</u>
>Novel - pending

<u>Volume of Poetry</u>
>Poetry - prospect
>(part-written)

<u>The Man Who Waited Until Wednesday</u>
>Novella - unknown

Good progress in last 12 mths.

Next...

Target list:

1) Volume of poetry
>11 pieces drafted
>13 more needed

2) Gisella
>3 / 20 drafted
>17 letters to go

3) Publish Mirrors on KDP

4) Losing Moby Dick
>20% done?

5) The Man Who Waited
>embryonic

1,   Poetry
>2 poems/week
>written by Xmas
>publish by end 2015
>- doable

2,   Gisella
        1½ letters/week - so 3 months
        publish by end Jan 16
                - doable   *(24/12/15 - DONE)*

3,   Mirrors
        publish by end Nov '15
                - easy?   *(24/12/15 - DONE)*

4 + 5 need to be planned out and one chosen.
        ~~~~ end of Q1 '16 to draft?

(24/12/15 - #4 DONE)

~~~~

What a year 2015 proved to be!

By December 24th, not only had he finished 'Losing Moby Dick' (the last 80% written between 15th November and Christmas Eve), but also two other novellas - 'Riding the Escalators' (by 15th November) and 'Writing to Gisella' (of which only 15% had been written by mid-November). In addition, he also could boast a short story - 'How Does It Start'.

But most significant is the sudden news, coming completely out-of-the-blue, that he had finally finished 'Mirrors'! After over thirty years of planning, stopping and starting, false dawns and - presumably - truly painful lows, there is the acknowledgement: "WRITTEN". What must that have felt like, adding the final full-stop to the final line - and to see all these projects marked as "published", taking full advantage of the KDP platform?

It had been a little over a year since his last review of unfinished things (September 2014), fourteen months since he had drawn up that short-list of projects on which to work. Had he expected the see them through this time? Reading through this history, would we have expected him to do so - especially when he suddenly threw in the new (and then later abandoned) 'Funerals' idea? How could we not have assumed another spin in the hamster-wheel?

But he __did__ make progress and at pace; consider what he must have written between 15th November and Christmas Eve! He had gone from nothing to something in the highest gear possible; finally there was tangible output.

What had been the catalyst - because surely something must have triggered such a wave of creative output? The notes give us no clue. The only thing of which we can be certain is that by the middle of that November he had discovered KDP. Was it that which opened the floodgates, and which - in giving him a means to share, the potential to make his voice heard - finally released the breaks? Is it credible to propose that he had never had a problem with production and that it was the immoveable blockage downstream which resulted in his enthusiasm and motivation backing all the way up to the pen in his hand? Remember, there was no issue in writing his professional books, scenarios where all the downstream channels and processes were already in place, looked after by someone else. Perhaps knowing that whatever he wrote he would still be staring into a dead-end, he had subconsciously thought "what's the point?" - and in thinking that, excused himself from the efforts he would otherwise need to make. There was no 'contract' in place with all the affirmation that provided. Knowing he was fundamentally stymied in terms of the ultimate goal - the books themselves - were the plans he drew up essentially 'safe' because he understood they were impractical, that he could never execute against them? It is a theory which holds up in the light of his professional volumes; gifted publishers who offered a mechanism to allow his words to reach an audience - never mind the subject! - he obviously found producing the books themselves easy enough. You might object to this notion and protest that we do need to mind the subject, and that writing non-fiction is an entirely different ballgame. And to a degree you would be correct. But consider what he achieved between September 2014 and the end of the following year, the sheer volume turned out. In order to do so, surely he must have found that process 'easy' too? And all because he had found a way to breach the dam that had towered over him and his writing ever since he left University. Thirty-three years of angst and anguish, frustration and disappointment; the source of what amounted to creative impotence, writer's block of a very particular kind.

All of which surely begged a question for him on Christmas Day 2015: could he kick-on? Was 2015 just a flash-in-the-pan? Would the boost given him by KDP fade? Might something else arise - or indeed be manufactured - to arrest the flow once again?

~~~~

The Man Who Waited...

only remaining fiction idea (of those shortlisted)

...'Who Was She?' - short? play??

...Poetry?

What about comedy?

'Finding the Time' - short story?

Series of short stories à la Dubliners?

~~~~ Anne - the Museum Curator

Commonality of <u>theme</u>
        <u>TIME</u>?

How about:

"THE MAN WHO WAITED FOR WEDNESDAYS and other stories" ?

- Anne
- Who Was She?
- Martin and Ruth

? Interleave shorter stories between parts of TMWWFW?
? Use a different style in each story?
? Do they need to have an explicit link?
? Size range for the stories? >1000 at minimum?
? Are the stories all set in the same time window e.g. 1 day / week / month?
? Could there be a cascading link between them i.e. a char. in A appears in B, B in C etc.?[40]
? What about the authorial voice? Can 'I' be used a) at all; b) once; c) more?
? Each story examines a single event?

---

[39] Obviously it was as he was writing this entry that he annotated the earlier entires for July, August and November.

[40] Subsequently taken up in a project in 2018.

? Framework needed? e.g. one story per month / set in a specific month: so 12 in all - or day ∴ 7 in all?
? Based around a defined list of virtues or vices? or the major Greek gods e.g. war, love etc...? A god reference could then provide the link + the theme of the events. Also the notion of the immortal + what that means re time. Stories are actually perpetual + ever recurring...

INTERESTING...

Notions of myth too in relation to fiction.

Zeus
Hera
Athene
Apollo
Artemis
Hermes
Ares
Hephaestus
Aphrodite
Poseidon
Hestia

Themis - Iris - Hebe - Ganymede?
(see Z.)   (see Hr)

Use characters of the gods to define the theme / incident / character for each story. e.g. Zeus = 'Alpha male'; Aphrodite = love story etc.

✽

ZEUS   (Zachary)

omnipotent; all seeing/knowing; tied to fate; dispenser of good/evil
embodied in whispering sacred oak
sceptre; thunderbolt; eagle
first wife, Metis - Wisdom (swallowed)
second wife, Themis - Law (renounced) PLOT?
then Hera (sister)
many mistresses/children
ability to disguise to get what he wants

duplicitous alpha male; not trustworthy boss; driver of specific culture;
favouritism
event:

>renouncing 'law' in order to achieve personal goal / personal
>protection? insider trading? (supports all-knowing)
>deception, blackmail

<u>S</u> ow W?   Tube: Temple

❊

<u>HERA</u>   Helen?

idealised wife; goddess of Women, marriage, maternity
cuckoo, pomegranate, peacock
Hebe, daughter
Zeus' sister -> wife
Ares, son ; Hephaestus, son
tried to chain her husband as punishment for infidelity
once had anvils tied to her ankles
vengeful & vindictive
Paris chose Aphrodite above her -> end of Troy

spiteful/disappointed older woman?
event:

>discovery of husband's infidelity (historic)
>her attempt to take revenge*
>wronged & wronging
>seen by others as 'perfect' wife
>Q? what drove husband to stray?

>*what shape does her 'chaining' take? + who is most impacted by it?

<u>S</u> or W?   Tube:

❊

<u>ATHENE</u>   Anne?

warrior-goddess; of art, peace, prudent intelligence (owl); weaving
protectress & guardian; patron architects & sculptors
given birth to by Zeus (after swallowing Metis) his 'favourite' loved a fight

protector of Hercules, Perseus, Bellerophon, Odysseus, Telemachus (in finding his father)
totally chaste + modest (punishment for Teiresias)
helped Jason (Argo)
challenge of Arachne (spider)

the museum curator story
event:
> the debate over the content, layout of an exhibition (what is subject?)
> protector of the things she believes in
> not 'modern'?
> provincial curator who goes to Brit. Mus. for inspiration / ambition (which is?)
> [is there actually an 'event' here?]

S or W?   Tube: Tottenham Court Road

❋

APOLLO   Anthony?

sun god; of prophecy; shepherd; musician
'beautiful young man'; beardless
bow & quiver; shepherd's crook; lyre
mother Leto (before Hera), Zeus' wife
Artemis (sister) born at the same time
kills python with arrow made by Hephaestus
gave Cassandra ability to foresee future, but no-one would believe her
the 9 Muses: history, flute, comedy, tragedy, dance, poetry, mimic art, astronomy (love + epic) - daughters of Zeus

politician or pundit? perhaps in TV/radio?
weatherman? producer? critic? dilettante?
Cassandra figure a colleague or rival?
give someone something they want but then render it completely valueless...
event:
> gives out valuable personal info in exchange for something, then renders it worthless somehow? or secrets of success, tips of trade etc.

S or W?   Tube: Great Portland Street?

❋

184

ARTEMIS   Audrey?

agricultural; chase; forests; sudden death
bow & quiver
Apollo (brother)
severe beauty; chaste virgin
punishes indiscretion, observation (Actaeon changed to a stag + killed by
hounds)
tricked into killing Orion whom she loved
also liked song & dance
Amazonian

'old maid'? event in history (Orion) that has made her so?
event:
> something that causes her to relive or remember the past (constantly?)
> deathbed reflection?
> hit and run from years previously? (as she was trying to escape
> attention?)
> tricked into breaking off with 'the one true love' and never recovered?
> the desire to replay time, change the past

S or W?   Tube: Euston Road? (for UCH?)

✻

HERMES   Harold? Henry?

god of travellers; souls of dead to Hades; commerce; messenger of Zeus
athlete god, winged hat & sandals
stole Apollo's heifers but became friends
inventor of the lyre
always helpful, to gods + heroes (Perseus, Hercules)
protector of flocks
father of Pan

'bad news' messenger - but if helpful, unintentionally deceitful? how to fit with
being protector?
event:
> reflection on helping someone which led to their death (accidental)?
> train involved? (travel) or coach crash
> gave someone their ticket?
> is there a sense of the imperfection in the message? trying to 'pad it
> out' or second guess in order to be more helpful?

<u>S</u> or W?   Tube: Waterloo / Embankment?

❀

<u>ARES</u>   Auguste? Alex(ander)?

god of war; no specific depiction
son of Zeus / Hera
not well-liked; brutal & violent
rarely victorious
lover of Aphrodite

bully: full of self-importance + self-deception
event:
>   some kind of 'contest' where he should actually win but fails to do so
>   because of his methods
>   darts? cricket?
>   story told by observer; protagonist never present?

S or W? Absence of both?   Tube: ?

❀

<u>HEPHAESTUS</u>   Herman? Hobart?

divine blacksmith; artisanal god
often with hammer and tongs
lame in both legs with twisted feet (make metaphorical?); hidden as an infant
because of it
husband of Aphrodite; he made Pandora

talented 'engineer'
event:
>   construction of something remarkable that has unintentional
>   consequences (or fails, like his legs??)
>   comes from creative family, hence name (Sydney, brother) or is it a
>   design for something? e.g. a building that collapses…?
>   event happened not in UK; brings secret with him
>   parents Australian, moved to Singapore; secret lies there?

<u>S</u> or W?   Tube:

❀

186

APHRODITE   Angela

goddess of love, all forms (noble & ignoble) - drove the various depictions of her
daughter of Uranus? aura of seduction
Paris chose her as fairest vs. Hera and Athene (bribed him with her nakedness)
magic girdle used to entrance/enslave men
'a divinity without courage'
son, Hephaestus; father Hermes

all gloss/veneer? absence of substance?
beauty queen (ex-) trying by all means to recreate her past 'successes'
event:
        success/failure of conquest (or both?!)
        "my friends call me Angel"
        image of a decline (would no longer be 'fairest')
        lack of courage in not accepting reality
        hint at degrading/falling into prostitution?

S or W?   Tube: On journey from Mayfair to Soho

✢

POSEIDON   Pincher? surname?

god of sea (= to Zeus); fecundity, veget.
horse & bull sacred. Trident
'rough cut' image (horse races?)
son of Cronus, swallowed; freed by Zeus
Once tried (with Hera & Athene) to dethrone Zeus
thirst for possession
god of earthquakes
fought alongside Z vs. Titans & Giants
built the walls of Troy
seduced Medusa - as a result Athene made her a monster

as a result of 'victory', vanquished paying ultimate price?
winner / loser rollercoaster?
event:
        reflection on the cost of success?
        driven by the desire to possess
        theft and its repercussions? real theft?

impact on the 'rough cut' perpetrator?
'insider trading' i.e. stable staff (lass) + what happened to her
afterwards
virtual theft; scam

S or <u>W</u>?   Tube: Bond / Regent Street?

✿

<u>HESTIA</u>   Hester? Honour?

homely and social goddess; protector of house / family / city
centre of earth / universe; circular form
oldest of Olympian gods; venerated everywhere
virginal, despite Poseidon & Apollo wanting her for a wife
Aphrodite never succeeded in exerting her power over her
sharing the fire/hearth -> continuity of the family (kind of live bequest); public
fire

the family saga? matriarchal figure?
what is it that is handed on?
event:
          visit of 'H' to relative to exercise bounty
          way she is treated / rejected?
          changing of the times & impact?
          expects to be venerated but is not
          visit relating to marriage / new baby
          first hand-off to married grandson/daughter
          sense of a generational shift

S or <u>W</u>?   Tube: Metropolitan line?

✿

<u>THEMIS</u>

ex-wife of Zeus. Remained as counsellor
regulated the ceremonial
helpful and obliging
goddess of justice; wisdom; deliverer of oracles
grave & austere; pair of scales

someone official / officious; Govt or Council?

is this about the straightjacket / paralysis of process, rules etc.
there is no event because progress/ doing anything is not possible
if so, story is talking about doing…(non-event)
? meeting over coffee?

IRIS
messenger of the gods (esp. Zeus)
devoted to Hera, often dispensing her justice
waited on the other gods

with Themis, justice, messenger - duality
courts' official?
? what is the event the talk is all about?
- an election?
- a change of taxation?
- a petty by-law?
absence of wisdom

S or <u>W</u>?   Tube: Westminster?
     -ve

~~~~

And as if we didn't have enough proof of the tremendous output from 2015, this Christmas Eve entry contains a well-formed idea for a collection of short stories based upon the major Greek gods. The utilisation of existing external structures - such as traditional virtues or vices - is something he has played with previously. In this instance he settled on a thematic framework using the gods' individual characteristics to shape the primary protagonist in each story. Not only that, but he embellished the idea by adding further elements of his own: firstly, each of the stories would expose - in one sense of another - something that could be regarded as examples of either secrecy or wisdom; and secondly, they would take as their geographic locus a tube line or station on the London underground. In the final product, 'Secrets & Wisdom', the underlying foundation is largely invisible; to enjoy the book requires no knowledge of the Greek gods at all, nor recognition that they were used as templates for his characters. As previously noted, 'Anne' makes her reappearance here after debuting in his idea for 'This Time Tomorrow'.

'Secrets & Wisdom' would come to represent his first successful foray into the world of the short story. He had toyed with the form often enough, having

previously made it half-way to short-form fiction with his three novellas, 'Losing Moby Dick', 'Riding the Escalators', and 'Writing to Gisella'.

Biographical note.

At this point I feel the need to interject with a biographical note. As I have said previously, my effort in annotating his notebooks is in no way an attempt to replay his life; indeed, some of the entries have been edited to remove any superfluous references. In the context of his considerable output during 2015, I was forced to ask what had been the catalyst, because surely something must have triggered such a wave of creative output? In doing so, I settled on his discovery of KDP as the only evidential contributor to his sudden surge of productivity. And within the confines of the notebooks, this is indeed true.

However, 2014 was also witness to an extraordinary shift in domestic and personal circumstances; a shift so significant that it would be remiss of me not to provide that context here. I do so not to draw any specific conclusions you understand, but rather to provide you with all the pertinent facts behind his sudden and colossal productivity.

In March 2013 he began working for a global freight-forwarding company headquartered in Switzerland. As a consequence, for some ten months he commuted, Monday-to-Friday, between Yorkshire and Basel (door-to-door circa seven hours). Then in January 2014, he and his family moved to Singapore in order for him to take up a senior position there, with a view to remaining in the city state for four years. Due to a variety of circumstances (which, in terms of elucidation, is certainly beyond the remit of this volume), that posting failed to work out as anticipated, the result being that in around May-June of that year he had what amounted to a nervous breakdown and was advised by a specialist consultant to return to the UK. This was indeed what he did in July 2014, leaving the company in the process.

His notebook entry of September 2014 in which he reviewed his creative options and came up with the prioritised list that inspired his output over the next fifteen months, was therefore written perhaps as little as four weeks after his return home.

One can only speculate as to his state of mind during that difficult summer and whether the return from the Far East not only saved his sanity but potentially provided him with a new impetus for his creative work. Had he finally recognised how critical it was to him? Had he needed to go through the trauma of mental breakdown in order to reestablish a more healthy perspective in his life?

How could those events of 2014, six thousand seven hundred miles from home, not have had an impact on what was to follow creatively? He would have returned home in August 2014 a changed man.

~~~~

<div align="right">

End-April 2016 (PBB)

</div>

"Intersections" - novel

"Poetry volume" - found + other   ✓ DONE![41]

"The Empty Box"
↳ existing short stories plus...
   "The interview"
   "Candles"
   "Evening Class"
   "Recommended Books"
   "Secrets & Wisdom" stories
   "The Glove"
   "I knew she had a secret" in the Oracle book
   "Welshman"
   "My Dear Polly"
   "The Pepper Curse"
   "The Bay Tree"
   "Fourteen"
   "Vinno"
   "Twins" ?
   "Old-aged Travellers"
   "Funeral"

"Near Enough"

"The Man Who Waited" - novel

"Mita's Shopping" - novel

Kids / Mr Brindley story - novel

<div align="right">

December 2016 (BBG)

</div>

<u>Christmas '16 Review</u>

-----

[41] KDP-published as *Collected Poems - 1979 - 2016*, it was more a 'selection' than anything else, so was essentially mis-titled.

Looking back - a lot done in '15 and '16!!

★ Secrets & Wisdom (to finish)
★ Index of First Lines
- The Man Who Waited...? Who Made Plans...?
- Short stories*
★ New Novel?
- 'Overheard': half of stories

* there's that thing I started with the 'marry me' homework... What's that?

I like the idea of a new novel.

New novel: what's important?
　　　　　　　　what do I want to write about?
　　　　　　　　what are my core topics?

Ignorance & Wisdom
Loss
Regret
Optimism
A battle against existentialism / meaninglessness
Second chances
Replaying & changing the past (not really - but how?)
Parallels

S&W　　8 to write; 1 / wk
IOFL　22 to write; 2 / wk (=11 wks)

- based on first horizon being 13th March; so 10 wks.

13 wks to plan in detail TMWW?
The write it May → Dec
　　　　　　　　8 months
　　　　　　　　32 weeks; 4k / wk

• ideas
• characters
• threads

✿

' "Life," she said, "is a bit like peeling Brussel Sprouts." '

Mother, perhaps? Earlier? Formative?
Notion: that after all the effort, is it really worth it?

' "You can spice them up with tiny bits of bacon - but in the end, they're still sprouts." '

✲

' He had been sitting at the dining table worrying at a jigsaw puzzle that had too much sky. Increasingly blurry, uniform blue shapes stared back at him defiantly. The space he had to fill - awkward and irregular - openly challenged him. '   'teased'?

✲

Why had she said the thing about Brussel Sprouts? And why about 'Life'? What has led her to this conclusion [so prior events] and what impact does her philosophy have on him [future events]?

✲

' As if in defiance - of her, the puzzle - his fingers picked up a random piece and, undoubtedly more by luck than judgement, his eyes found its exact location. The piece dropped into place with a satisfying 'snap' as he clipped it in, tensing the card ever so slightly to get the effect.

' "How are you getting on?" she asked, prompted by the sound.
' "What do you mean about life?"
' "Don't you mind me and my nonsense."
' She smiled over her shoulder.
' But he knew very well what she meant. '

✲

She is bitter because her husband has left them [so here is a plot thread] - and thus the failure of her plans and the sprouts comment. He is coming to terms with his father's departure by putting even more structure into his own life i.e. he can see the point of peeling brussels.

She dies [how old is he then?] in a car accident.? He suspects it might have been deliberate (or not sought, if illness), she having never overcome her 'loss'. At that point, he has to be old enough to cope on his own. Does this see him go more into his shell? More planning? Or does he face his own disappointments?

Or she could just get sick, having 'given up'? Does she make any effort to get back on her feet for his sake - or if not, is that for him another betrayal, another reason for him to try and put in place structures that keep him protected?

Q> Is it, in the end, a positive story with a good outcome for him? Does it reaffirm? Does it demonstrate that she was right and he was wrong - i.e. you can't plan the future - but in a good way? Is she right about the sprouts?!

Q> Is one of his preoccupations to replay his own life events with a new, better plan overlaid on top of it, and imagining a better outcome as a result - thereby reinforcing his prejudices and beliefs?

Q> Does there need to be one random tragedy that touches him e.g. terrorist attack perhaps, or a quake (in NZ) that kills one of his friends? * another plot thread (and the relationship?) (A)

*

' She had debated - long, hard, and openly - about how to split her time. She had wanted to give both islands a chance - "the North! Volcanoes! Lord of the Rings!" - but her heart was irrevocably drawn towards the south. She had seen the gentle beauty of it and wanted those unspoilt hills and empty beaches.'

*

(A) potentially unrequited (and not meant to be?)

Stories: his - Mother's - Father's - friend who dies -

Q> Does he have two names: John and Jack? One formal, the other given him by his father: "Jack-the-Lad". A misnomer.

Plot threads:

John and -
        Mother (past)
        Father (past)
        Person who dies in NZ (female)

Love / salvation in the +ve outcome
Work -
        Colleague
        Boss
Old Uni(?) friend

Mother & Father

John and his past events he attempts to replay (possibly replaying them as 'Jack' to try and alter the outcome?)

John vs. Jack is a kind of Walter Mitty or Jekyll and Hyde relationship. Jack is who he wishes to be; John is who he is (the man who waits, plans...)

1: Opening - the 'sprouts' kitchen scene provides tone & framework. Leads to

2: reflection on his mother and father
      ↳ their relationship
     her impact on him
     his impact on him
establishes John vs. Jack

3: The need to root John in his reality. So something work-related; shows his John-like tendencies.
Opportunity to map this against his mother's 'sprouts' philosophy?
Need to give a sense of his own beliefs (and the need to plan, to wait) and what he expects that to bring.

4:? Need to establish (or is this too early?) what it is he is waiting for. What is the Wednesday event?
If near at hand (e.g. if 'today' is Friday) then a) much of the book is backward looking, b) what happens Sat-Weds? Or is it that 'Wednesday' appears as a deadline (personal) later in the book and is only hinted at here, if at all? Probably has to be later depending on the 'big thing'? <u>Really</u> - establish the tension up-front.

5:? [looking back] parental

6: Something professional that demonstrates the failure of John's planning; what derails him and how he handles it.*
Presumably this is a relatively emotionless experience. There is impact, but not on him. (If anything this supports his mother's philosophy - and his father's to a degree too?)

195

* and how this relates to the 'big thing'. Looking back.

Jigsaws: bringing order to chaos.

There is a parallel here with planning of course. How he uses his dining table i.e. not for social.
So his background must be chaotic in some sense. Needs to be reflected in his relationship with his mother and father.

What causes chaos?
> Inconsistency   Uncertainty over future
> Turbulence   Failure of past?
> Lack of stability / reliability

Can be a) personal i.e. via relationships b) real i.e. through the process of 'living'.

Fantasising is a means of escape too
↳ the replaying his past to get to a different outcome.

Is Life stable and reliable (in its unpredictability, inability to control it?). Life like Brussel sprouts...

There need to be some 'big things'...
A big project at work - one he has to care about
A big relationship (at work?) that is important to him - and in conflict with the professional 'big thing'?

The waiting for Wednesday must have a relationship with both these 'big things' - what is due to happen / should he make happen? #

7: looking back - parental

8: meet the personal 'big thing'. Someone brought in to help John because of his failure in 6?

9: Triggers a looking back / reimagining

10: Combination of 4-6-8 sees John setting up a regime that is super-structured, designed to be foolproof - but which at every turn demonstrates how flawed and vulnerable it is. John works his way out logically... (see #)

Problem: the professional 'big thing' is likely to be very dull - unless there is some kind of 'edge' to it; perhaps a sense of risk or danger (that John simply doesn't see of course).
Allows for an undercurrent to be present - and further demonstrates his naivety.
So an additional plot line. Good.
Also maybe allows for a parallel between his father (shady character?) and the modern day events, rather than just a remote / detached memory.
In this case, the failure of John's plans has a more profound effect.
Is the love interest (8) duplicitous, or 'under cover'. Or is she somehow swayed from the dark side by John's innocence?

* Need to work out what the big thing is - then how it ends - then work back from there.

or is there a reliance? e.g. project ends successfully; project party; he plans to declare himself there to 'X'. Makes project even more important. And personal. Boses notice a change in him; drive. He feels a difference. Book builds to this? Something gets 'switched on'?

So Wednesday is all about action, hitting targets, the here and now.

Tuesday therefore needs to see a culmination in all the past tensions, perhaps their resolution/exorcism. All except the 'big thing' to be worked out on the Tuesday.

Monday is about increasing the pressure, both of the present and the past. Need to establish a sense of crisis or coming hubris. Make it evident that things hang in the balance for John.

Sunday is a reflective day, clearly overshadowed by the coming week. He is waiting for a phone call from 'the project' to confirm that Wednesday is still 'on'.

Saturday delves into his past, triggered by random practical events such as shopping or watching sport on TV. A film perhaps. Also a project milestone.

Friday needs to be a practical day that establishes the timelines and dependencies for Sat-Tues. The reader needs to understand 'the plan' at this point.

Thursday is where we establish John and lay down the foundations.

Good. Check 1 - 10 against this. map out the sequence of events.

How far back does the full timeline go?
How old is John now? Old enough to be mature / disappointed - not too old to overcome his failure / failings.

Maybe 32.

Story with parents goes back 20 years?
Story with work goes back 8 years?
(need to articulate how he 'fell in' to what he does today. So add in a period post-university where he tries stuff out? So maybe 10 years?)

Story with current project: 8 months?
Story with "name" ~~~~ maybe 6 weeks?

[use a spreadsheet or cards to map out the timeline. Wednesday date: 21.5.08?]

Is there part of the parents' story that predates him i.e. >32 years ago?

[64 items in the plot (13/1). If avg at 2k words = 128k... Interesting... Nearly there?]

1. ('90 aet 14) Mother: the Brussel Sprouts scene.
2. ('90) Mother: her impact on him; establish her.
3. need to root John in his reality (work-related); map against the sprouts philosophy; a sense of his own beliefs - the need for planing & order (jigsaws).
4. a work scene that establishes the 'big event'; both outcome and steps to achieve it (i.e. prepares for the weekend).
5. need to start to get a sense of what project failure might mean to company.
6. Introduce Mark.
7. Introduce Colleagues.
8. Father: something from the past that contradicts living by structure (Jack vs. John).
9. ('90 aet 14) Father: his impact on him; establish him.
10. ('90 aet 14) Mother and Father: initial reflections on their relationship.
11. a professional failure from the past that enhances his planning approach to life.
12. Introduce Joanna.
13. reflecting on how Joanna was brought in (when? 1st April?!).
14. Drinking with Rick; drink after work.

15. walking home from pub; replaying the failure from 11 and turning it into a success.
16. Introduce Sal - their first meeting at Unit; the beginning of something (slightly chaotic?).
17. a piece about jigsaws.
18. the day starts with J articulating to himself that day's activities on the project; structures his day around that.
19. Father: something from the past; demonstration as to why J is drawn towards structure.
20. Something about reflecting on Rick's philosophy (Rick vs. Jack; Rick vs. his Father for example).
21. ('96 aet 20) looking back on an outing with Sal.
22. Mother: demonstration from the past as to why J is drawn towards structure.
23. update on the progress towards Saturday's deadlines.
24. something about the way he tackled the project before Joanna's arrival.
25. recognising the impact Joanna has had on him professionally.
26. Mother and Father: example of their chaos.
27. replays that outing with Sal; how it might have been different (John vs. Jack); but not full monty of realisation.
28. recognising the impact Joanna had on him personally.
29. update on the achievement of Saturday's deadlines.
30. need to start to get a sense of what project failure might mean to him personally (is Joanna a threat?).
31. Mother: something positive from the past.
32. Father: something positive from the past.
33. M&F: something positive from the past.
34. update on the progress towards of Sunday's deadlines.
35. he thinks of those working the weekend - and wonders what those not working will be doing (Joanna?).
36. reflections on he and Joanna working together.
37. ('97 aet 21) death of Sal in earthquake in NZ (23rd June) - around finals?
38. framing the decision he faces in relation to Joanna.
39. update on the achievement of Sunday's deadlines.
40. Mark is tense; impact of that.
41. M&F: reflection on his witnessing a relatively minor incident that foretells what is to come.
42. Father: something from the past; his Father's disappearance (something like a death?).
43. Mother: something from the past which demonstrates her falling / how she has fallen; how she is not coping.
44. update on the progress towards of Monday's deadlines.
45. drinking with Rick; a mechanism to work stuff out.

46. looking back, Rick reflecting on Sal / John (from a different perspective).
47. reflect on an incident that goes beyond the professional somehow, so suggest intimacy is possible (Joanne standing up for him? brushing his hand? promise of diner?).
48. Confirmation of his decision to act re Joanna (and explicit recognition that he could have acted sooner i.e. not waited).
49. update on the achievement of Monday's deadlines.
50. Mark beyond tense; cavalier; get the sense of what project means to <u>him</u>.
51. how is everyone else affected, especially by Mark?
52. M&F: how and why they split up; the final scene.
53. update on the progress towards of Tuesday's deadlines.
54. Father: where is he now? Does it matter? the realisation here is one of lack of impact.
55. ('95 aet 19) Mother: death of his mother in a car accident (suicide?)
56. working together (he and Joanna) on the final day; conflict of professional and personal. Timing. Stress.
57. provide a sense (ambiguous?) in terms of how Joanna feels.
58. reflections on Sal / unrequited love; needs to be some kind of realisation for J.
59. does he complete jigsaw?
60. update on the achievement of Tuesday's deadlines.
61. the 'go live'.
62. Mark successful (clearly the project is important to him personally / professionally).
63. off to the party.
64. the denouement at the party (or after at a railway station?). Saying goodbye to Joanna? Not going with her? "He would go tomorrow".

~~~~

Although he had mapped out the entirety of 'The Man Who Waited Until Wednesday', he got little further with it than drafting those opening scenes set in the kitchen with the mother, the Brussels sprouts, and the jigsaw.[42] Why was that? This was not the first time he had rejected an idea which had significant flesh on the bones, and we have already held up such examples as a kind of maturity, of not wanting to write something simply for the sake of it. He talks - increasingly so - about the need to 'believe' in an idea; perhaps he simply didn't believe in 'Wednesday', or felt it was too dull, or too close to home. Thanks to the notebooks, however, it is not lost as a concept, and perhaps part of their merit is

---

42 Though much later, in 2021, he would use that same material in a short story, 'An Irregular Piece of Sky' (unpublished at the time this footnote was written).

to provide an insight into what - for one reason or another - he regarded as simply not good enough.

<u>Note</u>. As we are about to discover, from 2017 he adds a new medium for self-examination and general theorising in that he establishes a 'writing website' and starts to post material there. The blog contains a variety of components from short reviews of books he has read, through philosophical musings about the nature of writing, to draft work (some of which he will eventually pick up and publish elsewhere). If the tone of these entries is different to the notebooks it is surely because he is consciously writing for an audience; his www.writeral.com posts need to be different from those which were always intended to be private. In order to try and remain faithful to the goals of this volume it would be remiss of me not to include some of the writeral.com posts (it would be redundant to copy them all). What follows from this point onwards therefore includes a selection of entries from that website. Interspersed with these are the traditional paper-based entires, though not surprisingly they become less frequent given his adoption of the public platform.

Was this shift simply 'modernisation' or was it more significant than that? Because he was now 'published' - admittedly largely self-published - did he regard himself as being 'in the public eye'? Did he feel he had earned his seat at the social media table?

Part Seven - 2017

17th February 2017 (w.com)

Having spent so much of the first part of 2017 focussed on getting my paperbacks ready and then drafting this site and putting it live, you would imagine that something of a pause would be welcome. Not so, I find. I guess it comes from being goal-oriented, and not having something to 'finish' in the immediate short-term leaves an undoubted gap...

Although I am continuing to work on contributions for "Index of First Lines" and 'Found' Poems, I know that I need to kick my prose writing into gear again; to re-energise my fiction production - even if I find that ancient question of 'Poet or Author?' once again raising its ugly head...

However, given that I seem not to be quite in the narrative writing space just yet, I have settled on completing a submission for a poetry competition (min. 50-page volume) which has a closing date in about three weeks. I have about 85%-90% of what I need already, so that's good. And it feels great (sadly?!) to have the submission date to aim for.

19th February 2017 (w.com)

I have just watched the 2016 remake of the 1960 classic, "The Magnificent Seven", [56 years - really?!] and I was struck by the question as to when a copy ceases to be a copy and becomes something else. Something original.

In "The Magnificent Seven" (2016), although there are echoes of the earlier film's music and some snippets of dialogue are lifted word-for-word from the original, the characters - and their characteristics - are different, and the situation is altered: the Mexican bandits stealing food are replaced by a ruthless miner who wants the land for profit... Having said that, the underlying skeleton and premise of the film is pretty much identical.

This question, 'when is a copy not a copy?', is particularly relevant in terms of 'found' poems of course, where you take a text - a collection of words and punctuation in a particular order - and rearrange/delete/supplement them to turn the whole into something else. At what point does the new 'thing' become a 'thing' in its own right? Is it as soon as you touch a word? (At the logical level it of course changes as soon as you amend the smallest element, even a comma.) Or would it be five words? 15%?[43]

---

[43] The somewhat philosophical question about when 'changed' writing becomes something else - different, original - continued to fascinated him, and was obviously particularly relevant with respect to Found Poetry.

Or is it when the new 'thing' is used to convey a different meaning? When the essence of the revision becomes something else? If so - and this is where I'd place my money - who is to say when that line is crossed?

If the new "The Magnificent Seven" were about milkmen delivering milk, well, that would be another thing entirely..!

22nd February 2017 (w.com)

The only reason I ask the question[44] is that I've been struggling with an unfinished story in my draft "Secrets and Wisdom" collection. That struggle has seen nothing much added for a while - and created a roadblock for the whole thing.

And now I think I recognise that I don't actually care about the character in this latest confection - a bit like the Strawberry Creme in a box of 'Quality Street'.

So why try and complete that one? Why not 're-engineer' it? Why worry about something to which one is not attached? The lack of emotional commitment generates 'the block'.

If I don't care about 'Anthony', then why should anyone else?!

March 2017 (BBG)

Where am I? What next?

1 - Poetry is good.
> But - 'An Index of First Lines' feels a bit like a busted flush.
> ☑ So, kill it then? ('Pause' maybe)

> But - 'found' stuff has been interesting and is a reliable mechanism for keeping stuff churning...
> ☑ So, think of a new collection for 2017 containing all post-HA work, found and 'normal'.

> ☑ Update Writeral with news of both decisions.

2 - Fiction is good too!
> And I need to get back into it.
> But - is 'Secrets & Wisdom' a busted flush too? Should I take the same 'pause' approach? Feels the right thing to do.
> ☑ Update Writeral [probably with a kind of 'state of the nation' post explaining 'stuff' - or even this lot, typed up...!]

---

[44] The title of the post was "Is there really 'Writer's Block'?"

So the big 'fiction questions':
- One project, or more than one?
- Short or long (size/duration)?

Output/turning stuff out as important (sense of progress, self-esteem). The poetry helps with that. If I need it in prose, then do shorts fit the bill? In terms of a longer piece... "The Man Who Waited..." is all planned out and ready to go. Great opening sentence...! Big question here is 'do I believe in it?'.
Other/previous options:

"Conversations" (more short story?)
"The Rites of the Dead"
"A Year of Funerals"

Or something new... Thinking cap on...

✳

What can you do with the 100-word challenge?!
2 per day = 1400/wk = 6000/mth! = 72000/yr

So, a book...
Needs 'intersections'. How many?
720 in above example. 36x20?
Or with a third dimension - perhaps Past Present Future - 3x20x12

	X1	X2	X3
T1	P I P I F		
T2			

What would 'T' and 'X' represent?
There needs to be some relation.
Could be 4-dimensional...

P I P I F	6x12x10
— — — —	2 different
I I	perspectives!!

How do you decide the sequence for writing?
Random number generator?
The book would 'emerge', a bit like a jigsaw puzzle picture, though all the pieces are the same size and with flat edges!

No need for a complex plot either.
The 'plot' is framed by the contents of the two axes - 'T' and 'X'. It would grow organically almost...
Nice idea for 'tight' fiction.
So X and T...?
Where do people come into this?
X or T? Or one of the dimensions inside the box?
Need to have tangible things to react to (in X or T), and potentially some intangible things too - like feelings - 'fear' - 'love' etc.

Need to work up some ideas for the grid...

<u>People</u> - 3 to 6
How many?
Do people interact with:
      other people?
      things? (including place)
      feelings?

[200 word challenge...?]

<u>Place</u> - 4 to 6   <u>Things</u>
          <u>Time</u>?
          (PPF)
<u>Feelings</u>

One of the axes needs to provide the narrative flow? i.e. the story that is being told. So this needs to be worked out in advance.

The characters should have different voices. "I remember."
One talks only in the spoken voice. 1 3rd party. 1 is the narrator. 1 voice not a person at all, but 'factual'...

      story

      voices

??

~~~

Was his worry about 'Secrets & Wisdom' being "a busted flush" simply because of the difficulty he was having with one particular story? (see the previous Writeral entry) If so, it clearly wasn't sufficient to disillusion him in terms of writing fiction. As ever, it was all about settling on the 'what?'.

During late 2016 / early 2017 he had set himself the challenge of seeing what he could accomplish in truly short-form fiction: "the 100-word challenge". Over several months - and in order to test himself - he produced a number of vignettes adhering rigidly to that constraint, many of which he posted on Writeral. His consideration of an 'intersections' novel (which never materialised) came from the idea of taking those 100-word segments to the next level; to create a pattern, a matrix, which would allow him to weave dozens of them together and create a different kind of novel, fluid, fragmented, sparse.

~~~

19th March 2017 (w.com)

Question.

If you set yourself the task of writing a single blog entry / post every day and had these two options, which would you choose?

1 - You could only write forwards, in anticipation, at the end of previous day / very early on the day in question - and only cover what you were expecting to happen that day. No looking backwards. At all.

2 - You could only write backwards, in retrospection, at the end of the day in question / early the next day - and only cover what had actually happened. No looking forwards. At all.

Which would you choose? Does it depend on your perspective on life. Glass half-full/-empty perhaps?

Given such a constraint, personally I could only write backwards. It seems to me to be the natural perspective for a writer; to review, analyse, interpret, dissect, make meaning of... And the frustration of writing forwards, setting the scene, and never being able to say how things turned out..!

"Today is the day our future arrives!"

or

"Today was the day our past began..."

I need a new word...because it occurs to me that, in spite of its formal definition, 'Found' Poetry is too derogatory for some of the poetry I write. It implies a kind of laziness, of putting in no effort, of simply stealing. In the early, raw days that may have been pretty much what it was: lift and put some lipstick on the fragment you'd found.

I wondered about 'Curated' Poetry, as there is an element of museum-like display about the work; words - fragments - are rearranged, presented in new displays enhanced with additional elements to explain them, make them more accessible...

But then a) 'Curated' has already been used (no surprise) in some contexts, and b) it still sounds a little too passive.

Actually, to an extent I feel a little like an Archeologist sometimes when I'm working in this way, raking over something older, dusting off the fragments, trying to recompile history / meaning / understanding from the elements I select...

There should be a word between Curated and Archeology that better describes my version of 'Found' poetry. Maybe I'll have to find one...!

Having become 're-energised' - self-publishing books via Amazon, joining the local Writers' Group, even entering competitions! - I have also re-made a discovery that is both 'good' and 'bad'.

Yesterday I was doing some research on indie publishing spurred on by a concern that Amazon's KDP may not be the best platform for me, and sniffed around some community forums on the subject. On Tuesday, I attended the latest meeting of our bi-weekly Writers' Group where I read a short poem, 'Exodus' - the only poem in a forest of short fiction and memoirs. I've also been checking out various poetry competitions, with the upshot being that I've just entered one, snuck under the wire, closing date today.

And all these related threads demonstrate something that is both brilliant and daunting. And it's all about maths.

Take the Writers' Group. How many such groups are there in the UK? 500? 1,000? 5,000? And if each one has on average 15 attendees...? Or self-publishers. Hundreds if not thousands in the UK alone. And competitions: there are lots - and lots of past winners, and even more entrants.

The good news - the brilliant news - is that there are so many people being creative with words. Millions and millions of words.

The bad news - especially if you aspire to 'stand out' in some way, be 'different' - is that there are so many people being creative with words...

My guess is that lots of people write as a 'hobby'. But lots of people write because they think they have a special talent for it. Even if, in reality, they are 'hobbyists', they may still believe that they are one of the talented few - "waiting to be discovered". After all, isn't that what we really want? (And isn't our greatest fear finding out that we aren't 'special' at all..?!)

But the truth of the matter is that talent - the ability to put one word in front of another - isn't enough. You need talent, hard work, the kind of imagination that lets you see things - then through things and around things. You need time, perseverance, tenacity, intuition. You need friends, supporters. All that.

But most of all you need readers, and you need luck. Someone who happens to come across something you've written. Someone who lands on your webpage. Someone who picks up your pamphlet; a judge who likes your work; a friend who has a friend in the publishing industry...

Good news AND bad news. And incredibly daunting.

Think about it too much and it could make you cash in your chips and give up.

So, I'll stop thinking about it now and keep plugging away. Here's another blog..!

~~~~

Fuelled by a growing concern that KDP tied him to Amazon as his sole selling medium, he questions for the first time whether it is the best route-to-market for him. Although he has taken full advantage of KDP, he is less than a year into using it, so how much of this questioning is related to him trying to establish his position and status as 'a Writer'? You can tell from the entry above that he recognises he may end up just another "hobbyist" like millions of others; but there is something in his phrasing - the use of "they" - which suggests, whilst doing so might be his "greatest fear", he actually believes he is better than that. And therefore possibly 'better' than KDP.

~~~~

30th April 2017 (MWD)

Redrafted "Twins" for "The Empty Box"

Redrafted "Old-Age Travellers" for "The Empty Box" (though this may end up in a non-fiction pile somewhere)

Redrafted "Funeral" for "The Empty Box" (it may need to be re-titled)

Redrafted "Recommended Books" for "The Empty Box"

Redrafted "Candles" for "The Empty Box" (but will need some major surgery!)

We have recently had some work done on our house which has necessitated me packing up my study and returning the room to its naked state whilst it was re-painted and new carpet laid. Then came the exciting part of rebuilding, reconfiguring, 're-imagining' it (ugh!! fake news, fake words...) in a slightly changed context. In turn, this meant going through all my 'stuff' to make decisions about where - or indeed, if - it should have a place in the 'new' room.

Unpacking boxes that have been sealed for far too long - so long that you can't recall what is actually in them! - is something of a rite of passage that most writers should go through, either literally or metaphorically. [It's just easier to do literally!] I was amazed what I uncovered; what potential lay there. It was personal archaeology of a kind.

For example, I found thirteen (thirteen!) short stories of various lengths, written over the last ten or twenty years that have lain untouched, patiently waiting to be resurrected, dusted off, given access to the light of day. Some of them may be complete rubbish, of course, but even so, that's something of a treasure trove. It could be half a collection... And seeing the subtle differences in style compared to how I write today; at first blush, that might be really telling.

And then there were the half-written novels. A huge chunk of a kids' adventure story about a young boy who discovers he has a phenomenal talent for remembering things - and then gets mixed up with aliens... Maybe 30,000 or 40,00 words right there. The beginnings of a sci-fi novel called "Time Credits", which has been surpassed by the 2011 Justin Timberlake film "In Time". I may have got the idea first, but no prizes for coming second (or two-hundred-and-fourth). Another sci-fi/political novel called "The Test", with the first couple of chapters written out, all the characters defined, the plot detailed... And at least one - if not two - false starts on 'thrillers', born from when I had the notion about producing something commercial...

There's whimsy of a kind too. A kind of semi-diary with all sorts of internal musings and angst. And the odd nugget like a sharp non-fictional travel piece which starts: "Never go to Talgarth. There is no bus stop. Shops boast 'Home Killed Meat' and combinations of 'Carpets & Flowers'. There are two 'open-til-late' shops: civilisation." [Apologies to the residents of Talgarth. This was written years ago; I'm sure it's changed now...][45]

All this is, for me at least, quite exciting stuff. It offers timely confirmation about imagination, the ability to put words on paper, and - just occasionally - a whiff of quality that helps to keep me going. In thinking about resuscitation, it also adds to the long list of the things that I might do; those projects that just need to be undertaken because, one way or another, they really are important somehow.

---

[45] The entire Talgarth notebook entry was included earlier in this book.

But then that's what a new study is for, isn't it? To be a catalyst, an incentive, the incendiary that starts the next creative explosion.

~~~~

The discoveries referred to in the entry above were probably the trigger for the review he was to document in one of his notebooks over the coming months (see the entries below). In parallel, he also continued to post to his website; occasionally the subjects would overlap. These parallel streams of output pose a difficulty for this volume in terms of sequencing; the notebook entries are not always specifically dated (so have to be reproduced en masse), whereas the timings of the Writeral postings are absolutely explicit. As a consequence, it is almost inevitable that some of the comments below may appear out of kilter from a 'time perspective' from here on - though in reality, they weren't of course! It is an issue further compounded by the fact that he wrote in two different notebooks during the year.

In order to combat this and ensure as great a degree of clarity as possible, it may be necessary for my commentary to occasionally project forwards i.e. to be a little more explicit as to what would eventually happen to a plan, an idea.

~~~~

May-December 2017 (BBG)

Re-re-review…

Can't see the wood from the trees…?

So much on the go. Focus needed.

Website: blessing + curse.

So choose![46]

- Writeral
- Poetry volume
- The Empty Box
- 2017 - H1
- Near Enough
- The Man Who Waited
- Intersections

---

[46] Echoes of his list and its prioritisation from September 2014.

Wild cards:
- Mita's Shopping
- Mr Brindley

? Starting something else is not a good idea? Just adds to the confusion!
- Writeral is here to stay, so that's a keeper...
- Near Enough: not sure the timing's right
- Poetry volume: YES
- The Empty Box: Probably

? Is 2017-H1 a brilliant idea or just a cop out?
Ask yourself the question: How many conventional books are written /
published / unread? Millions. How many like 2017-H1??

2017-H1 offers flexibility i.e. I can work on everything - but does this just
duck the focus question? is it a bit too dilettante?

~~~~

*Having previously rejected both "The Empty Box" and "The Man Who Waited",
he was obviously happy to give them one more chance. Perhaps his reluctance to
cut the cord was down to familiarity, not wishing to let go, or - in the case of
"Waited" - the fact that it was all planned out and ready to write...*

*"2017-H1" was an idea to which he actually gave a whole page on Writeral.
What was it? His notion was that, rather than be tied to the completion of a
single project - a collection of poems, a novel etc. - he would instead be bound by
time. "2017-H1" would contain everything worthy he had written during the first
six months of the year: poems, short stories, parts of novels. It was a scheme he
thought might liberate him. If he wrote half of a novel in the first part of the year,
he might finish it in the six or twelve months after that. Eventually he would - or
would not. It was a way of making it not matter. Or matter less. In any event,
there would be two volumes per year, a continuous stream of creative outpouring
unfettered by conventional notions of what a book should contain: lots of
'beginnings', a fair number of 'middles', but far fewer 'ends'.*

~~~~

Branding question: poetry or prose?
↳ does it matter? why one or the other?

Take to its logical conclusion, you wouldn't write prose or you wouldn't write
poetry.

Not acceptable.

Q. What goes on Writeral? And where does this fit in terms of 'formal' output?

Scenarios…

1   2017-H1 (then 2017-H2)
      ↳ amalgam of prose and poetry, probably intermingled (slightly larger than 5¼ x 8?)
      + Writeral for:
      odd bits, like 100-word promotional, pre-release
      (2017-H1 becomes a bit like an individual Granta…)

2   Human Archaeology (HA)
      - poetry volume
      The Empty Box
      - short stories
      + Writeral

If 1, 6 weeks or so to deadline.
If 2, poetry deadline = ?
      The Empty Box deadline = ?

If 2017-H1, does everything go in? i.e. Near Enough, The Man Who Waited?…

If 2017-H1 is big, what happens if there's only enough work to make 2017-H2 really small?

Is 2017-H1 actually a bad idea for a title?! Makes it time-bound. How about HA for the collection? Could be ready anytime; as soon as there's enough material. maybe 250 pages or so…?

Would I have to assume that I don't win the PS[47] prize - or keep that material for the book that follows… idea.

Big question though: do people buy combo-books? [Would they buy them anyway…?!]

Maybe check with PS that I'm not going to win…?!

---

[47] Poetry Society, for the National Poetry competition.

Thinking about it, the fiction stories work with the HA poetry too as there's a similarity of subject...

What does this mean for the content & structure of Writeral? Would need some rework...

Work out current size: PAGES

140	Empty Box	= 62	
15	Poems	= 15	
24	Found	= 24	
60	Other Stories	= 58	
		= 48	Near Enough 10
		= 7	more poems + Vinno
_3_	100-word	= _5_	
242		219	

If this is c. 250, is that it?

"Human Archaeology"
↳ sequence
↳ rework
↳ cover
↳ Ingram account

WOW!

~~~~

For clarification, the "PAGES" count above refers to the volume of material he had already drafted and available. Perhaps the "WOW!" was his reaction to the realisation that there was already sufficient material at the time of this entry (presumably around May/June 2017) to make '2017-H1' a reality.

There is some potential for confusion, however. Although considering it as an alternative title for '2017-H1' (until as late as mid-2017), 'Human Archaeology' was to eventually be chosen as the title of his first volume of poetry since 'Collected Poems', and which contained entirely new work.

'Human Archaeology' debuted at the inaugural Ripon Poetry Festival (in October 2017) where he shared a launch event with Andy Croft (of Smokestack Books) and his friend David McAndrew (who sadly died in 2019). Although the

launch was well-attended and he sold a few copies of the book off the back of it, he was disappointed with his own performance - his first public reading since 1980? - regarding it as stilted, contrived, compromised by nervousness.

The reference to "Ingram Account" is also worthy of note. 'Human Archaeology' also marked the beginning of his move away from KDP, and was the first volume for which he was to use Lightning Source / Ingram Spark as his print-on-demand production partner.

~~~~

Disappointment[48]	Rebel
The Grand Tour	The Grand Tour
	(poet's looking in…)
Looking Back	Running
Extra time	Uprising
Beyond the B.	The Perm. of Shrap
Ripples	

Mirage

Failed Understanding	Archaeology
The Chef	I + II + III
	IV
Camouflage	Not Unlike Cleo

Journeying

Romance		Landscapes
Standing in Doorways		Exploration
The Grain of the Wood		Terra Firma
The Diss. of Lock	Rose	
Love-locked	Guilt	Abstraction

✽

"When he awoke he already new he was too late. He had missed his flight. That is, he was suddenly sure that he'd supposed to be on a flight - to home, presumably - and that it had left without him."

But <u>not</u> amnesia

—

In a country where he doesn't understand the language.

---

[48] Grouping potential poems for *Human Archaeology* into themes.

"It was as if it was written in a strange font he couldn't decipher."

And it is...

❀

What Next?

A new novel!
Current options:
• The Man Who Waited
• Intersections
• something else

TMWW
      boring?
      passion for the theme?

Inter
      n x 200 words (maybe)
      chop'n'change timeline / voices etc.
      ↳ has some attractions

Something else
      need the theme, the premise
      "there are two reasons for everything"
      something 'big', 'philosophical'?
      something difficult or challenging?
      exploring dichotomies / opposites
      e.g. selfishness - selflessness
      bravery - cowardice
      (these could be multiple plot lines?)
      (multiple characters)
      lost - found
      love - hate
      staying - leaving

Does the book articulate the struggle to make a single decision - and the book ends with the resolution? e.f. "He left." FIN.

History - what it is
      the impact of the choices made
      setting / closing off directions

two reasons for everything
↳ two outcomes…
all impact the pressure on the decision-making process

Book starts with a decision that needs to be made.
Book ends with the making of that decision.

In between:
reflections
considerations
other decisions
looking back at past decisions - past history

Interesting…

The key thing, then, is to focus on the decision.
<u>What is it?</u>
↳ then build out context and plot from that
(maybe use mind map to flesh out?)

⇶ character CORE IDEA character ⬱

or by event?

Start? "blah blah blah. That was the question…"
+ something about "easy to articulate with words, but…"

If so, is the real timespan between the beginning and end, just moments?
↳ story would need to be told in some kind of associated flashback.
How not to make it from a single POV
↳ or should it be a single POV?

It can be multiple POV, but these views would need to reside in separate chapters.
Potentially multiple reflections on some events
↳ there are two reasons for everything
↳ showing multiple / rippling impact of each decision made

Plot reflections need to show how we arrived at the point of being able to ask the initial question.

Is there some kind of 'origin' that needs to be uncovered?

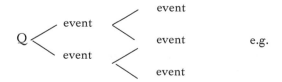

'Big' questions:
> "Do you love me?"
> "Are you going / staying?"
> "Who did... is..." etc.
> "When...?"

Let's say it starts on the Coniston Launch and the question is "Do you love me?".
Prompts:
> 'love'
> the other person
> trapped (on the boat)
> Coniston / travelling on water
> Lake District
> "two reasons"
> the question
> the answer

Each of these then fans out e.g.
> "two reasons"
> ↳ what does it mean?
> ↳ does he believe it?
> ↳ who said it?

- and again, these fan out...

So one question in one location by one person generates an infinity of possibilities...

<u>All</u> questions need to be posited, outlined in the first chapter - then answered in the rest of the book.

"Do you love me?"
> - question asked of Mac
> (current writing is therefore part of the history that fills out his character and leads to the final answer)
> [fits "After the Rehearsals"]

- question to whom?

- question asked by Jess (ditto)
different circumstance & location, different motivation
- parallel strands, same theme

Questions asked by different reasons.

Could it be that the person who asks Mac is Mags or Rosie?!

If dual questions, the Mac-Jess relationship provides the link between the two threads. A kind of lynchpin, datum point (even if a somewhat unstable one).

Is the end of the story the answering of both questions and a resolution of the Mac-Jess relationship?

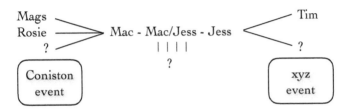

spin-offs from past (Mags etc.)

~~~~

I have already pointed out how difficult it is to allocate a timeline to the 2017 BBG notebook entries. We can only assume that the last in the sequence immediately above comes towards the tail-end of the year (and probably <u>after</u> the one PBB entry, a little way below). In it, 'After the Rehearsals' seems to be presented as a project already in motion, presumably in accordance with the schematic he had drawn out above. Clarification will undoubtedly follow, but for now - given we are about to see the remaining Writeral entries for 2017 - we need to be prepared for a little 'time travel' as elements presented in the long May-December segment above, may re-appear in one of his on-line posts as if for the first time. [Note: 2017 is the only year where this potential confusion exists, all future entries - hand-written and blog-posted - are accurately dated and thus avoid any material overlap.]

~~~~

Redrafted "Spinning Plates" [poem] - needs some work!

Redrafted "Evening Class" for "The Empty Box"

5th May 2017 (MWD)

Completed "Love-locked" [poem]

Completed "Spinning Plates" [poem]

6th May 2017 (MWD)

Working on an as yet untitled short story, probably for 'The Empty Box'; added 950 words to the draft

7th May 2017 (MWD)

Working on an as yet untitled short story, probably for 'The Empty Box'; added 1247 words to the draft (a candidate entry for the Bridport Prize?)

8th May 2017 (MWD)

Added another 633 words and completed the first draft of the 'as yet untitled short story'; rework to follow

9th May 2017 (MWD)

Started work on two new (short) 'found'/'curated' poems

10th May 2017 (MWD)

Further work on the two new (short) 'found'/'curated' poems

Redrafted "My Dear Polly" for 'The Empty Box'

11th May 2017 (MWD)

Completed "The Permanence of Shrapnel" [poem] - and it's not often I go 'wow', but 'Wow!'...

Completed "Gauntlet" [poem] - title may change...

13th May 2017 (MWD)

Attended an all-day Ripon Writers' workshop on the subject of "The Dark Side" led by an external speaker, Steve Toase. A number of pieces of flash fiction might make their way to this site.

---

[49] For an explanation of these short MWD entries, please see the "My Writing Diary" introduction in the Addenda section at the end of the book.

14th May 2017 (MWD)

Published "The Natural Light Alarm Clock" in the 100-word challenge series, this partly inspired by yesterday's 'Dark Side' workshop.

Completed "The Superiority of Nature" [poem] - title may change...

15th May 2017 (MWD)

Started work on a new 'found'/'curated' poem, tentatively titled "Murder Mystery"

Published "Carbon Dating" in the 100-word challenge series - along with the much longer original. Comments welcome!

16th & 17th May 2017 (MWD)

Continued work on a new 'found'/'curated' poem, tentatively titled "Murder Mystery"

Started redrafting "The Interview" for 'The Empty Box'

18th May 2017 (MWD)

Completed "Murder Mystery (or Archaeology V)" [poem]

Finished redrafting "The Interview" for 'The Empty Box'

Started redrafting "Vinno" for 'The Empty Box'

19th May 2017 (MWD)

Finished redrafting "Vinno" for 'The Empty Box'

Started redrafting "The Bay Tree" for 'The Empty Box'

20th May 2017 (MWD)

Published "The Blackwood Convention" in the 100-word challenge series

Finished redrafting "The Bay Tree" for 'The Empty Box'

21st May 2017 (MWD)

Decision taken on publishing 'Human Archaeology'; blog published

22nd May 2017 (MWD)

Draft content for 'Human Archaeology' selected and printed ready for editing

Started work on sequencing 'HA' material

23rd May 2017 (MWD)

Published "Wallpaper (1)" in the 100-word challenge series

Sequencing 'HA' material

Published the "Anything's Possible" blog post

24th May 2017 (w.com)

At my local Writers' Group, we were given the challenge of producing a story that had to contain the following six words: rules, postman, lamb, cripple, shotgun and sixpence. To make it harder, I thought I would try and do so within the constraints of 100 words. Here's the super-short story output (99 words):

"When the Postman delivered mail to 'The Lamb and Flag', he always did so remembering the past. He had been there all those years ago when the argument broke out about the rules for Cheese Skittles, Jack and Tom getting overheated about a friendly game spiced up by their traditional sixpence wager.

"Tom's departure and subsequent return with his shotgun took them all by surprise, none more so that Jack who, fielding a fair chunk of Tom's first round, ended up a cripple. Tom is no longer able to drink, shoot or play skittles where he is currently incarcerated."

25th May 2017 (MWD)

Sequencing 'HA' material (this could become a theme..!)

26th May 2017 (MWD)

First round of sequencing completed. Now to 260 pages of revision...!

27th May - 5th June 2017 (MWD)

Proofread / edited 88 pages

6th June 2017 (MWD)

Published "Wallpaper (2)" in the 100-word challenge series

7th June 2017 (MWD)

Published "The Fortune Teller" blog post

8th June - 20th June 2017 (MWD)

Proofread / edited 219 pages

21st June - 27th June 2017 (MWD)

Proofread / edited 270 pages - and breathe!

28th June 2017 (MWD)

Started work on setting up my title(s) with my publishing engine...

So it's now the 9th July and I suddenly realise that I haven't been keeping this diary up-to-date... Why? Largely because I have been so absorbed in getting 'Human Archaeology'[50] and 'Secrets & Wisdom' ready for the printers... The latest is:

'Human Archaeology' - the proof copy is due to be delivered to me tomorrow. If everything is OK, then I can promote and release it! First book with new publisher/printer, so everything's crossed! 'Secrets & Wisdom' - final copy is ready for one last read through, and the cover is prepared. As soon as I know that the quality of the finished physical article will be good, then I'll be striving to be able to order a proof copy ideally by the end of next week.

Ages ago I set myself the target of being done by mid-July. Looking good for that!

Hopefully I'll be able to resume regular updates to this page once I get into writing again!

21st July 2017 (MWD)

'Secrets & Wisdom' is published tomorrow; 'Human Archaeology' was published on Tuesday. WHAT A WEEK!

4th August 2017 (MWD)

Published "Veritas" - a poem

17th August 2017 (MWD)

Published "Making the connection", "The Seeds", "Knocking-off time" - three pieces of 'flash fiction'

23rd August 2017 (MWD)

Published "Islanders" - a poem

September 2017 (PBB)

- Work towards new poetry volume for end '17, early '18.

- Something else… (prose?)

- Publishing Co << Coverstory Ltd >>   ✔
  ↳ what do I need?
      - Ltd company (presumably)   ✔
      - website (Wordpress)   ✔
      - legals

---

[50]*Human Archaeology* now refers to his new collection of poetry.

- logo & style sheet ✓
- first books - mine (take from Amazon)

- My books into Waterstones?!
↳ Nielsen book data ✓

- re 'Something else'...
↳ 'low brow', trashy, 'popular'?
    ↳ designed to fit in publishing co and sell?
        (who am I kidding?)
    would need to be some kind of 'thriller'? "filmic"...

Website structure:

    About (is this the home page?)
    Contact / Submission?
    Our Books
    News (is this featured articles first, then moved to page?)
    How we work

About - News - Our Books - Now We Work - Contact

About - Our Books - News - Now We Work - Contact

- and 'featured content'

✽

About:
~ Coverstory books:
        - what?
        - why?
        - when?
        - how?
        - who?

Our books:
~ work on a template for promoting a book

How we work:
↳ maybe split out by process?

1) what we offer i.e. the high-level premise
    ↳ selection - formatting - cover - submission to printer
      'text-to-volume'

cost: time + set-up fees with printer
cost to author: dependant on 'state' of electronic manuscript
c. 50% of set-up fee (from £50) ebooks extra
payment 50% of royalties
    ↳ give examples

process
- init. query
- expression of interest
- submission
- acceptance in principle
- the quote
- payment
- set-up work
- publication + promotion
- monthly reports + royalties

publishing exclusivity

contact:
        questions
        query - step 1 of process
        ↳   book info
             type
             size
             words (no pictures)
             subject matter

~~~~

Having become familiar with the process of self-publishing, the next logical step for him to consider was not only a 'brand' for his books but also the creation of a vehicle that could potentially be used as a commercial endeavour to publish others' work too. The 'ticks' against one of the lists above suggest he made quick progress on these. Only time would tell if this secondary ambition would play out.

Also worthy of note is his comment "first books - mine (take from Amazon)". By the latter part of 2017 he had published a number of things of Amazon that were

candidates to move to the Ingram Spark platform under his "Coverstory books"
imprint: 'Mirrors', 'The Big Frog Theory', 'Collected Poems: 1979-2016',
'Riding the Escalators', 'Writing to Gisella', 'Losing Moby Dick', 'Human
Archaeology', 'Secrets & Wisdom'. If nothing else, this catalogue proves just
how much the discovery of KDP had liberated him.

Eventually he would remove the majority of these from KDP and move them to
use Ingram's production under the 'Coverstory books' label. The three novellas
were eventually collected together in 'Losing Moby Dick and Other Stories', and
other work - two small collections of poetry, 'Walking Thru Fire' and 'Second
Sight', and a number of short stories - were removed and never transferred, their
contents being absorbed into new books (the short stories would make it into
'Secrets & Wisdom', for example).

~~~~

At our writing group this week we had a panel-led session on "Publishing - Then
and Now". Even though I've been fortunate enough to have seen both sides of this
particular coin first-hand, it struck me how irrelevant the 'Then' part of the
conversation feels now. Like many things, it seems a world away; a world without
the internet and computers; a world that took time to get things done... Funny, it
doesn't even seem romantic any more.

Inevitably, when it came around to the discussion on self-publishing, the impact
of 'the indie publisher' on traditional publishing came up, as did the question as to
why we - people like me - chose to publish in the first place.

I played the vanity card immediately. Why lie about it? There is a big part of me -
'us', I assume - that publishes our work not only because we now can, but because
in doing so we are playing to our ego, finding a way to justify our obsession/
passion/hobby (delete as appropriate!), and leaving some kind of mark on the
world. There is nothing, I confessed, like the feeling you get when you open that
brown parcel the postman has just delivered and cradle your book - YOUR BOOK!
- in your hands for the first time. Nothing. And no-one can take that away from
you.

There is a price, of course. Because you can, everyone can - which means, to be
frank, there is an awful lot of really poor material out there competing with you to
be heard. And, of course, we can never afford to see ourselves as one of the weak
links... Not us. Surely...

In the end, I suggested, it didn't really matter. Not at some profound level. One
sale or 10,000 sales didn't change the fact that it was your book, that you had
those feelings, and no-one could steal that from you.

Then the question came... But surely you want people to read you work? Surely that really is important too?

And of course it is. Absolutely. Because for all the vanity and the self-massaging that publishing gives us, having someone read what we've written, having someone say they like it or get something from it, that's the thing that gives what we write true worth; that's the thing that really makes us 'Writers'.

That's what we strive for too - the notion that somewhere along the line we've said something that means something; that's beautiful, or profound, or new, or moving, or deep, or passionate... and that we've touched someone.

It isn't, for me at least, about shallow entertaining, not really - even though we do try to do that. It's about the unspoken; as if we have taken our thoughts and somehow been able to physically touch the heart of someone else... That's why we want people to read us. To 'share' and not just 'like'. For me, that's why I hope, day after day, that someone has the courage, fellow-feeling, sympathy, friendliness even, to take out their plastic and buy a book. It isn't about the money. It really isn't.

It's about justification of who I am and what I do.

It validates my life.

17th September 2017 (MWD)

Published "Telling the time" in the 100-word challenge series

26th November 2017 (w.com)

Tomorrow afternoon I go away to my very first "Writers' Retreat". A week in a remote Pennines location with like-minded folk; four full days with nothing to get in the way of writing - and walking, talking, reading, and taking photographs.

Perhaps it's long overdue, I don't know. But I can confess to being a little nervous.

Not about the writing, per se - although the prospect of having all that time to dedicate to it, maybe up to 8 hours per days, is daunting enough. After all, is it possible / desirable to try and fill every available moment trying to be creative? Somehow I doubt it.

It's more about the environment and the company; and by company I don't mean the other writers on the Retreat with me, but rather myself. How will I perform as company for me - if that makes sense?!

I go away with a kind of plan in terms of what I'd like to be working on, but fully expect to come back with something I hadn't foreseen - which is fine of course. Success will, I suppose, be the production of something, progressing something already in-train, and whatever it is being of sufficient quality. Success may end up being other things too, of course: a great photo, new friends, finding answers to questions I didn't realise that needed to be addressed...

Exciting stuff.

28th November 2017 (w.com)

If I'm honest, I was worried about how slowly time would pass... but the day is structured so well with really useable chunks of time, that this just isn't an issue. And the company's great!

Day 1 summary:

- 1200 words drafted on a prose 'thing' I'm working on;

- 2 new poems drafted, plus some rework on some existing stuff, and the bones of another piece;

- an hour's walk in the gloriously empty Yorkshire Pennines;

- reading...

More of the same tomorrow, maybe with a little sketching thrown in too.

Oh, and a reading of some of my work after dinner.

Does it get any better?!

29th November 2017 (w.com)

It's funny how writing can abuse you, isn't it? Well, not funny exactly. In fact, almost the opposite. After a pretty buoyant day yesterday, today has been a real struggle to get going. Fewer words - and 'less good' words too! - on the prose piece; a bit more of a struggle to find momentum / inspiration poetry-wise; some minor editing.

Tweaking at the edges really.

After dinner we're going to have a little impromptu 'reading' session, really just to introduce to each other the things we're working on. Then on Friday evening, a bit more of a 'performance' to round the week off...

If you read my intro two blogs back, it won't surprise you to hear that I quite liked myself yesterday, but today not so much...

1st December 2017 (w.com)

Somehow I just knew the value of trying something like this would surface in multiple ways... On Wednesday I had a minor, innocuous encounter on a short walk from the house. During the evening 'reading' session, the conversation turned to what we write about, how those things manifest themselves, etcetera.

And it was at that moment that I suddenly realised my walking encounter might actually be a door opening onto a writing opportunity...

The result? Around 2,800 words - in one day! - of a short story based around that experience (the first draft of the story to be finished on Friday, the last day). Not only that, but it also suggested an idea for a new collection of linked short stories[51]. Nothing may come of it in the end, of course, but I wouldn't have had the story without the walk, the Retreat, the conversation.

So the running total is now over 5,000 words of prose, work on a number of drafts of poems - perhaps six - plus reading (I have a book to finish while I'm here) and the value of our daily interactions.

One day to go, so things to finish off - the World Cup draw to watch (sadly!) - and then the final 'end of Retreat' reading to conclude the week. Then home in the snow!

2nd December 2017 (w.com)

In the end it was all just marvellous. Not just the writing, but the company, the "me time", the time to chill... And the interaction between us all, being able to spark and bounce ideas off one and other.

The last evening was spent in a kind of 'performance': Amy's academic paper had moved further towards completion than perhaps she ever hoped; we were able to read some scenes from Julian's draft play, which enabled him to sit back and watch/listen to his own work; I read my 3,000 word short story (draft) inspired my a walk to the train station on Tuesday; and Hamish and Rebecca treated us to some poetry and music, which was a great way to round off our week and their first season at Garsdale.

Priceless - in the most profound sense.

It will be great to get home and see the family. And to see what impact this week has made when I get back to the normal hurly-burly...

---

51 Eventually these stories would appear as *Degrees of Separation*.

Part Eight - 2018

January 2018 (BBG)

Here's an idea...

The plot / narrative of Rehearsals[52] is absolutely fine - but what if a) my prose isn't that great or b) I need the 'quick fix' of poetry?

Is there another format that allows me to tell the narrative?

A kind of prose poem, with a style to fit the subject / episodes?

Structure / Poems / Chapters all equiv. e.g. Coniston question is one piece; Saltburn is another piece.

Would need to be told in chronological sequence - except for answering the Coniston question - because it wouldn't make sense any other way...

Late 2017 / early- or mid-2018? (PVR)

"Write something big"

"Intersections"
↳ novel composed of a series of fragments, each strictly limited to maybe 150 words.

Characters in story each have their own unique voice:
- 1st person   "I"
- 3rd person   "he/she"
- 1st person   all verbal or stream of consciousness
- narrator   dispassionate and uninvolved, but not necessarily

There are a number of core 'themes' within the story e.g.
- centred around relationships between the characters
- ambitions
- 'first times' / 'last times'
- etc.

There are a number of core points of intersection along the journey. These could be:

---

[52] The idea first referenced in the entries from mid- to late-2017.

- places
- events (meetings, parties, births, deaths, achievements etc.)

The intersection points are where a theme and an 'event' / 'place' meet (e.g. birth in Barcelona) and at each of these intersections, all four (sic) characters express their thoughts, views, opinions.

The story is therefore built up like a tight mosaic.

If chars = 4 and limit = 150, that's 600 words per intersection. Aim for 80k, required 140 intersections (maybe 7 themes and 20 events).

The intersections are told in a completely random sequence, so comprehension comes gradually over time.

1Q> Will this work or too fragmented?

2Q> How many characters and who are they?

3Q> What's the story 'about', its message, what is it trying to say?

4Q> What does the conventional timeline look like i.e. what happens?

5Q> re 1Q - or should the story be told laterally (i.e. A->B->C), but just the intersections are written randomly... Might make it more accessible.

5QA> Yes, laterally <1QA

❁

3QA> What's the story about?

Dreams? The nature of dreams: what they consist of; how they are formed; how fallible they are / how fallible the dreamers are; the impact when a dream comes true / when it fails.

Dreams in the context of:
a) people / relationships
b) ambition

Characters	Relationship	Ambition
1 Ben	✓	✓
2 Laura	✓	x
3 Cap	x	✓
4 Brillo	x	x

This would include the narrator as a character - and surely the x/x one. This would then influence how they told the story.

6Q> Is the narrator a character in the story or 'just' the narrator?

7Q> Are the relationship dreams complex and interconnected in such a way as to mean at least one person is unhappy (not a Midsummer N's D...)? But, if so, one successful relationship ticks two boxes, so too easy.
↪ this would mean that there would need to be peripheral characters outside the main 4... there has to be at least one pair of dreams that mean one ✓ results in one x...
        - narrator is x probably

2QA> 4, including narrator plus fringe characters as and when needed

6QA> has to be a character to make it interesting / insightful (but heavily disguised...?)

What to use as inflexion points? Place would be an obvious choice. Allows the possibility of a 'starting place' and an 'ending place'.

Characters:

'Brillo' - the narrator; a nickname (how earned?) Not immediately clear that Brillo is the narrator, appears in others' excerpts as an additional character. A big reveal @ the end?

'Laura' - not her real name but "Because she always wanted to be called Laura - so that's what they called her. A name invested with Hollywood romance?" Possibly something foreign there (or in a different 2nd level char).

Ben - maybe the main char. The ✓ ✓ man in 1st person. Should be a painter, not a writer...

'Cap'? - is the x ✓ philosopher. Successful professionally but not personally. Uses his x and ✓ as feeds off each other... Or photographer?

Laura would need to be ✓ x, a professional failure.
If ? is photographer, is Laura his muse (and his x)?

❋

Events need to be spaced out to allow things to change in between. Almost like
an annual reunion, but not.

First intersection needs to be either a) when they first meet, or b) when they
first separate (e.g. after graduation).

❋

"The town had two railway stations which, rather than divide it
geographically, seemed more as bookends as if keeping the buildings in place.
They did, however, serve to split the place psychologically, you were either an
X or Y person. Where you went to or came from said so much about you that
it allowed the entire population to make assumptions which might be precise
or wildly off the mark."

The High St equidistant. Market Square.

Beyond one, rough paths towards the sea. The other, manicured lane to the
golf course.

Story is about the importance of place and how people fit into place / how
place affects them / how they affect place.

Story about new arrival(s) to the town and where they choose to live... + story
about those already living there.

Newbies start in 'the centre'; that's where they work and where they have
rented / hotel(?) while they look for work.

Work colleagues are 'fixtures' for the town + and the two stations. (plus others
e.g. if hotel-based).

Does the job enforce meeting people from across the town? e.g. hospital. legal,
library etc. 'Social' role.

Is there a sort of 'ring road'? Character could be a runner and this could be
one of their routes...

"Checking out of 'The Unicorn'."

❋

OR

Keep the idea of the quay station as a place of arrival for a small town / large village. Now a request stop; trains hardly ever.

Arrival one day. 'Mysterious' woman.

Somehow base the story on the nine muses, each a 'theme' for a section of the book?

MAUNSTON QUAY

The woman who arrives is some kind of catalyst for change.

ravelling or unravelling (or both)

The other main character is the thread through the stories, the observer. Drawn in to her / the unfolding stories. The final story is about her and him.

Muses[53]:

Calliope	Epic poetry	Writing tablet
Clio	History	Scrolls
Erato	Lyric/Love poetry	Lyre
Euterpe	same + Elegiac	Flute
Melpomene	Tragedy	Tragic mask
Polyhymnia	Hymns	Veil
Terpsichore	Dance	Lyre
Thalia	Comedy	Comic mask
Urania	Astronomy	Globe & compass

Q> How much is the woman's past vs. those who live in Maunston?

Main char	Woman	Others
Love (9)	Love	
	Religion	Superstition

---

[53] As we have seen before, once again he displays here a penchant for structure provided through established external influences e.g. the mythological Muses.

```
                  Mourning
                  ↳ (Death)        Death
                  Writing
History           (History)
                                   Dance/Party/Music/Song
                                   Comedy


6      GRAND SCALE/WRITING/BOOKS
1      HISTORY: examination of past
9      LOVE: new attachment / emotion
2      MOURNING?
8      DEATH
4      RELIGION
7      DANCE/PARTY
5      COMEDY
3      SUPERSTITION?
```

✾

What will there be in Maunston?
church - pub - village hall - village shop - one rental property - old forge - station - boat house - a few houses

Most people who live in Maunston work in the local town.

What's beyond the quay? [Quay is a little detached from the body of the village] Where would the boats have gone to? - just old fishing boats?

Perhaps a small river that runs to the sea. A headland.

What is her connection to the place?
KEY QUESTION
Something in her past - or in the past of someone she knew (who has just died?).
What is Main character doing in Maunston?
Work there? Or in town? Retired? - perhaps some kind of 'invalid', living off an insurance policy.
Would need to be a not too debilitating injury, but probably visible…

Three cottages by the quay
1 - Main character
2 - Boatman
3 - Rental

Start with main character driving into village, held at crossroads by train. Sees her get off the train, pause, then walk towards the sea.
(no conversation)

He then talks with someone in shop; cleaner for cottage rental. Delivers groceries?

Characters

Column headers (printed vertically):

```
                          s
                          u
                          p
                          e
          m       r   r
      h   o   s   e   w
      i   u   t   l   c   r
      s   r   i   i   o   r
      t   n   t   g   i   p   d
      o   i   i   e   m   a   e   l
      r   n   o   d   n   t   r   o
      y   g   n   y   t   t   t   v
              n       y   g   h   e
```

(columns read as: history · mourning · superstition · religion · c5 · c6 · c7 · c8)

AGE	role	name	history	mourning	superstition	religion	c5	c6	c7	c8
35	Woman	Anna Woolley (Maskelyne)	❋	✓	✓	✓	❋	✓		
42	Main char	Lewis Airy	✓					✓		
61	Boatman	(Marlon) Bradley			✓	x				
49	Shop Owner	Oscar Ryle				✓				
53	Shop Owner	Shirley Ryle (Bliss)						❋		
58	Vicar / verger p-t	Richard Dyson			✓					
55	Old forge owner	Aubrey Rees			✓			✓	❋	
46	Publican	Tommy Christie					✓			
41	Pub's wife	Jenny Christie (Maskelyne)							❋	
	various									
	librarian	Maisie Wolfendale								

Halley . Bradley . Bliss . Maskelyne . Pond . Airy . Christie . Dyson . Jones . Woolley . Ryle . Smith . Wolfendale . Rees

She may operate under a false name ∴ hiding a link to one of the other characters (or via her dead husband?)

There has to be a reason she's chosen Maunston Quay…

Need to map out a character sheet for each of the characters, including timeline and major events - then need to insert where in the narrative each major event happens or is revealed.

9 parts. A quote on the title page of each part?

Tense? Quite like the idea of using the present tense. Tell the story as if you were watching a film.

Opening part.
The beach. the headland. the jetty. the 3 cottages. the path to the station. history of the trains. waiting at the x-gates. the train's arrival. the woman. where she goes. the gates opening. driving into the village. conversation with Mrs Ryle. something about the woman. delivery of the shopping. man and woman meet.

need to include something about the history of the quay / the village

1 - Mourning
Main: learn why Anna is there: death of son; death of husband
Also: find out about her writing, religion
          Lewis' history. Dyson re religion; Bradley (re history?)

2 - Comedy
Main: Oscar comedy moment
Also: Lewis/Jenny +hostility?. Bit more about village history
          Shirley & Aubrey; Shirley & Oscar
          Tommy & Jenny marriage

3 - Superstition
Main: Discussion about failure of village
Also: Lewis & his past; Bradley anti-religion;
          Shirley & Aubrey; Anna and DD 'belief'
          Tommy & Jenny

4 - Writing
Main: Anna
Also: Anna & Lewis; Anna + Tom/Ryan

5 - Party
Main: Event in pub (Tommy & Jenny)
Also: Everybody!

6 - Religion
Main: DD + Anna / Bradley
Also: Anna still mourning; Jenny's unanswered family question;
        Lewis + his past

7 - Death
Main: Anna + Ryan's death
Also: Anna + Lewis; Lewis + Jenny; Anna writing;
        Lewis his history/Anna's (Maisie), belief Anna/DD
        Tommy & Jenny; Jenny her family history (softening)

8 - History
Main: Anna, Lewis, Jenny, Maisie (Maskelyne, Ryan)
Also: Anna/Lewis; village failure/future;
        Oscar + Shirley

9: Love
Main: Anna/Lewis
Also: Anna death/writing/religion; Lewis his past;
        Shirley & Aubrey; Tommy & Jenny

~~~~

It would be useful to be able to locate this entry in time, though based on a later entry it must be prior to May. In echoes of his earlier planning for 'Mirrors', he has mapped out the significant elements of 'At Maunston Quay', though at this stage that is probably as far as he had managed to get.

Further muddying the water in terms of defining an accurate timeline is the fact that he likes to have more than one project on the go at any one moment, and references to these can flit in and out of the notebooks almost haphazardly. Of course, 'Mirrors' is the example par excellence!

~~~~

So what comes next?
It would be good if it could be a little experimental.
Voice (unusual) needs to be that of a particular point of view or perception of or relationship with the world.
~~~~ possibly something inanimate?
        ↳ a story of possession?
                and loss?
                and searching? - success / failure

237

"Misappropriation on the Journey Home"?

A painting?

   Vauncey - name?

A painting can be sold, have several owners, be moved, put into storage. Its perspective will always be factual and unemotional (correct?) and therefore +ve emotion can only come from what it can actually 'see'.

"You're right; the eyes really do follow you around the room!"
"Of course they do," I want to say, because I <u>am</u> watching them. ???

- opening?

There are other potential elements too re the painting (i.e. the narrator)
↳   authentic or fake?
       provenance?

So questioning the authenticity of the painting is therefore to question the accuracy of the narrative.
Questioning provenance means that we can't believe the painting's retelling of its past.

So the story - the long narrative thread throughout - is about the painting, not about what the painting 'sees'.

So does that mean there is a collection of short stories, or is it possible to have consistent thread running through what the painting recalls? If so, would it have to be familial in order to make sense? And if so, that story would need to be worked out.

Two narrative streams in parallel...

   ✱

'Orchestra'
       as if hearing the word for the first time
       ✱ how does someone understand what it means?
       ✱ how to translate reality into the word's meaning

'The River'
       'rapping' suicide note

* form as the important thing

'Rachael/Rebecca/The Affair'
     laughing girl in pub
     short skirt
     "go on; look at my legs"

- back to the painting...

Story told backwards? i.e. starts in the present and traces its roots back to the brushstrokes even?! - does it then become a story about the intent of the artist, which is reflected in how the painting is perceived through the years, and how it is <u>valued</u> (£).

If so, at what point does the painting cease to be able to tell its own story? Is there a degeneration of language as it begins to unravel (i.e. was originally formed)?

*

'The Man Who Bought the Pier'

*

Title story:
     "... Portrait..." or
     "A Question of Provenance" #
Also
     "The Man Who Bought the Pier"
     "Orchestra"
     "The River"
     "Rachael, Rebecca and Ruben"
     "The Box"

the authenticity of the painting
the authenticity of the story it tells
the authenticity of the human subjects
↳ need to map out the story and the timeline that goes with it

Vauncey family

"The Box"
     a story about both escape and entrapment

"The Man Who Bought the Pier"
	is this about
	- doing something impossible?
	- fulfilling a dream?
	- failure (perhaps the pier burns in an arson attack, or is destroyed by the sea)
	- rides? one chapter each?

"Orchestra"
	what does the word mean?
	trying to explain something
			signifier & signified
			understand the difference
	what's the story?

"The River"
	'the water looks cold'
	'racing under the bridge'
	'someone told him/me of the difference between a black and a brown river'

February 2018 (MWD)

I'm currently working on three things: a re-edit of my novel "Mirrors", to be published under a new title (probably) in the summer; a new collection of short stories, hopefully ready for the autumn; and a narrative poem, again targeting a summer publication.

I have discovered that the value of a page like this manifests itself when working towards a deadline e.g. the final stages of revision for a new publication. So whilst I am writing now (and quite a lot), these are drafts towards a couple of works-in-progress. On that basis, I am unlikely to be making a regular entry here until into the New Year.

mid-March 2018 (MWD)

"Mirrors" re-edit. I have reached Chapter 30 out of 41 and am scandalised by a) the number of typos I missed first time round, and b) the odd really clumsy sentence (where I was obviously trying to be too clever!). Fixing most, hopefully. I can't go too far with the awkward sentences as that would risk destroying the overall integrity of the style...it's an effort of its time, I'm afraid. Still on schedule for a summer re-publication.

Short story collection. I have made it to page 90 or 9 stories in. This should be about half way. On that basis, again a summer publication is on the cards.

Narrative poem. Progress is still good - though harder to judge than the two projects above. I'm probably just under half way through. Given I've no idea how long re-work/editing will take, this one's looking like the back end of the summer before it sees the light of day.

I'm hoping to be able to have some kind of 'event' later on this year to hopefully launch at least two of these. Watch this space!

17ᵗʰ March 2018 (w.com)

Nearly two months ago I wrote these three lines, straight into a draft post, certain that something would come of them. I've revisited them several times since, always with the expectation that somehow they would 'take off' and lead me to a different outcome, a more comprehensive 'thing'.

But nothing ever happens.

Maybe they're meant to be just as they are, who knows?

Anyway, rather than leave them festering, I think they deserve their chance of flight...

"Did he go quietly?
No-one but God knew,
but no-one was talking to God."

19ᵗʰ March 2018 (w.com)

I am conscious that for a website that's supposed to be a writing showcase, I have published little new material here recently; most posts have been book reviews (of sorts). So here's another 'non-writing' post..![54]

I just thought an update on all the creative action that's going on in the background might be of interest...

· "Mirrors" re-edit. I have reached Chapter 30 out of 41 and am scandalised by a) the number of typos I missed first time round, and b) the odd really clumsy sentence (where I was obviously trying to be too clever!). Fixing most, hopefully. I can't go too far with the awkward sentences as that would risk destroying the overall integrity of the style...it's an effort of its time, I'm afraid. Still on schedule for a summer re-publication.

· Short story collection. I have made it to page 90 or 9 stories in. This should be about half way. On that basis, again a summer publication is on the cards.

· Narrative poem. Progress is still good - though harder to judge than the two projects above. I'm probably just under half way through. Given I've no idea

---

[54] You can of course argue that this is a 'writing post'.

how long re-work/editing the first draft will take, this one's looking like the back end of the summer before it sees the light of day.

I'm hoping to be able to have some kind of 'event' later on this year to hopefully launch at least two of these. Watch this space!

~~~~

This is the kind of update that would have traditionally appeared in the notebooks. All three updates are significant - and a demonstration of his predilection for working on multiple projects simultaneously - as is his failing to give working titles to the last two. Was this merely caution on his part? As we may deduce from earlier entries, the "narrative poem" is almost certainly the one referred to earlier as "Rehearsals", but the short story collection? Is this related to his previous list including "Orchestra" and "The River", or something else? And from left-field, we discover that he is working on a 'Mirrors' "re-edit". Almost certainly this was initiated as part of the process of moving the book from KDP to Coverstory books.

He is clearly committed to the triumvirate a) because he talks about a "launch event" - another example of him seeing himself as a bona fide writer perhaps? - and b) because he is already clear that he will have completed "at least two of these". This is a type of confidence so obviously missing from the early part of his career; was it this lack of confidence which used to hold him back as much as the cul-de-sac of having no publication medium?

Remember his entries about self-esteem? It is surely not fanciful to suggest that his 'professional' volumes, the discovery of self-publishing, and the appearance of real physical books, all contributed to a rise in his self-esteem and the image he was beginning to build of himself as a writer.

~~~~

20ᵗʰ *March 2018 (w.com)*

This may sound a little weird, but recently I've come to appreciate the beauty of punctuation more than ever - especially when it comes to writing poetry. And I don't mean simply the use of standard punctuation - commas, semi-colons and the like - I also mean the absence of punctuation, the freedom to choose not to use it, or even to suggest it in other ways, for example with the use of space(s). In some contexts, I think how you punctuate something can be as powerful as the words you use, and can add as much meaning as the words you use.

"Eats shoots and flies" vs. "Eats shoots, and flies" vs. "Eats, shoots, and flies".

We're all familiar with his one, aren't we? The definitive Truss book on the mechanics of punctuation.

When it comes to verse, punctuation is what gives us pace and tempo, and via pace and tempo - as well as grammatical structure - meaning too.

In the narrative prose poem I'm currently working on I've been playing with differing structures to create alternate voices, if you will. By playing with structure and punctuation, it's truly amazing how much flexibility language can give you - and how much it can give back too!

Here's an example from an early draft.

It might have looked like this:

Shakespeare. You know what to expect don't you,
even if you hadn't read or seen any?
Almost as if it were gifted, imbued into your psyche,
part of your dna, your life force.
"The quality of mercy " and all that shit.

Of course it could have looked like this:

Shakespeare.
You know what to expect don't you
　　　　　　- even if you hadn't read or seen any.
Almost as if it were gifted,
　　　　　imbued into your psyche
　　　　　part of your dna
　　　　　your life force.
"The quality of mercy"
　　　　　and all that shit.

But here's where I've ended up:

shakespeare　　　you know what to expect don't you
even if you hadn't read　　　or seen any
almost as if it were gifted　　　imbued into your psyche
part of your dna　　　your life force
the quality of mercy　　　and all that shit

And not a single word changed. A myriad of possibilities, and each one different.

"The Beauty of Punctuation" ©　!!

1ˢᵗ April 2018 (w.com)
Update 1st April:

- 'Mirrors' re-edit is now complete and I am awaiting my proof copy. The book will be republished as 'An Infinity of Mirrors' on or before 21st May 2018.

- Short story collection: now 120 pages in and five stories left. Aiming to reach the 160 page target draft by the end of April / early May.

- Narrative poem: up to page 104. Seven poems left. Aiming for the same timescale as above. Hopefully published in June with a launch reading in July.

7th April 2018 (w.com)

Update 7th April: Great progress!

- 'An Infinity of Mirrors' as before.

- Short story collection: now >140 pages in and just two stories left. Should reach the 160 page target draft by the 15th April. Revision then through May with a revised publication & launch reading at the end of June.

- Narrative poem: draft complete. Revision starts next week. Hopefully published with a launch reading in June.

18th April 2018 (w.com)

Way ahead of schedule, so great progress!

Update 18th April:

- Novel - 'An Infinity of Mirrors': proof copy arrived, awaiting final review

- Short Story collection - 'Degrees of Separation': draft finished; proof copy to be ordered

- Poetry - 'After the Rehearsals': draft finished; proof copy ordered and awaiting delivery

I can now think about planning my book launch events for June!

~~~~

Now there are titles!

If you needed confirmation as to how far he had come since the end of the twentieth century and into the 'noughties', you need only to consider 'Mirrors'. Not only had he finally finished and published it, the further spur provided by his adoption of the Ingram Spark platform saw him reworking and relaunching it. Is 'An Infinity of Mirrors' appropriate reward for the years of anguish and toil? Indeed, is this is its final incarnation? Only time will tell.

Akin to the tremendous increase in output in 2014-15, it is clear that the following three years proved similarly productive: not only the reworking of 'Mirrors', but other migrations from KDP (his three novellas), a collection of short stories ('Secrets & Wisdom'), more poetry ('Human Archaeology'), and then two other volumes rolling off what was beginning to look like a production line. He had found his 'mojo', and a pace at which he could work, spurred on by the emotional rewards - self-esteem! - doing so offered him. None of his endeavours garnered any profit however - which made his pursuit of them either 'honest' and driven by the love of creating, or commercially naïve. Perhaps a combination of both.

There was another motivation, too. On Writeral his 'strap-line' was "Furiously writing until the light goes out", and surely one can only interpret the 'light going out' as the anticipation of that moment when - for whatever reason - he is unable to write any longer. Perhaps most of all it offers a sense of him racing against mortality. All the time he can write and produce books it is proof that he is still alive.

~~~~

May 2018 (BBG)

Currently planned:

- 'First-time Visions…'
↳ not really a 'novel' collection of poetry in any real sense.
A good title, and a title poem plus some candidates.
Is this really a repository for a new collection in late '18 / early '19 rather than anything 'new' (thematically or otherwise)?
If so, that's fine. I just need to accept that's what it is.
I think it's highly likely to be much more rigorous than previous collections though (also good).

- 'At Maunston Quay'
currently conceived as a novel told in the present tense.
two key questions:
        1 - is the plot strong enough?
        2 - is the format correct?
        Leave 1 for now…
        2: options   - carry on
                        - revert to 3rd p-past or 1st p-past
                        - turn it into a 'hybrid'
        Need to answer 1, actually.
        Key question:
               IS IT A STORY I WANT TO TELL?

Is there any merit in the old 'intersections' idea? i.e. one story but multiple viewpoints.

Or what about something slightly post-apocalyptic ∴ to the brink but not quite over?

The only(?) other format option is the play (radio?) with a sole focus on the spoken word. Subject could be anything ∴

Is it possible to work up a plot idea irrespective of the mechanism for delivery? I would imagine so.

What do I know about?

How about the story of a man who is forced, through circumstance, to go and 'find himself'. (A bit like Ironmonger's whale.) He washes up somewhere and starts to accumulate attachments.

'At Maunston Quay' could be the man who gets off the train…
Could go for multiple POV too.
He, lost his wife in childbirth => depression.
She, recluse, painter — has a history.

'Quay' is not play material.
Would need to rework the plan…

    POSSIBLE

+ try a play at the same time?

How about not having any plot or outline and just letting the characters go and see what happens…?!

10ᵗʰ May 2018 (PBB)

Fiction: 'At Maunston Quay'   ✓
Poetry: 'First-time Visions…'   ✓

Something else?

How about a play?…

~~~~

These two entries were almost immediately followed by a very public restatement of them. We have previously seen evidence of a reluctance to commit to projects in such an overt way until he was somehow 'certain'; remember his delay in divulging the titles of works-in-progress until he was satisfied he would get them over the line? The affirmation on his blog of his next two books surely points to commitment to them, as if he were talking to a captive audience desperate to know what he would be producing next. Proof of his heightened perception of himself as 'a Writer' or merely self-deluding? In a way it was almost as if he were in a stadium playing to a crowd which had not yet arrived; as if he were laying down a trail for the benefit of posterity and those who would come after.

~~~~

Having been so focused for the last six months on getting my most recent books completed, edited and published, I'm suddenly hit by 'the void'. OK, it's my own fault for not spreading the work out to ensure I always had a blend of writing whilst editing whilst preparing for publication - but I didn't. I'd targeted June latest for all three which resulted in three final drafts, followed by three lots of the other stuff. All now done.

Early May arrives and the volume of really new writing in the previous few weeks is actually pretty poor. [I like being hard on myself!]

Although that feels a little bit like a failure (even though it shouldn't), in a way it turns out to be a good thing. A pause. A chance to take stock. A rather hackneyed 'recharging of the batteries'...

The very cheering thing is that I found myself desperately keen to get writing again - and that I've started.

Very rough at this stage, but:

- 'At Maunston Quay' - potentially a novel of about 120k words. I've already drafted 9k and have the whole planned out. Tentative due date would be May next year, depending on how much free time I have. [Loads right now, but I expect this to reduce.]

- 'First-time Visions of Earth from Space' - a new collection of poetry that's likely to be a traditional, 'informal' collection rather than anything with a particular theme. Maybe 10-12 pieces drafted thus far. Aiming for roughly the same timeframe as above, but this one could come in much earlier if I suddenly get a wiggle on...

I'm also thinking about a play (stage or radio), partly to do something different, partly as a test. It's been years since I wrote a script of any persuasion (and the last one was unadulterated rubbish, long since - deliberately - lost...55). Nothing

---

55 Although I am sure he believed this to be true at time of writing, the manuscript of that play - rather preposterously titled *China Geese Never Fly South in Winter* - was subsequently located.

more than a vague notion at this stage. But the novel's feeling pretty good just now.

Maybe I'll rattle off another few hundred words before lunch...

19th May 2018 (MWD)

'An Infinity of Mirrors': published 1st May

'Degrees of Separation': published 14th May

'After the Rehearsals': published 14th May

Starting work on one or two new things, tentatively...

10th August 2018 (w.com)

I now have the grand total of six ratings on Goodreads.com for 'Losing Moby Dick'. Not many, I know, but you've got to start somewhere. I had hoped - after a 'Goodreads Giveaway' - more of the 100 people who'd received the e-version of the book would have read and rated it, but beggars, choosers and all that...

And what do they say? One '5', one '4', three '3', and one '2'. Overall that's about 3.4 so far.

Disappointed? Only if you're naive enough to think that every book - especially yours! - deserves to score a 5. In the Goodreads lexicon, a '3' means 'I liked it'. Personally, I've scored lots of books a '3', many by some of the most well-known authors of our time; I liked them, but I didn't 'love' them; they weren't, for me, 'awesome'.

On that basis, I think 3.4 is pretty OK. The '4' and '5' are great, of course, and perhaps 'Losing Moby Dick' was good enough to get a few people reading other things of mine.

Maybe I'll average a little closer to maybe 3.75 for the next book that collects reviews.

12th August 2018 (w.com)

When I was out jogging this morning - early, in the rain - I saw something that my mind immediately translated into words:

"Green. Round. Spikey.
On the black roughness of a pavement improperly made
the first horse chestnut."

I love it when that happens. It's something I have no control over. Luckily I only had to remember it for a little under 1 km! When you have a moment like that but can't get to write it down soon enough and then forget what it was... well, it's like losing something precious.

And then, as I dipped in and out of my breakfast, I opened Wordpress, looked at my site and it's pathetic traffic, then browsed 'Discover' for the first time in ages. And I thought: "I should blog a little more".

So...

Oh, and I checked on Goodreads (like I do most every day, sad individual that I am!) and I discovered that someone had rated one of my professional books. 4 out of 5! That's pretty good!

26ᵗʰ August 2018 (w.com)

I can't help myself. Even though I am striving to be a writer - a better writer - I often seek measurement of my success through numbers. It is, I suppose, something to do with upbringing, or education, or profession; but there is a solidity in numbers which is satisfyingly concrete - especially when one spends so much time and creative effort trying to get words to work.

1+1=2 is gratifyingly correct and unambiguous; deciding where to place an adjective on a line of poetry - or whether to have one at all - is completely at the other end of the spectrum. And never mind the torture of trying to choose the adjective in the first place! There is no 'rightness' involved there, it's only feeling, instinct, gut, sound, sense, taste, and hopefully a little talent - and all of it mine alone.

Which is what you see all the time when you look through the blogs of people who write; the trying to make sense of things, of both themselves and their craft. Trying to harvest some proof that others feel positive about our work, that it has 'value'. And most of us are using our blogs as a Segway into something else, perhaps hoping for the day when we don't need to blog because we have been taken seriously, have become mainstream, successful, vindicated.

And how do you measure that? Probably with numbers. The number of followers, 'likes', dollars made from the last book, stores stocking your work, invitations to speak, shelf inches in the local bookstore...

This is my **200**th post on Writeral. In **18** months. Is that good or bad, I've no idea. I have some followers - to whom I am always grateful - but do I have enough? Can you ever have enough, I wonder?

So some more numbers - just for this double-century post today:

80% - 115,000 - 250 - 8

I am about 80% of the way through the first draft of my next novel which should top out at around 115k words or 250 pages. When will it see the light of day? Probably in about 8 months. At the moment it feels like a complete 'thing' as I accelerate towards the end; gentle and understated, but hopefully worthy and worthwhile.

I have reached page 62 in my next collection of verse, aiming at 100 pages cover-to-cover. This is likely to be delivered in the same 8 month timeframe. Worthiness? To be honest, I'm not yet sure.

And beyond that, some unknowable numbers exist. Answers to questions that, in truth, we never want answered. How many more words / books / poems will it take, will I write, will be good (or good enough)? How many more times will I feel that frisson of excitement having written something of which I am truly proud? How many people will read, will share, will buy, will like?

Of course in one very real sense, it doesn't matter. As Mr Holmes might say, it only matters that the game is still afoot...

~~~~

"Furiously writing until the light goes out" - he is aware that there might come a time when he will cease to be motivated, or until he gives up. Nothing to do with mortality, this one. Is he also asking what if he realises the quality is never there, can never be there? What if one day he wakes up knowing in his heart-of-hearts that what he has written has no value - commercial, intrinsic, literary or otherwise - and never will have?

~~~~

1st September 2018 (w.com)

September 1st. The first day of autumn, at least for us in the northern hemisphere. Where I live they say it will be warm again next week. Kids back to school, of course...

As time gets shorter - both in the sense that it seems to travel faster, and that there's inevitably always less of it to look forward to - I get an increasing sense that one should not make resolutions just at the beginning of each year. Because of time's tyranny, each quarter becomes ever more important and precious, so why not a resolution at the beginning of each of these? But where will that end: resolutions each month? Each week? Maybe that's how we should live our lives, a resolution every day...

But then I don't do resolutions any more. And I certainly don't use them when it comes to writing. Not that I haven't succumbed in the past. I mean, who hasn't? But I'm struck, when wandering through the Discover section of Wordpress, how many people do: 'a poem a day', 'a thousand words a week', 'flash fiction through the alphabet' ("I'm on P" they say...).

We know why people adopt such regimes. Because they want to write; because writing's important to them.

And why don't I? Because I want to write, and because writing's important to me.

In the past I found that you can become a slave to your routine. You have to write something that starts with the letter "K", is at least 300 hundred words long. Or this week Maisie has to have another wacky adventure. Or you have to write sonnet 48 in that 200 sonnet sequence you've planned. If that works for you, fine; but I found I ended up writing for the wrong reason, to satisfy the pattern. Most often what came out was drivel. And why? Because I didn't believe in it; I wasn't emotionally invested in it. I think you can see a lot of things written which are more wheel-turning than heart-turning. And we're not hamsters.

Maybe I'm lucky. Maybe as time has shortened and I now understand how important writing is to me   - at long last! - I don't need to be put into a straitjacket. When I'm on a roll, writing fiction, I can turn out over a thousand words an hour, especially when it's dialogue. I'm not saying they're all good words - they aren't! - but it's a start. And when I'm writing at that pace, by the way, it's because I am invested in what I'm writing and who I'm writing about. I can go three weeks without writing any poetry and then 'find' three new poems in as many days.

It's magic really. And maybe I'm just lucky.

Why I am I telling you all this - other than because it's the 1st of September? I don't know really. I've just been browsing through the cacophony of noise that Wordpress inevitably generates and thought I'd chuck in my two-penneth.

4th September 2018 (w.com)

One of the things I have learned over the last few years - especially recently - is that, when trying to write the concrete things we call 'books', they have a dynamic all their own.

Sitting down and writing a short story or a poem off-the-cuff is probably the most relaxed kind of writing there is; after all, there is no commitment other than to fill the page or get to the end of the story / poem. But writing a book involves a whole different set of disciplines.

At some point - even if it starts out innocently enough as a couple of stories and a few poems - there is a need to plan. For me planning a book is when the first commitment is made, the first obligation arises. In the early days, it is still just a nice idea, and it is the idea that warms you.

After a while - maybe as early as a quarter of the way through - I start on the cover design. I find this gives the book an identity, a form. You start to imagine what it might look like, or feel to hold in your hand. This ups the ante in terms of your stake in the game.

Somewhere between a third and a half way through I find is the most dangerous time; that period where the writing can become more of a chore and you can feel a slave to the plan. It is a time when you can easily chuck it all in. I have, somewhere, at least three 'novels' that made it to about 30,000 words and then I simply stopped. This is when you need belief.

And then there arrives - suddenly and almost without realising it - that wonderful moment when there is so much momentum, so much thought, dedication, effort, that you suddenly realise that you *will* finish the book. There is suddenly no doubt. You will finish it because you have to, because you owe it to your characters to see them through to the end, over the line.

I'm over 8ok words into a 100k novel and have recently arrived at that sublime tipping point. I will finish it. I know there are weeks of revision and rewrite ahead, but I will cross the line. I can almost feel my cover dressing the pages, the weight of the thing in my hands. It may still be six months away, but that day will come.

Glorious feeling! Isn't that why we do it?

~~~~

There is a shift in these last two posts away from the 'what?' of his writing towards the 'how?' and the 'why?'. Does this demonstrate evidence of progress, of his transition from frustrated ideas man to a 'finisher'? This analysis recognises one of the most critical moments in his creative process - "that sublime tipping point" - when he knows he will finish something. And it is surely interesting that, when it comes to fiction, part of him feels completing a story is payment of a debt owed to the characters he has created; he has breathed life into them, and they into him too.

Given all the procrastinations and false dawns of his past, I wonder if by this point, heading into the Autumn of 2018, he hadn't also moved further along a spectrum stretching between starting and finishing; i.e. he was able to know earlier, perhaps when working on an original idea or in drafting those first words, whether a particular project was going to be something he would see through. If so, then how would it have been had he started Mirrors in 2018? Would it needed to have suffered a gestation period of over thirty years?

~~~~

7th September 2018 (MWD)

It has been far too long since I updated this page. Indeed, since I updated a number of my pages. A job for the weekend, then. For here:

'At Maunston Quay' - a novel where I have about 16,000 words to go before the first draft is finished. Aiming for publication in the spring 2019. A new poetry collection is about 60% completed. It will be easier to finish once the novel is drafted. Again aiming for a spring publication.

I think that's enough, don't you?

Five days ago I made an offer of a free book to Wordpress readers. A number of people liked the post and checked-out the link, but no-one signed up for either of the books.

This bothered me somewhat as my audience is largely driven by fellow writers and readers, people who search for things tagged as 'writing', 'reading', 'poetry' and so on. What was the problem? I had assumed - naively as it turns out! - that the prospect of being given a free ebook would be snapped up; after all, where was the risk? Read a page and like it, read to the end. Read a page and don't like it, just stop.

There will be no visit from the Not-reading-my-book Police...

So I thought I'd expand my offer to another of my social media networks, one that is not writing-centric but where I have over a thousand direct connections. And guess what? Exactly the same. Lots of 'browsers', but no takers.

Given the breadth of the audience I approached - friends, colleagues, fellow writers and book-lovers - what does such a response, such a lack of take-up, say about us all?

Perhaps not surprisingly I can't think of anything particularly good. Does it demonstrate that these days we are inherently suspicious - even of someone we know?! That at some level we don't really care about others? Or that we're not prepared to take a risk - even when there is none? Is there a fear in making - risking?! - a new connection?

I felt like a man in the street unsuccessfully trying to give away money...

But in the end my conclusion was that the reason people weren't interested might probably be because I wasn't 'a name'. If JKRowling or Tom Clancy or Charles Dickens had tried such a stunt, would their offer have fallen on fallow ground? I don't think so. How cool would it be to be able to say "I've just got a free book direct from Dan Brown"? [insert the name of your favourite author].

Well I can't do anything about that right now. Maybe if enough people were to read my work I might become a name one day. Isn't that the journey we're all making here, though "more in hope than expectation"....

I have just read Ted Hughes' poem "Chaucer" from the volume 'Birthday Letters', a vast collection of pieces written for / about Sylvia Plath.

The thing that struck me about "Chaucer" - indeed as it has about many of the poems I have read thus far in the book - is that they read like drafts rather than finished pieces. Is that sacrilege? In any event, it occurred to me that one could edit the poem to create something tighter, leaner, more impactful. Not necessarily better. Obviously.

Now. Is that acceptable? And if not, is it because it's Hughes?

Chaucer

Swaying at the stile's top, arms raised,
you declaimed Chaucer to a field of cows,
to the Spring sky with its laundry of clouds,
the new emerald of the thorns,
your voice over the fields
to become lost somewhere else.
The cows watched. Appreciating, approached,
you wrapt in the Wife of Bath.
Making a ring, they shoved and jostled
to gaze into your face, snorts of exclamation
renewed their astounded attention,
catching inflection, remaining six feet distant.
Disbelieving, you could not stop
fearing attack, the potential shock of silence.
So you went on, you and they hypnotised
until they reeled away
while my own commitment
was already become perpetual.

Mine or his? Acceptable or not? And if acceptable, how few words need to be changed to make it mine not his?

I don't have an answer. Obviously.

~~~~

This was probably his first - and very public! - statement in relation to the 'ownership' of words. Given he regularly dipped his toe into the realm of 'found' poetry, we should not be surprised. The question he is asking is when does something stop being 'his' and become 'mine'? When do you cross that threshold - and who is to say? Later he was to suggest that, if you followed some arguments about plagiarism to their logical conclusion, as soon as someone put two words together - say "and the" - no-one else would ever be allowed to use those same words in that same sequence. It would be stealing. But if drawing the line at the bare minimum possible of two words is ridiculous (as it clearly is!), then what about three words or four? During conversations in one of his writing groups much later (in the Spring of 2021, in fact) it was suggested that what allowed someone to 're-use' others' words was actually down to tone, message, sentiment etc. Essentially all the intangible things. If that were the case, then his editing of Hughes' "Chaucer" would be simple plagiarism if it were published under his own name. But if credit was given to Hughes, what then? And what about those 'found' or 'curated' pieces that never actually saw the public light of day? Still theft - or do they only become contraband when someone else sees them?

~~~~

Having recently finished the first draft of my new novel - "At Maunston Quay" - and having drawn a line under what may well prove to be my next collection of poetry - I am in editing mode again.

It's a strange time in many ways. I like it because it's a period filled with promise, where the joy of having something new to offer - physical and real - is so very close; where the reward for months of hard work will soon be manifest in a new, tangible 'thing'. It's not working on the words again and again which embodies my sense of anticipation the most, but rather finalising the cover. Perhaps that's because the cover is what you first see; the envelope which encases, protects, and delivers the words I have written.

What has also struck me this time around is that it's October, and I'm likely to be publishing early in the new year. Again. As if it were some kind of personal biorhythm, this cycle I seem to have found myself in; a twice-yearly round of writing, revising, publishing.

Of course what's not so great about revising is not writing. I find writing something new whilst editing for publication more than difficult. It's as if there is a danger of contamination. Which there is. If I start writing something new whilst editing - perhaps adopting a completely different style - the fear that this might bleed into the editing process and contaminate that which is already 'finished' is a real one.

But not writing is hard. Reassuringly so. It's actually wonderful to feel the absence of creating so keenly! And so I plan while I hibernate, mapping out the next episode on the journey. I tease at titles, ideas; I write down fragments of unvarnished and isolated 'things', sometimes in the middle of the night. I compile clues and snippets; I latch on to names for characters, images to develop, knowing that there might be something in this idea or the next that could prove to be really important. Not unlike a sleuth, it's a little like trying to solve a mystery, Holmes on the moor surrounded by fog...

Thinking about it, maybe this isn't such a bad part of the cycle either!

~~~~

One of the challenges of self-publishing is a book's cover, a key component of the end product - the first thing people see, after all! He took cover production very seriously, and this note demonstrates just how important it was to him. Rightly or wrongly, he felt that many self-published books gave themselves away as obviously just that because their covers were crude and amateurish.

As much as possible he tried to use his own photographs for his covers. Where that was not an option, to find suitable images elsewhere and seek the photographer's permission to use those (as in 'At Maunston Quay', for example). Using the Canon he had owned for a number of years, he took many photographs - thousands, in fact - and it is interesting that nowhere in his notebooks does he make any material reference to doing so. It was a creative channel he failed to explicitly link to his writing and only acknowledged the overall activity via a dedicated website - www.photorway.com - to which he would irregularly post.

Of course, the main take-away from the entry above is the confession to an instant sense of 'lack' when not writing. How far removed is that from his earlier years?!

~~~~

After about a month's work, I have just completed the first screen-based revision of my next novel, "At Maunston Quay". Now I can put it down (metaphorically) for a few weeks before a second screen-based review in December and then a proof review during January. Publication date is now the beginning of February 2019.

It's a great place to be, knowing that essentially the book is 'written' and all that remains will be the filtering out of silly mistakes: inconsistencies in tense or timeline; annoying repetitions of the same word in close proximity which makes the text clumsy; simplifying the over-complex; identifying the rogue words that always trip me up - like typing 'form' rather than 'from'...

And having completed the first review, I am free again to start writing prose once more. Because the next thing I write will be stylistically different, I have to be confident that I can avoid 'cross contamination' between pieces. I think I'm on safe ground now.

In addition to starting prose again - and I already have a working title for my next piece! - I have a slim volume of new poetry to edit. More anon.

That's how November's shaping up...!

I wrote my first story when I was five. I can still remember writing it. I had my first poem published in our local museum - framed and hung on the wall - aged about twelve.

That was the beginning, the beginning of a lifetime of writing, on and off...

Indeed. But what I realise now, and what haunts me every single day, is that it has been more 'off' than 'on'. I have written in phases, spasms almost, sometimes years apart. The University years were prolific, and then the real world took over. My writing took a back seat, relegated there by the imperative of needing to earn a living and then the practicalities of the living itself. There were triggers along the way that prompted sporadic literary activity, but I now know these were far too few.

I feel as if I have let myself down.

How much more might I have written? What have I missed or failed to write in all those years? Who knows? How might my life have been different if I'd recognised and then remained true to my course?

If there is regret, it's there in spades. Thinking about it, regret is the wrong word. It feels more like grief. There is a sense of loss, of mourning almost. Yet having rediscovered my passion, 'born again' if you like, there is a new intensity and purpose driven by that loss. With time running out, I feel as if I have to work doubly hard, partly to make the most of the time I have left, and partly to make up for all those lost years.

This is all rather self-indulgent, you might say, and perhaps it is. But it doesn't feel like that. It feels like a purpose, a calling, blinkered and focussed; a making the most of things.

And still, in spite of all the recent and ongoing effort and this strange compulsion I feel, there is no escaping the nagging doubt of worth. In the first instance I write because I must, because now I have no choice. In the second, I do it because I am trying to convey something intangible, or to create something - a feeling, perhaps no more than that - in others. I can measure the impact of my drive because it is tangible; it's the number of words, or poems, or stories, or books. I have no control over the second. That's driven by readers; how many there are, and what they think.

If I crave feedback, then it's not (I hope!) for any kind of glory or reward, but to answer a question, to balance an equation. Recognising this, I can only throw myself onto the mercy of others.

~~~~

And so here it is, in a nutshell. Remember the strap-line for his blog: "furiously writing until the light goes out"? Here he gives us an insight into the reasoning behind it: "How much more might I have written? What have I missed or failed to write in all those years? Who knows? How might my life have been different if I'd recognised and then remained true to my course?"

He is trying to catch-up, to make up for lost time, to redeem himself - first and foremost in his own eyes: "I write because I must, because now I have no choice."

And in doing so he is also clear that he is seeking external confirmation too; not for self-esteem's sake per se, but because he wants to be told he is not wasting his time, that he has a modicum of talent, and that what he is writing is worthwhile. A couple of months earlier he had said "Isn't that the journey we're all making here", suggesting that he is part of some global cabal of unrecognised writers. Is that a false step? Clearly he doesn't want to be an anonymous member of an amorphous mass; he wants to be a recognised unit of one.

~~~~

24ᵗʰ *December 2018 (PVR)*

Is 'A Question of Provenance'[56] a single long story - long enough for a short novel?

Is 'The Man Who Bought the Pier' a return to Nev-like world of strange magic?

What about the short stories?

And is it time for another single-theme volume of poetry (like 'Rehearsals')?
(or like The Sonnets...?)

Things to do ∴

1 - start to map out the timeline of provenance

---

[56] The Vauncey painting story.

2 - map out the topics for pier

3 - create a workable series of sonnets: endings? themes? can these be a journey too?

Let's not make the same mistakes next year...57

Perhaps that should be the only resolution any of us make when facing into a new year. After all, it is bound to cover a number of bases..!

Twelve months ago - almost to the day - I posted a review / preview of my writing years, '17 into '18. The stand out? That I had rediscovered my 'mojo'. Heady stuff. And guess what? Twelve months on, and the mojo's still going strong!

In three days 2019 starts with the publication of a new collection of poetry, "First-time Visions of Earth From Space". Am I happy with it? It's funny, that's the kind of question I have been asking myself more and more. Having rediscovered a passion and found a medium and method, the first priority was to leverage that as much as possible; to do something with it.

'Being published' became a mantra all its own. That was the motherlode.

But is it? Really? I am co-editing an anthology under my Coverstory books imprint which will be published in March or April next year. My co-editor has persuaded me to include a small number of poems alongside his and nine other poets' work. I'm enjoying the process and really looking forward to getting other people into print too.

The personal challenge I had was in selecting five poems to include as my contribution. Not that many - and so many to choose from... Four of the selection come from "Visions" (a publicity-driven necessity, possibly), and one from "After the Rehearsals", published this year. What was interesting as I sifted through my work to make my choice, was how few pieces I thought were candidates. Shouldn't they all have been? And if they weren't, why was that? Perhaps I'd set the selection bar particularly high, but as I reflected on it, I knew I wanted all my pieces to be able to jump it. Naturally. And, naturally, they can't.

You want every single thing you produce to be a winner, a masterpiece - but that's just not possible.

And perhaps that's the learning, the mistake not to be made. Having proven the process, a level of ability, should volume become secondary now? Is it time to focus much more harshly, single-mindedly on depth, sophistication, quality,

---

57 This was the title of the blog post.

'newness'? Is there therefore something else - something fresh - to be proven here? Do I want - the next time I have to filter for an anthology (and I hope there will be a next time!) - the choice to be much, much harder? Absolutely.

It's not just poetry, of course. On the 1st February my new novel, "At Maunston Quay", hits the metaphorical shelves. And how do I feel about that? Is it - kicking the tyres on the new mantra - 'good enough'? Hard to say. And I am biased. I think the story is solid enough, and in places there are passages of which I'm really proud. The sentiment is positive and optimistic (if a little too sweet for some palettes, probably), and there are parts of it that make me cry - and I wrote the damn thing!

If it were an exam it would be 'merit' pass - but what if you wanted a 'distinction'..?

I am currently kicking around some ideas for 2019: two for poetry collections, two fiction. I suspect there are the 'easy' options, and the 'hard' ones. Toss a coin? In 2017 I knew which side it would have fallen. But now? It's still in the air...

Part Nine - 2019 to 2020

Not sure "Provenance" works as a story told backwards. Logically perhaps, but from a narrative and 'readability' perspective, not.

The idea, at its heart, is possibly sound enough, but the setting / plot / storyline is probably not strong or inventive enough.

So the germ of the idea is ok, but...

And "Pier"?

I wonder if I've gone beyond that kind of story, and whether it's too 'simplistic' for me these days...

Well there you are then...

Or, looking at it another way, if the sequel to "Maunston" is sitting on a table in Waterstones, what would I want it to say, look like, be about?

Maybe I need to imagine that...

Does it need to be a more complex, sophisticated story?
Both in terms of plot and style?

What do I <u>want</u> to write?

Must there be fiction? I think so; a counter-balance to verse is a good thing.

But think of the Robertson book, a hybrid which has been successful - but as poetry. There are no successful hybrid fictions? True or false?

And if false, how?

What about a kind of internal monologue like this?!!

Idea that.

A twist on the first person.

A more dynamic approach to the 'I'. Almost a soliloquy, play-like.

Nice…

And breathe + and think.

You would think, wouldn't you, that when you announce to your friends and family that you have a new book out, a good number would buy it. It may only be out of a sense of loyalty - misplaced or not - but there would surely be a few dozen sales you could count on.

Evidently not.

It surprised me when it first happened - or didn't happen, depending on how you wish to construct the sentence in your head - and it continues to surprise me still. And that leaves me trying to answer a simple question. Why?

I think there are only two possible answers.

The first is that they don't read books. Clearly rubbish. Okay, so they may not read poetry, say, but the vast majority of people do read books. And even if they only read Grisham, or pot-boilers, it doesn't seem too much of a flight of fantasy to think they might just try yours... So perhaps we should refine this answer: they don't read your *sort* of books. It's nothing personal.

Well, maybe.

The second answer is more subtle in a way. Because they *know* you, a person in their immediate circle, what you write can't be any good, can it?! After all, they don't know Rowling or McEwan or Amis or Ludlum; but you... You! You're just their friend from work / the pub / church / the badminton club. They *know* you. How can anything you write be good enough to read?! It's not personal.

But it is, of course. Intensely personal. Whether it's because of the first answer or the second (and, to be honest, in most cases it will be a combination of both) it is intensely personal - to *you*, as the writer. Not as their friend / colleague etc., but to you as an individual.

I often wonder what might happen if, one day, I were to get 'picked up' by a *proper* publisher and have my books suddenly appear on the tables of Waterstones or Barnes & Noble. The books won't suddenly be any better, will they? They will be the same books; the same words, in the same order - but I wonder if my friends might just start buying them...?

It would be nice to find out!

At work today I was reviewing some CVs for a role I am likely to need to fill in my team. As I was doing so, I wondered what my own CV - in a writing context - would look like...

- Wrote my first story - about a boy's adventures in space - including illustrations, aged 5.

- Most Christmases thereafter either longing for or getting a new typewriter. Didn't stop writing, always intoxicated by the potential of those two little words: "CHAPTER ONE".

- Early teens, had a poem published in the local paper, and then another poem framed and hung on the wall of the local city museum.

- Not really knowing why, I decided I wanted to study English at 'A' level. Fell in love all over again.

- University was a profoundly productive period. Lynchpin of the department's Writing Group, I was also one of the founders of a new University magazine, "The Definite Article". Wrote a tremendous amount of poetry, most of it mildly average and/or hopelessly romantic, the odd piece better than that. Performed at one or two public readings; had the odd thing published.

- After University - and a difficult period teaching in West Africa - wrote my first play and my first novel. Both cringingly atrocious and long since lost. Thankfully!

- Although work and 'life' started to get in the way, had sporadic bursts of creativity; whenever I finished something, I tried to get it published. The feedback from agents (when they bothered to respond) was never very complimentary...

- Twenty-four years ago, wrote the first book I felt reasonably happy with: "The Big Frog Theory". Failed to find a publisher (though I'm not sure how hard I tried).

- Then, responding to an ad in an industry magazine, I found myself with a contract to write a book - with a real publisher! - on IT Strategy and Management, thereby combining twenty years of industry experience with over thirty-five of writing. Four years later and I had written and published - two through an arm of Bertelsmann, no less! - three such books. University libraries in Europe started stocking them; in Sheffield, one made it onto a course reading list..!

- Kept plugging away at prose and poetry, and then, around 2012, discovered Kindle Direct Publishing. Dusted off "The Big Frog Theory" and pulled together collections of poetry going back years.

- I was suddenly liberated!

- Since then - and having swapped KDP for Ingram Spark for my print editions - I simply haven't stopped. Ten books in three years: novels, collections of short stories, volumes of poetry.

- I feel like I'm making up for lost time, racing toward a brick wall with no intention of putting my foot on the brake.

- I try not to think about all the years when I wasn't writing enough. Try not to imagine all those wonderful lines of poetry I might have written, or that missing lucid, fluent, insightful prose.

- I try not to, but sometimes you can't help it.

Maybe it's not much of a CV, I don't know; but I do know that it isn't finished. I know that there are still unwritten 'chapters' to come. I hope that more people will read my work because that's the ultimate validation. Not pecuniary; I just want people to read something I've written and say "that was really good".

~~~~

Is this a reasonable distillation of his writing life based on the evidence contained in his notebooks and blog posts? At a relatively crude and high-level view, possibly. And might it also be a triangulation point for all the conclusions drawn in reading, analysing, and annotating?

But of course it isn't a CV. It is more a potted 'writing Life' than anything else, with him mapping out the way-points on the journey. This is something his notebooks do to an extent, and, using those as my guide, as I have tried to do too. Perhaps given those three perspectives - the reality, his interpretation of that reality, and our analysis of his interpretation - the notion of 'triangulation' is an appropriate one.

~~~~

11th March 2019 (w.com)

Nothing to write about? You're not trying...[58]

In fact it's almost the opposite; there's almost nothing *not* worth writing about..!

I'm sitting in the casual bar of a reasonably up-market hotel as I write this. In front of me a panoply of characters and interactions, of dialogues and intrigues, of mystery and emotion. Actually there's a whole short story collection right here!

---

[58] This was the title of the blog post.

Take the couple opposite. She came in first, solo. Short hair, male cut. Comfy shoes. She sits down alone. A few minutes later, a man - huge, bearded, older - appears with two pints of lager. There's a frisson. Ahhh.

Not what I was expecting. But what's the story there - because there is one. And of course, I don't know what it is, but I could make it mine. I could steal them, make those two complete strangers mine.

Or the two businessmen across the way. Middle-ranking in all probability. Sharing stories; indulging in that little commercial indiscretion beers in hotel bars always seem to induce. Are they really on the same team, or is one playing the other?

Or the couple a little way to my left. He, older, greying but still with a ponytail(!); she, of indeterminate age. There is no frisson there but rather aggression, voices too loud, arguments about onion rings. Playful or not? What lies beneath the surface? An under-current of threat perhaps..?

Sit in any cafe or bar or restaurant for perhaps half an hour. Go in with a notebook and leave with the bones of a collection of short stories. Perfect material - and so wide open for you to do with as you will. Characters on a plate.

Almost literally...

12th March 2019 (w.com)

I was in the kitchen at work the other day when a colleague said something about writing books being "a nice hobby to have".

Work (defn.) - what you have to do to pay the bills when you'd rather be doing something more meaningful..?

It was, of course, small talk, and it was good of them to both know and then comment - but I was surprised how much I bristled internally. It's **not** a hobby. It's something I've been doing compulsively, religiously, almost without choice since I was five years old.

What's the most appropriate word for that I wonder..? It's neither work nor hobby that's for sure.

In the end, I'm pleased my colleague knows and felt comfortable enough to comment. Small acorns possibly..?

17th March 2019 (w.com)

There is a fantastic moment in a 1971 sketch with those late greats: comedian Eric Morecambe and conductor André Previn. Previn is conducting a small ensemble in Grieg's piano concerto; Morecambe is at the piano.

The musical intro is great - unlike Morecambe's playing. Previn stops 'the band' and comes over to the piano:

"What are you doing? You're playing all the wrong notes."

"I'm playing all the right notes - but not necessarily in the right order."

More and more it strikes me that writing - especially poetry - is just like that. Often I find myself looking at drafts and thinking 'that's ok - but are they the right words?'

Sometimes you want the words to tell you that they're not to the right ones or that they're in the wrong place, but they're complicit in your failure (if you can call it that). They sit where you put them and wait. They offer no clue, no assistance. If you're lucky they resonate somehow, usually silently in your head, but that's about it.

"What arc you doing? You've written all the wrong words."

"I'm writing *some* of the right words - and almost certainly not entirely in the right order."

It's the striving to get all the right notes in the right order that keeps us going.

You should check out the sketch if you don't know it; it's very funny.

April 2019 (PVR)

"Life on a Lease"
↳ verse collection for the Autumn of '19 ✔

"Liam"
↳ a 'slow burn' novel; the 'follow-up' to Maunston - probably running slowly through '19 until the plot emerges from the vignettes

"X"
↳ what about this hybrid idea - or is that simply too much to take on?

MARKETING
↳ do I need to address the 'selling' question?
↳ how much am I prepared to 'invest' in that?

- requires some research (what have I got to lose?)

✿

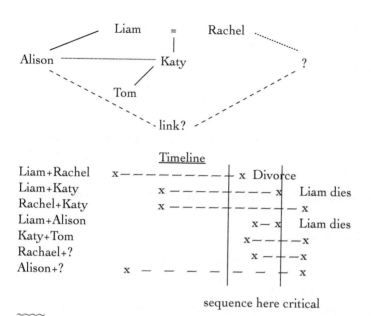

Timeline

Liam+Rachel	x — — — — — — — — — x Divorce
Liam+Katy	x — — — — — — — x Liam dies
Rachel+Katy	x — — — — — — — — x
Liam+Alison	x — x Liam dies
Katy+Tom	x — — — — x
Rachael+?	x — — — x
Alison+?	x — — — — — — — x

sequence here critical

An odd portmanteau entry which poses a number of questions. Given his focus on Writeral and its somewhat more 'general' posts, we've had nothing at all from him recently in terms of what he is working on. There are new ideas here - "Life on a Lease", "Liam", "X" - so where did these come from, and how long has he been thinking about them? "X" is perhaps the most intriguing of the three if only because it is essentially unformed and we can have no clue as to what it might be about - unless by "hybrid" he means a blend of narrative and poetry. At least with "Liam" we can assume not only that it's fiction he is considering, but - based on the diagram and table sketched out - that he has already given it some thought.

The "Marketing" observation is an interesting one, presumably referring to a lack of sales, something he has touched on in his blog on more than one occasion. When he says "invest", does he mean time or money, or both?

~~~~

12th May 2019 (w.com)

I don't know about you, but when I grew up and learned to write, all my stories were in the third person past tense. Perhaps that's the easiest way to teach children English. Later, as we become more sophisticated and get a greater sense of self, we move on to first person narrative - but again in the past tense. Everything has already happened; that's what makes it easier to re-tell - right?

It was only very recently - with my novel *At Maunston Quay* - that I decided to try writing something of scale in the present tense.

It was difficult at first, and I found I would lapse back into the blue blanket of the past tense. Somehow you felt safe there. But soon - and surprisingly quickly - I warmed to the present tense; it gave the story something of an immediacy, the characters life. I actually enjoyed it enormously.

But now I have a problem; the opposite one I had when I started "Maunston". Now, when I try and write in the past tense, the present slips in under the covers. It has become my natural voice.

"But", you may say, "isn't that all fine and dandy? Just write in the present all the time."

If only it were that easy.

My current endeavour spans a number of years, and multiple characters. Although all of the story is set in 'the past'/has happened, for one particular character I'm keen to generate that degree of immediacy the present tense gives so am writing the sections seen from his perspective in that way, using the rest of the narrative to give the context of time, that his 'present' experiences have already happened.

Does that make sense?

The problem - I discover - comes where there is a chain of events, chronologically and immediately sequential: a first chapter told from the perspective of a 'past tense character' immediately followed by a related second from the viewpoint of 'present tense character'. Past tense followed by present for what is essentially a single event? I'm not sure that really works. But then switching my present tense character to the past for that particular event - well, I'm not sure about that either...

There are options. Leave it as it is and rely on the Reader to sort it out. Make it all past tense. Make it all present tense. (At the moment, the first of these is probably the front-runner.)

25th May 2019 (*w.com*)

I'm now thirty thousand words in to my latest expedition in fiction. That's probably about a third of the way through, though I'm not sure yet. If my rough plan's about right, I should be done with the first draft around October.

What I said in a recent post about that magic tipping point when, as an author, I become as much a Reader as a Writer still stands, but today I realised something else too - something that also keeps the fires stoked.

Every time I write some more, I learn something new about my characters.

For example, I hadn't realised until a couple of days ago just how insecure one of them was; and then I discovered how they tried to process that, and the things they did in order to compensate or overcome it. I didn't know just how much they would see it as a weakness - nor where they would begin to lay the blame.

Of course all this fits perfectly with the story I'm trying to tell, and when something seems to come from nowhere but fall perfectly into place, I find myself wondering just how much of the story I already have lodged in my subconscious. These magic moments, incidents that seem God-given, are almost too good to be true.

Perhaps that sense of being subservient to the story supports the notion of Writer as Reader. Or perhaps 'Translator' is a better term, I don't know. But these are real people now. I can see them, almost as if they were scenes from my past and harvested from my memory.

The folklore is to tell people to write about what they know - and the complaint from writers is often that they don't really know about anything. In a way we actually know about *everything*. If you have a sense of the individual - and you will have spent an entire lifetime getting to know people - then you can put characters in any situation and explore how they would react. Most of the time you will know, and sometimes you will find out.

As a writer, both experiences are, of course, absolutely brilliant..!

~~~~

How can we possibly know what those experiences are like? Not the fundamentals of being a writer or a reader, but when the characters created take on lives of their own and, as their author, we move into a subservient role, almost becoming their puppet. Isn't that what reading is about, putting oneself in the hands of another to be guided along a journey? How profound and complex must the author's emotional experience be when they are simultaneously mapping out that self-same journey? What comes first, the chicken or the egg, because there is a sense here that in some strange way - in a 'fictional' way - the characters are as responsible for what happens to them as he is. His description is very specific: "I discovered how they tried to process that, and the things they did in order to compensate or overcome it. I didn't know just how much they would see it as a weakness - nor where they would begin to lay the blame". The effort is that of the characters, the actions theirs, the perception of weakness and how it might be excused away is owned by the fictitious people created. What he describes sounds symbiotic, a relationship not between independent organisms but rather two 'halves' of the same being i.e. him as writer / reader. More than that, there is a third party involved i.e. the triumvirate is completed by the conglomerate we might term 'the characters'.

Is such an experience unique? Who can say? But it is powerfully expounded here, not just in the way he describes it, but in the absolute clarity of knowing it is a fact of writing, a blessed byproduct, to which he is profoundly committed. There is belief here; a faith even.

~~~~

7th July 2019 (MWD)

In case anyone were to be misled by this page, it isn't a true reflection of my writing efforts; it's actually a dereliction of duty! I write virtually every day. Really. But I have failed to keep a record. Must try harder. 1/10

Later, Part 2:

More work on the draft of my next novel. Now up to just under 59,000. Final total looking like it will be in the region of 85k-90k.

Reviewing / tinkering some 'almost finished' poems, including selecting one - "Brachiation" - for Tuesday's Stanza poetry group.

Entered three poetry competitions - as ever, with little expectation...

8th July 2019 (MWD)

Another writing day - of course! A few hundred words added to my draft novel, plus the beginnings of a poem; a poem which started with two lines that came to me in the middle of the night about a week ago that I had to get out of bed to write down! We'll see what comes of that...

8th July 2019 (w.com)

Years ago - but maybe not so many years ago - my process of writing poetry was relatively straightforward. And immensely naïve. I used to think (subconsciously at least) that the first words written had some kind of 'sacred' quality to them; that because they had come first, were the outpourings of 'the Muse', had been gifted to me by some mythical force, then they should be left pretty much alone. In those days, editing perhaps involved changing three or four words. How could it be anything other than that?

Complete rubbish.

I'm not sure exactly what triggered the change, my departure from this romantic notion of being a poet. I suspect it was two things: the first, publishing, and the rigour of wanting to ensure that what you launched into the world was as good as it could be at that particular moment in time; and the second, going to writing groups where there was a standard to be measured against, where the 'ante' had been 'upped', where people could - in the nicest possible way - call your bluff. And actually, thinking about it, there was a third: starting to write the occasional 'found poem' where the words aren't yours in the first place. Indeed, this may have been the greatest influence.

In any event, the end result of this unconscious transformation is that now the first words I write in a new poem are often no more than way markers, like a painter roughing out a sketch on a canvass. Over time, words are added, taken away; how they look on the page has become more important; there are questions of style and tone; intellectual questions about voice and meaning. It's less *random*. The work - and it is work - is much more artisanal, if not like a painter then possibly like a sculptor. Because there is chipping away involved. Often I will draft a poem and then tweak it every day or every other day for potentially weeks on end. Although a poem is never truly 'finished', I find my measure of completeness is if I haven't altered a piece in the last three of four times I've looked at it, then it's probably good enough - for now at least.

This may sound a little - I don't know - 'excessive', but it's actually very liberating. I no longer feel enslaved to the first words I write; indeed, quite the opposite. So even the smallest adjustment - like the removal of a single word during the twentieth brief edit - is to be celebrated.

So it isn't magic. It's lots of hard work and practice. Patience and practice. And - hopefully - one day the magic will arrive..!

9th July 2019 (MWD)

The monthly Stanza meeting, so little time to write. The tweaking of a few poems, partly inspired by the group tonight - and the desire to write more, but just too tired to do so.

10th July 2019 (MWD)

Novel draft now up to about 59.5k words. About 25-30k remaining.

Last night's Stanza not one of the best. Feedback on what I had submitted confirmed my suspicions that it wasn't up to the requisite standard; a little confused I felt, even before the meeting.

Which is fine. That's what the group's all about. Need to bring my 'A' game next time!

11th July 2019 (MWD)

A busy day, so just a little tweaking of the few hundred words I wrote last night - and the inclusion of a really important sentence! - plus some minor re-tuning of a poem of two.

Little activity. Some minor editing.

Maybe 500 words on so on my novel. Edging over the 60k mark.

Again, another few hundred words on the novel plus - as ever - reviewing of that written the previous couple of days.

A few hundred words more edges the total over 61k. These small bursts may seem insignificant (larger chunks of drafting tend to happen at weekends for obvious reasons) but at the end of the day they all mount up...

More of the same to edge me towards 62k - plus a blog post about writing. What else?!

Sometimes, as a writer, you get those moments when you are bowled over by what you have written. It's almost as if it had come from someone else.

Those moments can be as a result of modest things - a line in a poem, perhaps - or something much larger - a paragraph or even a page or two. Very rarely, I would argue, is it truly much more than that. None of us are that good...

So this morning, writing a little at breakfast before work, one such moment. It may not look like much - indeed, it may not **be** much - but just then it was something special. A short little paragraph, four sentences, that simply said what needed to be said:

> From somewhere Katy thought she saw lightning. It may only have been imaginary, figurative, but it meant thunder was coming. She wanted to close her eyes and close her ears, to hunker down under a duvet somewhere and ride out the storm. But she knew she could not, for she was at its centre.

~~~~

It can be moments like this, paragraphs like this, that end up launching him into something else. Four sentences could become eight, or two paragraphs, or three pages, four chapters, an entire novel. If you consider the one above as the opening gambit - page one, line one - it does many of the things such beginnings are supposed to do i.e. ask questions which require a story to provide the answers. Who is Katy? Did she see lightning? Was there thunder coming? And if it was a storm - a metaphorical one - what was its context and why was she at its centre?[59]

Does such an example at least partially align itself with his earlier views of reader vs. writer, of his characters becoming 'real' and taking over? If so, I wonder at what point Katy would become 'a person' in her own right, an individual who compelled him to write her story. Or has she - in those four simple sentences - already achieved that goal?

~~~~

20th July 2019 (MWD)

Bits and pieces over the last few days with the completion of another chapter. Eight to go, around 60 pages and 20k. End of September?

22nd July 2019 (MWD)

Some inroads over the weekend sees the word count nearing 65k... And all at the cost of having written no poetry for a little while.

22nd July 2019 (w.com)

I have always liked to have multiple projects on the go: poetry *and* prose; differing themes and styles. I like to think the variety keeps things fresh.

There comes a time, however, when striking a workable balance, juggling more than one thing, simply doesn't work - and that happens when I'm getting close to finishing something. It's as if all my energy needs to go into that final sprint, the winning line in sight. Back both horses if you want to, but only one can win.

Which is where I am now. About 65k words into the draft of my next novel (and about 20k-ish to go), and poetry takes a back step. I start to get consumed with the need to **finish**. Whatever it is I'm writing, when it reaches that state I become creatively myopic. I can only see one thing.

But actually, in the case of prose, that's not entirely true because I actually start to get ideas about the next thing I'm going to write. Or, in the present circumstance, the form which it is going to take. The next prose piece - whatever it is - *feels* like it will be first person. Time to ride that old nag again..!

Anyway, one step at a time. Finish the draft; take a break; start the editing process - which, bizarrely, I find frees me to start writing other new stuff again.

---

[59] The excerpt ended up in the middle of *The Opposite of Remembering*.

Another chapter finished and 65.5k words. Six more chapters to go. They're short, so perhaps 25k more words? Looks like the book will be over 90k and a few more pages than the 240 I was envisaging. A few, not many. I also have a nagging feeling that there's a chapter or two missing that will need writing and inserting when I go through my first review. We'll see. Oh, and I finished a poem that was half-written - which is nice.

Tiptoed over the 67k mark this morning - probably with more to come later today and over the weekend. Into the final furlong. I find myself wondering if I can get the draft finished before we go on holiday on the 3rd...one final manic push, perhaps...

[Later: make that 67.5k...]

At 68.5k, I'm about 4 and a half chapters from finishing my draft... But today I also managed to write a really rough paragraph or two. At least I'll know where to look for the bodies when I start editing..!

Just over three-and-a-bit chapters to go; touching 72k words. We're off on holiday on Saturday and I had vague hopes of getting this across the line before we went...But unlikely. I should finish it during the first few days in France, and then we'll see what stimulation from a new environment surfaces...

Just started the third-last chapter and broken through 73k. Within a week now the first draft will be done..!

Someone's moved the goal posts. The Holy Grail has shifted. It used to be that writers dreamed of being published, because 'being published' meant something.

Now, thanks to Indie Publishing and services likes Amazon's KDP, lulu, Ingram Spark etc., getting published is a piece of cake; having your words turned to into real physical books (or virtual electronic ones!) is not the big problem it used to be. Anyone can do it.

Today's biggest challenge is being **read**...

There are lots of reasons probably, but the major one is, I think, that the market-place is flooded with books in a way it has never been before, and so navigating between what's good and what's not is almost impossible. As a reader, how do you take a chance on someone you've never heard of? Maybe 30 years ago, being published - through a literary agent etc. - was more of a guarantee that you might be read; someone had already done the filtering for you.

Today, as a 'published author', the thing I seek more than anything else is to be read. Not because I want to be a mega-bucks JKRowling-type superstar, but just to know there is someone at the other end of my literary handshake.

1st August 2019 (MWD)

Seventy-four thousand... Edging closer, ever-closer.

3rd August 2019 (MWD)

I think I may have finished..! The third chapter from the end reached such a logical conclusion that I may not need the last two chapters I had been planning; they would only be duplication.So pen down, breathe - and leave it alone for a while...

6th August 2019 (La Rochelle) (MWD)

Having spent a large chunk of last night 'imagining' the beginning of a new story, I was up at 7 this morning and 70 minutes later had drafted 1,877 words. They may end up being nothing of course, but boy was I in the groove!

7th August 2019 (La Rochelle) (MWD)

I started my 'holiday piece' on Sunday, and after another solid session before breakfast, have now reached the dizzy heights of over 4,800 words. It feels a little like a novella at this stage, but let's see where we go with it. I slept badly (again) last night, creating (again) the next sequences in the story. I have at least another eight identified. I won't know for while yet whether or not it has merit.

23rd November 2019 (w.com)

When we write fiction - and especially when we are steeped in revision - it would not be unreasonable to assert that our primary goal is to land on the 'right' words, that elusive combination which tells the story we want to tell and does so in the perfect way. Not unreasonable, surely?

Indeed.

I am in the second phase of revision for my next novel, "The Opposite of Remembering" which is scheduled for publication at the beginning of February next year. The way I work? First stage is a review on the computer; the second is a paper-based re-read; the third and final phase is another re-read, this time through a proof copy of the final book. All of which sounds like a thorough process which should give me the best possible opportunity to 'get it right'.

But there's a flaw in the argument.

What I discover every time I go through this activity - and especially during the second stage - is that the degree of revision undertaken is dependant on two rather more emotionally influenced criteria. First, the quality of the material I have to review is entirely dependant on how I was feeling when I actually wrote the first draft i.e. if I was 'in the groove' when I first put pen to paper, the quality is usually good; if I was struggling, then it's inevitably not so hot.

Maybe that's not surprising. But secondly - and crucially - irrespective of the quality of the draft, how much I choose to revise the text is profoundly dependant on how I'm *feeling* when editing it. Take two copies of the same paragraph and edit it on different days, and I **guarantee** that you will end up with different outcomes. Given that, how can there be a 'right' answer?

It's common to acknowledge that a poem is never finished. I would argue that you can say the same about fiction too.

~~~~

We learned in May (six months before this entry) that he was making good progress on his "latest expedition in fiction", but he gave us no clue as to what that might have been. Perhaps back then he wasn't confident he would be able to see it through; perhaps he was getting to that 'dangerous' stage where a novel sinks or swims. By July he had clearly got past that point - and written thirty-five thousand words in two months!

The origin of the novel was the "Liam" idea he floated in his April entry; which means he had gone from the sketch of an idea to sixty-five thousand words in six months. And if that was not impressive enough, he did so whilst working full-time - not that any of his notebook entries nor blog posts make any reference to that fact. Considering what has gone before, how significant is the absence of any work-related acknowledgement? When was the last time he talked about his 'profession'? Might this not also demonstrate how far he had come on his writing journey, how his priorities had changed, how he had established a new balance? Does the commitment to 'The Opposite of Remembering' further indicate maturity and belief, backing up his mission to write "until the light goes out"?

~~~~

29th November 2019 (w.com)

It's that time of year again. As seems to have been the case for - what? - the last two or three years now, I arrive into December putting the finishing touches to the final drafts for new books that will see the light of day in February; all that remains is the generation and checking of the physical proof copies. One book is a novel, "The Opposite of Remembering"; the second is a collection of poetry, "The Myths of Native Trees". [I'm also working on a three-handed collection of verse - "Triple Measures" - with some very old friends, and this too should be out in the New Year].

If this pattern is to repeat itself in twelve months' time, I need to be deciding what comes next. Custom and practice demands that I should be thinking about my next fiction project in the coming few weeks and then putting 'pen to paper' as 2020 dawns.

Probably like many writers I keep a notebook (read notebooks) in which I occasionally jot down thoughts and ideas. Not only are these entries remarkably sporadic - they tend to only occur when I have a creative decision to make - but they are also spread across numerous notebooks. Numerous notebooks!

With the (highly unoriginal) notion of harvesting old ideas, I have just spent a few minutes skimming through the (was it six?!) volumes that contain these somewhat nomadic musings. In one, the first entry goes back to the nineties; in another 2013 can be followed by 2017 because thoughts from the in-between years have been lodged in another one or two. The whole process is, I confess, disorganised and somewhat fickle; I think I choose which notebook to write in based on the mood I'm in, the kind of paper I feel like writing on (i.e. lined, plain or squared), and which of the various covers takes my fancy at that precise moment.

Hardly a scientific process!

Many of the ideas I remember well. Some have even been mapped out in enough detail as to contain a list of all the chapters, or excerpts of draft text, or comments on character traits. For some I confess to now wonder what I could have possibly been thinking!

There is something cathartic and necessary in all of this. It seems to me to be an essential part of 'The Process'; a kind of 'navel-gazing' that - probably more often than not - throws up something to run with. If I am honest with myself, it is also one I enjoy and find profoundly satisfying. Maybe I like to think it proves something about me.

I have a small number of things started that could end up being 'The Thing'; seven thousand words here, ten thousand words there. But I'd like to be doing something different next year, to take on a new challenge stylistically. Just thinking about the opportunity is truly exciting...

Time to pick a pen and choose a notebook!

~~~~

Here he provides us with a considered introduction to the notebooks upon which this volume is based. The use of them - in terms of the physical books themselves, the timing of the entries - is, as he acknowledges, haphazard ("disorganised and somewhat fickle"), but their importance to him is clear: not only do they serve as a repository for ideas, they also have a role at an emotional level permitting the overall process to be somewhat "cathartic". He doesn't over-emphasise the latter, but the notebooks' use as a sounding board has benefit on multiple levels.

What follows - the very next day in fact! - is only the third notebook entry of 2019 and squarely in the tradition of very many of his earlier musings i.e. absorbed with the dilemma of what to write next.

~~~~

30ᵗʰ November 2019 (BBG)

Fiction options:
1. the French story
2. 'Confession'
3. Pier
4. something else

1
+ lots of words   -ve not sure if I believe in the story
+ it's broadly planned out

2
+ve it's a slightly different construct and a new style
need to work out the plot but at its centre is the relationship between the main characters, Matt and Anne.
- clearly a possibility

3
+ve probably the easiest to write
-ve a bit formulaic - and possibly doesn't represent that much of a progression from Nev.

4
? chance for a new style of writing (à la confession): something more 'modern'

need to settle on some kind of central theme or event to drive the action; there needs to be something to which the story builds
and multiple background themes such as the failure of words, the definition / blurring of truth vs. lies =>

Indeed I quite like that truth vs. lies conundrum because it goes hand-in-hand with language. Words are the means of delivery for both, the difference between them can be minuscule, or influenced by how the words are delivered (or the 'physical' context from which they come).

It is also an opportunity to play with the reader; to present a lie as truth and vice versa. So how can the reader trust what they are reading? How can they know what's true? A way to represent the breakdown of language, or at least its fallibility.

Characters can represent either side of the argument. We might invest in one the greater likelihood of telling the truth because of who they are / what they do. This is very subversive. Who can you trust?

And what role does the narrator play in this (if there is one)? Or the author come to that? We instinctively trust the author because of their role, because it is their story; why would they lie?

If we were to take this approach then it would make sense to start the story with an untruth - but one presented as truth so that the reader then builds their interpretation of the story around that i.e. A leads to B, B to C, C to D etc. But if A did not lead to B, then this causes the rest of the chain to collapse. Makes the plot really important therefore. It needs to be written in such a way as to have dual interpretations. 'I offer you this, and please read it in this way. I'm going to put you off reading it in any other way; even deny that it can be done. Accept my truth.'

So who would lie, why, and about what??

It would need to be non-factual, something that cannot be checked therefore it probably needs not to be a matter of record or measure. It probably needs to be personal, emotional - for how do you prove any of that?

Do you need multiple viewpoints for the same 'event' in order to throw up the doubt / illuminate the dichotomy? If so, then perhaps that introduction needs to appear about half-way through the story (to allow time for the conceit to gain traction and not be challenged).

Does the 'Confession' story lend itself to this i.e. question => answer. And why should anyone assume the answer is a lie? e.g. what if we don't hear Matt's side of the story until much later? The challenge to 'the truth' would come then...

Where do these ideas come from? As we have seen, there is always the "something else" option! "Pier" is not a new idea, of course; he has previously made reference to it - and questioned its validity. Given what he says about "Confession", does this demonstrate that this notion has been around for some time too? Perhaps he had been working on it subconsciously. From an archivist's perspective there is a degree of frustration when a reasonably dressed notion such as this arrives out of nowhere, its source obscure and unacknowledged.

The same might be said about "The French Story", but in this case it is possible to provide a little historical context outside of the notebooks.

In the summer of 2019, he and his family enjoyed a two-week holiday in France: a week in La Rochelle followed by a second week a little further inland. Whilst in La Rochelle he started work on a new idea that arose from nothing more than spending time around the harbour and planting a new character in those surroundings. During that holiday he drafted perhaps twelve thousand words of what he calls here "The French Story" (and later on, "The French Thing"). And remember, all this during the period when he was also writing those tens of thousands of words for "Liam".

'Confession' told from the perspective of the interviewee. The veracity of what they say is immediately established, and the Q&A approach goes some way to achieving the 'ring of truth'.

The first part of the story is about establishing the plot. Then undermine what we have learned by hearing from Anne and Matt. Format? Not Q&A; possibly more as a statement, a testament. Would further complicate the authenticity of the 'I' persona in the story.

The invisibility story: is that a metaphor? i.e. his invisibility stands for something else both in the sense of context / his story but also being 'invisible' permits him to get closer to the truth...

Q> is he the only person who is invisible? If not, what does this do to his status?
The rocket story is about choice (deciding whether or not to hit the 'return' button). It's all about the 'point of no return' - but also has the astronaut asking questions about the two 'realities' he has been presented with: which of these are true / lies?

It becomes a question of belief for him - an internal war ranged and raged against the only reality / truth he has i.e. inside his rocket. The 'big red button' therefore becomes symbolic of something else too.[60]

❋

Poetry - options

1 - totally 'found'; using all those National Geographics
2 - formal / stylistically consistent ~~~~ but what form?
3 - something more radical?
e.g. W__ _____ _ ____
         O____ __ _____ _
         R__ _____ __ _ _
         D_ _____ _____ __

And then there's the question of subject...
4 - a narrative poem i.e. a bit like rehearsals / 'The Long Take'

Subject? Subject? - because it might be interesting to try a 'theme' rather than a random collection.
What could be the basis?
         historical?   a life?
         contemporary?   political?
         allegorical?   a re-imagining?
                          (à la Eliot)

❋

Perhaps I should start with an event, or a theme.

"Write what you know about"

How about the homelessness of a child? Chapters punctuated by loss, of absence, of being deprived of all those things the other children took for granted. It could be a harsh portrait, stark. If so, it would need to be told looking back - a story imbued with wisdom and hindsight (the setting up is therefore critical).

---

[60] "The Big Red Button" became the title for a short story he did indeed write - but which, to-date, he has not published.

It would also be a confession of sorts. An apology.

"This is what I am. This is what life sculpted me to be."

So what is the 'event'? Both event and trigger. The trigger starts the story; the event is the story, the thing toward which we journey without choices, variance. Perhaps there are way points, where things might have turned out differently if another decision had been taken, another door opened.

Perhaps it is a story about the gradual accumulation of blame and in the end the making of a decision not to help, not to forgive...

"The Homelessness of a Child" is a collection of poems. A kind of autobiographical snapshot. Could pull out things / events that provided the framework for those first 20 years? Notion that only when home was 'left' was the notion of homelessness defeated; how could you be homeless if the default position was to be without a home?

This alongside something fictional, the 2020 plan...

~~~~

There is some confusion here when discussing "The Homelessness of a Child"; at one point he refers to "chapters", and then "a collection of poems". He is clearly working things through, though what he has established is that it is likely to be an "autobiographical snapshot" - the first time he has ever really considered such a project, in whatever format.

~~~~

What about 'exclusion' as a theme? à la Brexit. The idea of the effect of a change of status, and how that can impact people. The changes would need to occur at a fundamental level e.g.:
- Religious (finding or losing)
- Political (rights and status)
- Liberty (gaining or losing)
- Emotional (love and friendship)
And the changes can be both positive and negative.
- 'Winning' or 'Achievement'
- Self-esteem

One advantage of something like this is that it can be multi-threaded and apply to many people, connected or otherwise. A single narrative or a collection of stories. So the Rocket Story is possibly one such idea which is more about looking at the tipping point which leads to a change of status, in this case a truly conscious one.

Interesting!

A little like ' S&W' and 'Separation' there is a thread here - much more comfortable than trying to weave everything into a single narrative: the family / village from hell? Totally unbelievable because of so much coincidence. 'Understory' shows how such an approach can be done well.

So in the majority of cases the stories will be about the effect of the change - or exclusion if all are negative. Some about the leading up to. Some about making the choice to be 'in' or 'out'. Some like 'the Rocket'...

Religious: the losing for faith - the exclusion from God, a community, a routine or way of life. Isolation? Vulnerability? Fear? Being alone?

Political: a change of status, of rights. Practical impacts; the can't / must do e.g. rules, forms etc. how you are treated when an 'outcast' - but should be subtle. Brexit? e.g. no longer 'European'. left with no choice, powerless, unable to do anything about it - unless driven to (the verge of another exclusion because of crossing a legal boundary? another choice? ties to liberty?)

Emotional: the falling out of love or out of a relationship (two different things) Parallels to the political exclusion perhaps?

Winning / losing: (the latter only?) - in a commercial context probably. A 'failure' and isolated because of it. Also could be isolated because of being a winner?

Intellectual - what about exclusion if one is not as bright as - or brighter than - everyone else?

Hmmm.

- 'The Big Red Button'
- Can the French story be used? What exclusion would that represent; liberty? freedom?
- What about the story of the man incarcerated because of what he had done? the exclusion from love and the reaction to it?

For the first time in a while he appeared to be seriously considering another collection of short stories. Perhaps "The Big Red Button" was the spark. Once again what this proposal had in common with both 'Secrets & Wisdom' and 'Degrees of Separation' was the idea of taking an external theme to provide the framework that would join the stories together, in this case the notion of 'exclusion'.

It is unclear whether his addition of "The French Story" to the list of potential candidates was because he thought it might fit or because he didn't want to lose all the effort he had put into it thus far.

1st February 2020 (w.com)

It was a little over two months ago I wrote the first version of the post below[61]. Given the books I was working on were finally published today, the questions posed below become even more relevant. I'm heading into the bulk of 2020 without a firm plan.

I have been through the start of the notebook process, shortlisting four possible projects, and rereading the beginnings of things that are already written. The result? Well, fog...

I may have settled on my next poetry collection[62]: something with a consistent 'theme' throughout. But as far as prose is concerned, my next novel? I haven't a scooby-do...

The danger is, of course, that I end up 'settling' for something rather than land on something I actually believe in. I have come to realise that there are two key components which need to be in place in order for me to see a project through to the end: the first is that I have to be writing about characters I am personally invested and interested in (I need to care what happens to them); the second is that there needs to be a story I want to tell. With the three pieces where the potential beginning is already written, I have to say none of them qualify quite well enough... Could they? I guess so. But right now, I'm not feeling the love.

This uncertainty is, I have to say, a strange feeling.

---

[61] A post entitled "Published Today!" but not reproduced here. He would always announce his publications on writeral.com with such posts. In this case he was referring to *The Opposite of Remembering, The Myths of Native Trees*, and his three-handed collaboration *Triple Measures*.

[62] The "Homelessness" idea.

"The questions posed below"? There were none in the "Published Today!" blog post to which he refers, so presumably he is talking about the implied rather than stated questions in this entry i.e what does he write next? If 'belief' and 'investment' have become the cornerstones for such decisions, does this indicate that he has reached a point - after a hugely productive three years - where 'turning the handle' in order to generate output is no longer the primary concern it once was? He had previously floated the idea of another short story collection and already has three candidate pieces, yet seemingly prepared to discard these perhaps demonstrates that, although they might meet the 'investment' criteria, they fall short in terms of 'belief'.

~~~~

<div align="right">

15th April 2020 (w.com)

</div>

On the 19th December I started work on something that - as is often the case - was no more than a vague notion, a few opening sentences. On Monday, just under four months later, I finished the first draft of a new, relatively small novel (c. 52k words, about 150 paperback pages).

I have spoken before about reaching the point in writing fiction when I become 'reader' as opposed to 'writer', when the compulsion to finish the work arises out of a need to find out what happened rather than the original need to write something down. I reached that point towards the end of March - after that it was plain sailing!

Now I have to put the work away for a couple of weeks before I begin the process of revision: first on-screen, second and third iterations on paper. My current target is 1st August to have the book completed.

~~~~

As if to confirm there is no problem generating output...

~~~~

<div align="right">

18th May 2020 (w.com)

</div>

Perhaps it's an inevitable question. Having just completed the first stage (on-screen) of a three-cycle review and proofreading activity, the default question I always ask myself - perhaps more subconsciously than not - is do I like what I've written?

Reasonably short at c. 140 paperback pages and around 52k words, my next novel represents something of a stylistic departure, and so any question about 'liking' is made harder to answer. Perhaps it's more about it 'working' than anything else i.e.

does it succeed not only in terms of narrative cohesion, but in the way said structure and style support the story?

I think so - or at least I think so sufficiently to have printed the whole thing out ready for the on-page step 2 review. And it's often step 2 which proves the most critical.

The other bell-weather is when I start to think about firming up on the title (I have a working one) and then work on the cover. It's only when I have a draft of the cover that the book truly becomes a book...

So by early June I should know. After that? Well, it's plain sailing, isn't it..?!

July 2020 (PVR)

"The Last Quarter..."

So where are the projects?

1. Finish "A Pattern of Sorts"[63] (pub. date? not 1/8?)

2. Continue working on "Homelessness"

3. Decide on / commit to "Sonnets"

4. "Context Q121"
   ↳ decide on this as a publishing venture - or not

5. Think about the next piece of fiction.

Is the French story actually valid because it can be commercial?
↳ use nom de plume!

Would multiple personas allow multiple projects?

A new story - question of subject

1 = 10th August

3 = yes: one per week

4 = 200 pages; 400 submissions @ 2.5 = £1k...
   ↳ cost of Submittable??

---

[63] This is the novel to which he referred in his previous two entries.

5 = reread draft thus far

5? What about the notion of having a character who runs consistently through a series of novels (or stories)?

There would be a consistent range of sub-characters too...

Allows for the exploration of themes; avoids the need to keep building character; creates an "oeuvre" à la Amis or Bellow...

Would require a great deal of pre-work in terms of mapping out a 'history' to ensure consistency across multiple books.

1) voice of a woman as a trigger back into the past.

Opening sentence immediately raises three questions:
1 - who is the current woman?
2 - who was the past woman?
3 - why has it become easy for him to go back into the past?

Which question do we answer first?
- about the voice
- why it's a trigger for the past

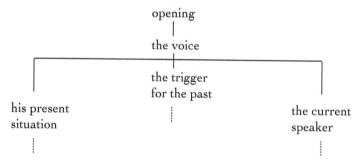

Are there two or three narrative streams here?

also:

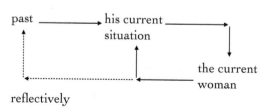

reflectively

Need to map out the three narrative streams therefore; three plot lines that have a connection - and not just the voice (which is merely a trigger).

And the three critical moments:
1 - from the distant past
2 - from his recent past
3 - for the present

How might the story be told:
1, linearly   2, interwoven

1x Needs to be some kind of failure from which he is determined either to learn or not repeat. This therefore influences the narrative thread for 2
↳ and perhaps 2 isn't a specific thread but rather a philosophy that is interwoven in the present & how he lives his life.

3x Therefore should be something which challenges both decision & philosophy, and which threatens a reoccurrence of his experience in 1x
↳ the voice therefore is more than a trigger for memory, it represents danger, the possibility of history repeating itself.

HISTORY REPEATING ITSELF

Is this something we can control or prevent? Is it out of our hands? Is his life lived on the basis of preventing it happening? And if so, what is it he doesn't want to experience again?

Original idea was that it was about hurt - caused by him and his dishonesty - and his cure was to be honest (with himself and with others) but the new woman threatens that not simply because of herself but because he finds he cannot help himself.

Will - struggle - honesty* - decision etc.

~~~~

"Where you end up"

~~~~

*honesty - integrity - truth - 'bravery'**

↳ philosophy because of the pain and hurt of lying

voice -> memory -> past pain -? present philosophy -> new situation -> challenges philosophy

recurrence:
- of choice[1]
- of memory
- of decision
- of pain

[1] Different choice vs. same choice

So what was the choice he had to make and $\therefore$ the outcome that triggered?
↳ must be a joining or a breaching
      joining would be less conventional...

** does he regard himself as a coward? because of the 'wrong' decision he took

Did she give him an ultimatum where he knew the right answer but chose the one he thought she wanted / that would be the 'easy option'?
↳ and proved quite the opposite.
Did he think it would free him but in the end it merely proved a trap?

Has he shunned 'love' because of the trouble of the past? If so, why is he so much in peril now? What is different about this new woman? And the passage of time?

Names?
      Cath - Nick? - Fliss? - Beth? - Neil?

What happened to the first woman? Was it 'just' the pain of separation / divorce? suicide
How did they fall out of love?
Who transgressed?

"He wasn't Don McCallum, but he had a certain reputation."

Photographer. Colour, glossy, 'romantic'. Part of what wins Cath over. The slide into 'glamour' & infidelity. After her suicide he 'reinvents' himself in B&W. Beth makes him want to go back into colour.

And what did he do about 'love' in the interim? Something transactional? 'Fliss'?

Can start to draw the timelines:

Cath	Photography	Interim	Beth
↓	↓	↓	↓
Era 1	Era 1		
	Era 2	Era 2	
	Era 3		Era 3

Why is it easy for the voice to drag him back to the past? "especially now"...
What has happened to make him suddenly susceptible, vulnerable?

Is it the failure of his philosophy?
Time has, perhaps, eaten away at it. This questions its validity. Was it never
going to work for him? And if not, has Beth's interview acted as a trigger for
self-questioning? Is she then both the catalyst of the problem and its solution?
Cath was earlier a catalyst for his 'first' problem, but could never be the
solution, even though he thought she could be. Back then he was the only
solution, but he didn't recognise it; now he wants to be the solution - perhaps
knows that he should be - but he has reached a point (the failure of his
philosophy?) which means he is at the mercy of another. All he can do is to
submit to that; this is the decision he has to make.

❖

"The Nine Commandments"

- Time   "Don't waste time"
- Honesty
- Action / Execution
- Planning
- Governance
- Relying on others
- Goals / Outcomes

~~~~

*There is so much to go at here! Perhaps it makes the most sense to return to the
beginning of this entry and consider the five topics he outlined - before
addressing the throwaway "Commandments" list.*

*1, Finish 'A Pattern of Sorts' - Quite simply seeing the process of revision and
production through to completion. Another example of how far he had come: no*

idea what his next piece of fiction was going to be back in February, then five months later he is working through the second revision of a slim novel.

2, Continue working on "Homelessness" - The autobiographical collection of poetry of which he has previously spoken.

3, Decide on / commit to "Sonnets" - Back in December 2018 he made reference to "The Sonnets" but without any further explanation as to the project. Sometime earlier he'd had the notion of taking the last word at the end of each line in Shakespeare's sonnets and, using them as a prescribed framework / rhyming scheme, create a collection of 154 sonnets of his own (though not intending to keep to the theme of the original). It was a background project on which he occasionally worked, using a little of the output in 'The Myths of Native Trees', including one piece - "Pilgrimage" - submitted to and published in the on-line edition of "The Aesthetic Apostle" in February 2019. He had struggled to commitment to the idea, however, though it was never clear how much of that was down to 'belief' and how much to an inability to execute technically.

4, "Context Q121" - Partly as a reaction to unsuccessful submissions to poetry magazines and competitions, and partly in response to others' work that was being commercially published, he had been toying with the idea of using his 'Coverstory books' imprint for a new anthology. Having successfully produced the 'Oak Tree Alchemy' anthology for the Poetry Society's North Yorkshire Stanza group, it was a project he knew was well within his compass. Other than in the early days of 'Coverstory books' when he was outlining what its website and offer might look like, he had generally refrained from making any reference to it in his entries - though largely because it was, to this this point, almost solely his own vehicle[64], and because it had its own specific voice via www.coverstorybooks.com.

5, Think about the next piece of fiction - After regularly questioning the suitability of "the French story" and briefly kicking around one or two other ideas, he quickly landed on the "voice of a woman as a trigger back into the past", a proposal he was able to rapidly expand upon in this entry [which was almost certainly multiple entries spread across July 2020]. By the time he gets to August, the outline seems well-formed in his mind.

---

[64] He used Coverstory books to publish *Triple Measures* of course, and in 2019 had published *A Kind of Making* for his old University writing partner, Tom Furniss (who also contributed to *Triple Measures)*.

And "Commandments"? A brief flirtation with returning to a 'professional' book presumably driven by the greater likelihood of financial reward. It seems highly unlikely there was any real motivation at all behind this project.

~~~~

7th August 2020 (w.com)

I wonder if that's what 'Life' does, getting in the way, forcing us to take our eyes off the ball, allowing us to forget what's important... In many respects it's also the easy option, isn't it? A kind of abdication. Knowing what matters to us, believing in it, keeping the faith - all of that requires attention, dedication. To do it justice - whatever 'it' might be - demands something unremitting. It's a full-time job.

One of the outcomes of the current pandemic[65] has been, for me as for many others I assume, the opportunity to reflect and re-evaluate. Not needing to commute to an office, being able to "work from home" and not be 100 miles away from the family Monday to Friday, having more time to spend with both them and myself - and more time in my environment and not someone else's - all of that has promoted if not enforced reflection. And reflection leads to reassessment.

Some of that navel-gazing is what you might call "profound", I suppose. But that's too grandiose a word for plain and simple honesty.

Yet what value does that reassessment have, you might ask. Well, none - unless we do something about it. And, having rediscovered what's truly important to me, I feel as if I am about to do something about it. There are steps to be taken - many of them, no doubt - and indeed I have taken the first (of which more in a later post). Now it's all about having the courage to take the second, and then the next one after that...

I was out for a walk yesterday evening. Someone had been mowing grass along a riverside path and as I walked it was as if I was smelling the wonderful fragrance of newly-mown grass for the very first time. It was heady, intoxicating. In the context of this post's subject it's no more than a simple metaphor, of course, but all at once it seemed as if I had forgotten that smell, lost it along the way... It was sublime to be reacquainted with it.

4th September 2020 (w.com)

At the end of this month I'm giving up work. More or less by choice. It is a step that has been labelled in various ways by various people, me included: 'retirement' seems the most common, with the upcoming period a 'glide-path to retirement' - after all, I'm not officially qualified to be there yet...!

---

[65] The Covid-19 outbreak of 2020. This post was written during a short Cumbrian holiday between lockdowns, before vaccinations and before the menace of the second wave grew.

Is that what it is, though? I'm not so sure. It's starting to feel more like a cliff edge.

What's undeniable is a certain aligning of the stars that have presented me with an opportunity to step back from the professional life I've been leading for far too many years. An opportunity for - excuse the cliché! - some 'me time'; to be free to spend that time writing without the encumbrance of having to try and fit it in, or being too tired after a working day to do so.

I am gifting myself time. What could be more powerful than that?

And yet that 'freedom' is quite daunting. Take away the structure of a working week, the ability to abdicate responsibility for your time to other mundane matters, to the pressure and demands of outside forces, and 'time' looms large. And 'looms' is exactly the right word.

Fourteen hours a day, punctuated by the need to feed-and-water etc., which will be more or less mine to do with what I will. That novel I've started working on? Surely over in a jiffy. Others' books I'm planning to publish? I'll have more time to devote to them. Sounds idyllic. A rare opportunity. And it is.

Ignoring any questions about whether it's the right thing to do, or practical, or even sensible - and ignoring the likelihood that at some point in the not too distant future I may hanker after the old routine, the old structures - what strikes me as much as anything else (as much as looming time!) is what I will see when I look in the mirror at the beginning of October, November, December... And later what I have will have produced, what I will have to show for all that time...

Because as much as anything this is about reinventing *me*.

Throughout my life I have often called my own bluff: choosing to leave school at sixteen - and then go back two years later; choosing to go off to West Africa to teach when going to London was still an adventure; taking voluntary redundancy more than once because I was bored and fancied a change. I have always believed that there was something better round the corner. Maybe that makes me an optimist.

But what if this is the last corner? What if there isn't anything better around it? What if the only option proves - sooner rather than later - to be to turn around and come back? And what if I can't?

A bluff called - and beaten by the final card dealt...

So this next part of the adventure isn't really about time, or writing. It's actually about who I am - or who I want to be. If, come the 1st October, I'm the same person I am today; if I haven't worked out at least a plan of who / how / what I want to be...

~~~~

If it was indeed stepping off the edge of a cliff, he would only know if he had survived the fall six, twelve, twenty-four months later. Was it a brave move or one enforced? How much choice did he have in the matter? About leaving work, he suggests little; about what was to come after...he argues that was down to him and no-one else.

~~~~

Today is the first 'new Monday'; the first whole week where I can decide what I do with my time, how much I write. Staggeringly it is a month since I wrote "The Daunting Prospect of Reinvention"[66] - and what's more bizarre is that it feels as if I have been footloose and fancy-free for more than just the Thursday and Friday of last week...

The primary reason for this feeling is that the 'glide-path' during my last month at work saw me required to 'do' less and less; given there was no abrupt cut-off, you could argue I've had my time to myself for much longer than the middle of last week. Which is great, isn't it?

So why the angst?

Structure. Like it or not, 'work' imposes structure upon us: times we start and end; meetings we need to be in; things we need to do; people we need to see and with whom we need to talk. It provides us an agenda which allows us to abdicate responsibility for how we spend huge chunks of our time. Scandalous though that may be, if you think about it that's how we are conditioned to be. As babies, our parents imposed routine upon us (or tried to!); and then comes school, college. Work is just the next (final?) extension. So when you take that away..?

I'm trying to give myself a calendar of sorts, goals for the day: do this, work on that. It's helping - and it gives me a chance to measure myself - but it's also easy to cheat. On one level, it doesn't matter - even though I tell myself it does. For example: 11-12 every day, exercise (bike, run or gym); blog/post/tweet something everyday from at least one of my sites; work on my latest novel/collection of poems; work on my publishing ventures.

There's enough in that list to keep me busy, but this is where the rubber hits the road; this is where it all comes down to discipline, self-control, belief.

I've called my bluff. It was theoretical, romantic, idealistic when I articulated the proposition, but now...

---

[66] The 4th September post on writeral.com.

I confess to have been prompted to this mini self-assessment by Andrea Badgley's post "writing-more-means-doomscrolling-less", and as a follow-up to my own "Missing Work Already?"[67] It's not the kind of thing I normally do; I'm not a natural "look at me" kind of person - though I am belatedly realising that as an author I really do need to make a bit more of an effort!

So we're half-way through October. How is it going?

Well, the diary is working to an extent. I'm normally ticking off around five things a day from my 'list'. The biggest hitters are currently:

• working on the publication of a poetry and prose anthology - "New Contexts" - that I'm putting together for January 2021. I'm at the selection stage - which is so much harder than I'd imagined! There are, not surprisingly, too many Covid-related poems...

• working on the publication of a collection of original plays for an old friend of mine. Lots of enjoyment there!

• adding (slowly!) words to a short novel I'm trying to write. Even though I've got the whole thing planned out and am about a third of the way through, I'm still not convinced that I yet believe in it. I need to pick up the pace.

• working - again slowly - on a couple of collections of poetry. One will probably see the light of day next year, the second probably never...

• trying to be a little more 'out there' in terms of my social media presence, but as I say, I'm not a natural, and this is proving the hardest thing of all!

• going to the gym / running / getting on the exercise bike.

The rest of my time is taken up with normal domestic stuff. And I'm avoiding (I think!) wasting too much time on the TV or gaming and stuff like that.

So am I missing work? Not at all. And yet, in spite of the list above, my days don't yet feel full. I know I don't need to add anything else to my catalogue, I just need to do a bit more of them: an hour rather than thirty minutes, that kind of thing. And I probably need to turn the writing into a little more of a 'job' i.e. 9-11 every day, write X or Y.

But the interesting thing is that, given so many of my tasks are creative, there seems to be a limit, a capacity for creative thought. It requires a different mindset to a 9-to-5 job, requires a different type of commitment, intelligence. Just flicking a switch and saying "I'm now going to be creative for the next 90 minutes" just doesn't work. It's a bit like there's a daily allowance, and once it's spent...

---

[67] The title of the 5th October writeral.com post.

~~~~~

Two 'working weeks' into his new regime, is this a verdict of 'so far, so good'? The multiple projects of which he speaks must have given him heart following the concern that he would struggle to fill those "fourteen hours a day" - though it appears his first lesson has already been learned: not that relating to structure (as if he needed to be taught that!), but rather the daily limit on his 'creative juices'. One gets the sense of a juggler needing to re-learn his craft having had his juggling balls replaced by skittles perhaps. The objective is unchanged - keep three identical items in the air at all times and fill fourteen hours a day in a productive, constructive and engaging fashion - yet execution requires an adjustment in technique, a different level of concentration. Bluff-calling indeed.

Part Ten - 2021

24ᵗʰ January 2021 (w.com)

Why is it that so many of us live our lives - subconsciously or otherwise - as if there is a secret rewind button always available? A button that gifts us the opportunity to revisit past triumphs, to avoid horrible defeats; a button which permits us to take different decisions and make alternate choices. And because we believe in its existence - totally and profoundly - we can never truly live our lives 'in the moment', no matter how much we kid ourselves that we do; we never really accept that once this moment has gone then it's gone forever. It's as if the Arrow of Time simply doesn't apply.

You might argue that the minority who do understand - again, subconsciously or not - that there is no such safety net, are more likely to live life 'in the fast lane', to 'flame and burn'. Are they more likely to become well-known, a 'celebrity' - whatever that might mean? Are they more likely to be successful? That depends on your definition, I suppose. But are they any less likely to make those same mistakes as us and suffer the same sorts of defeat? Absolutely not! Will they too wish they could go back and change things? Of course!

If we find ourselves in the former camp, supremely anonymous within the morass of humanity (however much we kid ourselves otherwise!), then at some point - hopefully? - the penny drops; either in a flash of insight or, over time, gradually the truth dawns on us. One day we suddenly realise that we can't go back twenty years and un-say those things we said, do that thing we should have done, turn left instead of right.

And maybe even then we don't believe it...

In a way, perhaps language holds the key. Think about it. It's called 'the past tense' for a reason. If we can only describe something, articulate it, examine it in the past tense then that means it's gone, lost irretrievably. "I type this word" - I'm doing it; "I typed this word" - I've done it, and I can't un-type it. But in addition to giving us a black-and-white confirmation of how we stand - and how, moment by moment, the unavoidable fact that all of our experience has already happened, even that word I just typed! - it also offers us a means of revisiting, of reexamining, of trying out an alternative reality.

Of course we can't really go back to that night in the University Halls of Residence and do X or say Y, nor can we alter that life-changing decision we made to say 'No' rather than 'Yes', but we can interrogate and cross-examine that moment, we can play out how those alternatives might have looked. Given we have sufficient imagination and a modicum of talent, writing offers us the next best thing to changing our past lives - and that is to reimagine them.

Okay, so it's second prize, a silver medal if you like; but surely a medal of some colour is better than none?

The strap-line on this website is "furiously writing until the light goes out", and I make no apology for that. However much talent I may or may not have, writing is my rewind button, the only tool I have to look back into my past and ask the 'what if?' question. Not only that, it gives me the chance to undertake that examination through the lives of other characters, to place them in situations - historically similar or dissimilar to my own, it doesn't matter - and to explore and examine.

In my work there are lots of characters who are trying to come to terms with their past, to reconcile themselves to their histories: Lewis and Anna in "At Maunston Quay", Liam and Alison in "The Opposite of Remembering", the narrator in "A Pattern of Sorts". And, published in a few months, in "On Parliament Hill" Neil will experience an in-depth re-evaluation of who his is and what he wants his future to be.

And maybe that's the most important thing for all of us: deciding what sort of future we want for ourselves - because all too soon it's going to become our past...

~~~~

Philosophical, yes - and possibly not very good philosophy! These thoughts are perfectly in-tune with his status at the beginning of 2021; mentally, he has divorced himself from the world of work and given himself permission to write - but he knows he needs to grasp the "moment" in order to make the most of the opportunity. It may be melodramatic to view every minute he doesn't write as minute lost, but this is against the background of the barren writing years he sees as lost. Yes, he has moved on remarkably in the last five years or so: he has arrived at a position where he is proven, at least to himself; is prolific; has earned his stripes. But now there is another step needed.

He often talks about belief in his ideas and projects, and states that he needs to believe in a story (sic) in order to see it through; he revels in those magic moments of transition from 'writer' to 'reader', and the compulsion these generate. In some way, is he now - between the lines, as it were - making the same statement about his life? He has an idea about how to live, he has sketched out a rough plan for this new 'project', but does he believe in it enough in order to commit to its execution? From a practical perspective - "the Arrow of Time" - he doesn't have the luxury of a gestation period; he can't live his life by submitting himself to subliminal background machinations, hoping for a 'ta-ra!'

moment in twenty or thirty years time. Most likely he won't be around then. Is this at the heart of his 2021 dilemma?

We know from his own words that his fiction tends towards an exploration of how people experience 'time' in their lives, "characters who are trying to come to terms with their past, to reconcile themselves to their histories". It strikes me that he is intimately entwined with all those people too. 'Write what you know about' - and he knows all about the struggle to reconcile the past with the present. Aren't his notebooks an exercise in exactly that? But they surely go beyond that. They are about what comes next; at the practical level in terms of what to write - which in some respects is no more than a naïve puzzle to be solved - but more profoundly in terms of how to live. His decision to "gift" himself time (i.e. permission to take control over his future) has opened a Pandora's box filled with questions of much greater import than simply 'what next?'.

~~~

February 2021[68] *(PVR)*

Reflection on entry of July 20:

1 ✓   done & published
2 ✓   done & in review (Apr. '21 pub)
3 ?   still background task
4 ✓   published as New Contexts
5 ✓   On Parliament Hill (in review)

So that wasn't bad for 6 months' work, was it?!!

And the cycle comes around again… Let's resurrect the old questions:

? the French thing?
? Sonnets ?
? Pier ?

Then there are all the dormant ideas sitting in these various notebooks - <u>plus</u> the idea of turning the notebooks into a narrative of their own… Must be at least 3 notebooks covering ideas over a number of years.

Timing of this one?

---

[68] Started in February but most likely the multiple segments of this entry would have taken him into March.

How much will depend on success / otherwise in the search for an Agent?[69]

? a new thing?

So, in turn:

French thing
✓ commercial
~~~~ different
? do I believe in it?

Sonnets
? I think this is a question of belief, both in the quality and 'the project',
though the idea is clearly sound.
The sort of thing a 'known poet' does perhaps…

Pier
✓ planned out
✓ relatively easy to write
? but have I moved beyond magic realism?

Notebooks
? intrinsically interesting?
? but there is no narrative flow; would one need to be overlaid upon it? e.g. a
novel about a writer with half the text the writer's own notes; juxtaposition of
real life vs. imagined
? again, is this a question of timing (a last work?)
✓ easy to create the bones of a draft; it's just a question of 'typing up'

Something new?
[let's ignore New Contexts: 2 for now as that's a publishing prospect and is
also a question of timing…]
↪ Poetry? I don't think so; should probably start to build a new collection as
and when…
↪ Prose? Novel or Short Stories?
- would short stories need to be 'themed', perhaps taking or reworking known
ideas or plot lines (e.g. Shakespeare's plays). Either that or just a 'loose'
collection.
- if novel, then I need to have an idea for the story…
- or a 'hybrid' piece i.e. elongated prose poem à la "The Long Take".

---

[69] He had sent the opening of *On Parliament Hill* to seven random agents to see if he could generate
some interest in it.

And some other old ideas:

- A Question of Provenance (D)[70]
    - story where the narrator is a painting & narrative progressed back to its origins. P
- 7-16
    - what <u>was</u> that? Some kind of 'thriller'? Yes - interesting; needs a plot
- In Reality (D)
    - the reality TV story set on a train
- The Idea that fell to Earth (D)
    - idea but nothing drafted. P?
- The Impossible University (D)
    - some planning; minor start. X
- The Year of Funerals
    - fair bit planned
    - January drafted  Dull?
- The Man Who Waited Until Wednesday
    - planned out
    - 1/36 drafted  P
- 'X'
    - whatever that was supposed to be!
    - a little drafted
- Intersections (D)
    - which was that very fragmented multi-dimensional retelling with many perspectives

Are there any of these ideas good / still valid / worth resurrecting?

It's comforting to know there are a few kicking around, even if they never see the light of day.

After the last four, it might be good to do something different.

If I believed in any of those old things, then they wouldn't be lying dormant...

Is <u>form</u> as important as <u>theme</u>? Do I need to try and come up with something that is more radical in terms of style and structure? looking for an Agent again makes you realise that <u>they</u> will be looking for something that is outstanding...

Of all these unfinished bits I can't help but think the French thing has the greatest potential (it has sex in it for a start, and is a bit off-the-wall in a John Fowles kind of way...).

---

[70] There is no clue as to the meaning of the code here.

It has been sitting on my table, printed out, awaiting a review for an awfully long time. Maybe that's what I should do next...

Interesting question in terms of what comes first: plot or style? What influence does one have on the other?

Let's face it, my novels have a 'voice' don't they? (given that Nev and Pattern are slightly different) If P. Hill was to get picked up, then that's just dandy - but if not, then should I really just turn the same old handle again? There's that definition of insanity isn't there...?

Of everything I've written, Pattern is obviously different because of 'the voice', but it's not that risky. And I can never get away from the sense that Mirrors may be the 'sleeping giant'. If P. Hill were to get picked up I can see someone asking me to rework Mirrors in its entirety...

'What can I but enumerate old themes' - or whatever the Yeats quote is...

But I have to knuckle down! The prospect of having to work again soon is a bit of a spectre, the threat of stealing time. Maybe I should be a bit more disciplined - like the kids with their lessons - and say that 9-12, every day, is my writing time - would it matter too much what I wrote? The new thing, obviously plus some old things, sonnets, shorts, fillers.

You can't be a writer without writing...

~~~~

French thing is looking more promising as I review it - but I haven't got to the sex yet...

Interesting how plot gaps / ideas are surfacing as I review. How the (new) plan hangs together when it's finished will be the litmus test...

Let's say it proves enough to be my next fiction project, then what else goes alongside it if I assume the 2-projects-on-the-go approach? Clearly (or presumably) not fiction. And if not poetry, then what else?

Something 'different' and 'innovative'? The notion of transcribing my notebooks won't go away... Maybe I need to copy out a few pages to see what they look and feel like is the next step?

What was it Tom said about "scholars of the future"?

✤

French thing...

The story of Paul's grandfather (PG)

war (?) -> paper -> packaging -> wealth -> marries Paul's grandmother -> Paul's mother is born (PM) -> PG starts affair with Hélène -> Hélène gets pregnant (as does PM) -> PG finishes with Hélène (buys her off) -> generates resentment / desire for revenge -> comes across Paul's work, makes the connection, hatches plan -> GM dies when Paul is young; PG chooses not to reconcile himself to Hélène (PM dies when Paul is ?)?

And Sylvie - what is the relationship to Hélène? Is she part of the revenge plot or an innocent victim?

Hélène aims to destroy Paul as her only way at getting back on GP. Creating then breaking the relationship with Sylvie is a parallel to her and GF.

Hélène's daughter is ∴ related to Paul.

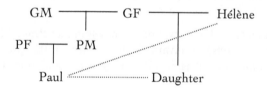

Is Sylvie's link through the daughter?

What about Sylvie's past? We know she needs to be careful about 'love' and letting herself go... Did she 'steal' a man from Hélène's daughter?

~~~~~

Should it be any surprise that, a little over four months into his new freedoms and his gifted "me time", he should begin 2021 with his habitual 'State of the Nation' address - one as inconclusive as these considerations have always tended to be. Does he pin his hopes on "the French story" because he has drafted thirty-eight thousand words and doesn't want to lose them, or does this represent a degree of 'straw-clutching'?

"If I believed in any of those old things, then they wouldn't be lying dormant..."

The question over form still haunts him; it is as if there is something beyond traditional fiction and poetry which offers the key he cannot find. He has tinkered before of course - 'After the Rehearsals' is no conventional collection of poetry, and 'A Pattern of Sorts' diverges to a degree from a standard narrative - yet you cannot help but get the sense he feels there is something more radical both within and just out of his grasp. Is that one of the gems he hopes using the notebooks as sounding-board will reveal to him: a change of form, a break from convention, something new? Or is it more than that? Along with his January writeral.com post, does he regard where he is as an opportunity to slay ghosts, to clear the decks, to 'empty' the past and allow himself to take the opportunity he has created? Does he regard his next step as an exorcism he needs to perform in order to free himelf to believe in his future, to allow him to have faith in it? "You can't be a writer without writing..."

~~~~

3 February 2021 (w.com) [71]

Every few months or so - usually at propitious or convenient points - I take stock of where I am with my writing. These reviews take the form of notes scribbled into one of many(!) notebooks, and essentially provide a snapshot of where I am with my creative work.

When arriving at such moments (as I do now, finding myself in that strange 'half-world' when I'm between projects), I invariably look back at the previous notebook entry to see how I measure up against the thoughts and ambitions I had sketched out then.

Back in July 2020, I set myself five goals:

- Finish "A Pattern of Sorts".
- Continue working on a new collection of poetry.
- Decide on / commit to Project X[72] (a long-standing work that has been on the back-burner for a while).
- Context Q121 - decide if this is a publishing venture or not.
- Think about the next piece of fiction.

So how did I get on?

- "A Pattern of Sorts" was finished and published. TICK

---

[71] Obviously written immediately after the opening salvo of his last notebook entry; a tidied-up version made suitable for public consumption.

[72] The "Sonnets" project.

- A new collection of poetry was finished and is currently in review; we're probably looking at April publication. TICK
- Hmmm. I think the reason I haven't settled on Project X one way or another is that I don't quite believe in it yet. I will complete it at some point, but for now it remains in the background; something I tease at from time to time.
- Anthology completed and published at the beginning of the year as "New Contexts: 1". TICK
- Not only thought about but drafted! (70k words) Currently in review. Probably publishing around May. TICK

So not a bad six months?!

But what about the next six months, you ask. How are they shaping up?

Well, it's early days, of course. Usually I will cogitate for a period of time - from days to weeks - before I settle on something. Sometimes the route I end up taking is out of my hands, driven by a sudden thought or idea which takes hold. I anticipate a "New Contexts: 2" anthology at some point in the year, but at the moment I'm not looking to any more formal poetry projects for myself. So fiction it will be - but what?

Yesterday I had a trawl through my archives and came across no less than eleven old ideas for novels, each at various stages from the most embryonic, through to a few thousand words drafted and the whole thing planned out. Is any one of them worth resurrecting? Perhaps. But if I had really liked the idea behind them why did I drop them in the first place? It could be a question of timing of course, but in most cases I'm sure it's more fundamental than that... Maybe I'll post bits and pieces of the stuff I have drafted and see if there's any reaction.

Yet having said all that, I think it's likely I'll land on something new - though what that will be, who knows?!

6th *February 2021*[73] *(w.com)*

Sounds obvious, doesn't it? But how many of us like to think of ourselves as 'Writers' (note the capital 'w'!) when - to be frank - we don't really put the hours in. Think about it. How could you be a surgeon without learning your craft and then operating on people day-in day-out, or a lawyer without knowing the law and then practicing it?

One harsh truth is that the vast majority of us do enough to get by and justify what is really more ambition than achievement; a poem here, a short story there. Perhaps we follow a weekly prompt, or try and post something small and simple (yet often not beautifully formed!) daily on our website / blog / Instagram / Facebook (delete as appropriate).

---

[73] The post was titled "You can't be a Writer without writing"

Another painful fact is that for the vast majority that's probably all we can do; 'Life' - jobs, family, domesticity etc. - steals time and energy from us.

Yet is there anything intrinsically wrong with how we handle all that? Of course not. We operate within the constraints imposed upon us; we try our best; we tell ourselves - and anyone else who'll listen - that we're a 'writer' (note the lack of a capital letter...). Fine. All good. As long as we're honest with ourselves at the same time...

Why do I raise this observation now? Well, not surprisingly this is more about me than anyone else (though the same criteria applies to us all). I like to think of myself as a 'Writer'. "Look at all these" I say, pointing to my five novels, six books of poetry etc. "doesn't that prove it?"

Well, 'yes' and 'no'. 'Yes' in that the output proves something, stands for something. It demonstrates that I can put one word in front of another, that I've a degree of talent, a modicum of ability (I hope!), and the skill and wherewithal to get books into print. But 'no' in the sense that, at another level - at the level of the lawyer or surgeon - I'm clearly not.

And this is relevant because? Well, I have the opportunity - for how long I'm not sure - to be able to dedicate time to writing, to treat it more 'seriously', to dedicate a volume of time to it. Indeed, to treat it as a 'job'. "I'm a Writer. It's what I do." And it's also relevant now because I am between projects; tidying up another novel, another volume of poetry, and looking forward to what comes next. And it occurs to me that what comes next - what must come first - is the commitment to the role; in a way it doesn't matter what I write next, it's how I approach it that counts.

Do I want to be a Writer or a writer? There's a world of difference.

7th February 2021 (MWD)

It's nearly eighteen months since my last entry here[74] - not that I haven't been writing! The draft I finished on 3rd August 2019 turned into 'The Opposite of Remembering' published at the beginning of last year, and this was followed by 'A Pattern of Sorts' (as well as another volume of poetry, 'The Myths of Native Trees'). So far from fallow.

Why the update now? Well, in my last post - "You can't be a Writer without writing" - I indulged in a little naval-gazing, the consequence of which was to persuade myself that I needed to do better... Not a score of 2 out of 10 as I had (harshly?) given myself a while ago, but probably nearer a 6. What's good? 8?

---

[74] In his on-line 'My Writing Diary'.

In any event, in trying to up my game I've wondered if going back to this public record might offer me a means to keep me 'honest' when it comes to putting in the effort - or another stick with which to beat myself! So let's see.

This morning I've been working solidly for two hours thus far, the bulk of that time reviewing the start of the 31k words of the story I started when on holiday in France. The aim is to answer the question as to whether or not it has the potential or merit to be picked up again and seen through. My immediate reaction is that it's better than I thought, and the opening is okay. I'll see what it feels like once I'm a bit further through it - probably in a couple of days.

Writing this counts towards 'working activity' as do things like planning - something that will follow as soon as I've posted this. I want to try and work three hours a day as a minimum. Day 1 is off to a decent start...

Of course, all this may come back to haunt me..!!

8th February 2021 (MWD)

Yesterday was a decent start, and I've spent another two hours today going through that part-draft of a novel set in France. It has been interesting in that, coming at it from a distance of a year-and-a-half, I find myself detached enough to a) hopefully edit a little more rigorously, and b) to identify the gaps, raise questions, surface ideas in relation to the story. At this stage, if it is to go on to be a project I decide to work through to completion then b) is the more important of the two - especially as when I finish reviewing the remainder of the 31k words, I will need to pull a plan together for the rest.

I've also started typing-up the entries from some of my old notebooks. 6 pages thus far from one that started in October 198something. I was never very good at dating the entries!! It is proving an interesting exercise thus far, and I wonder - should I carry on through all, what?, five notebooks - whether it will merely prove to be a more 'coherent' record of thoughts, or the basis for a truly radical narrative of some sort...

11th February 2021 (MWD)

Great progress over the past three days. I have now finished reviewing the 31k words / 90 pages of the French story. Next step is to type up the amendments - a job in itself! - and then work on the overall plan. It will only be once I've done that - and picked up the metaphorical pen again to try writing the next section - that I'll know if the thing has legs.

As far as the notebook work goes, I have typed up over forty pages now, and have come to the end of 1993 - a tumultuous personal year. I didn't realise how much! Still many days work to go on this one before I'll have a true sense of what I have on my hands; only then will come the meaningful internal conversation about what to do with it.

Often I am woken by words.

From somewhere I will suddenly become conscious that I am writing something in my sleep. It could be anything: a line for a poem, a sentence for a book, even a single word. There could be an idea for a plot twist - or an entire plot! - or the resolution of a 'writing problem' I've been wrestling with over the previous days. At some point my friendly other self says "This is too important to lose. Wake up!"

I'm never entirely sure if this is a gift or a curse. Whilst it often feels like the latter, I'm more inclined to the former - even if it does mean that all too often my recharge light hasn't managed to get all the way to 'green' before the first cup of tea of the day...

In one of Lawrence Durrell's poems there is a wonderful line:

"Give us the language of diamonds"
- The Death of General Uncebunke, *Fourteen Carols (V)*

That simple phrase - "the language of diamonds" - has always seemed to me complex, profound, powerful, beautiful. The subtlety of it comes in the unpacking of it of course, and drawing the parallels between words and diamonds.

Diamonds are tough and unyielding - the hardest natural substance currently known - yet they can also be shaped and facetted. In the right light, they can sparkle and shine, lure and entrance. Occasionally they can almost be without price.

Are words like that? A word is a word. 'Clock' is 'clock' and nothing else; in that sense perhaps it is as hard and unyielding as diamond. As soon as you change it - removing the first 'c', for example - it becomes something else and is no longer 'clock'. You might argue this proves words are not 'hard' and incorruptible, but at the most basic level you have done nothing to the word 'clock'; it is still there, when you need it...

Yet in spite of this inability to 'corrupt' words [was that partly what Joyce was trying to do in Finnegan's Wake?], we can still make them shine. We do this, not by grinding them into a new shape or polishing them as individual gems, but by giving them relationships to other words. What are novels and poems if not an attempt to make words 'shine like diamonds'? And like diamonds, the 'value' of our creations comes from how they sparkle, their uniqueness, the inventiveness of their juxtapositions - or if you want to pursue the metaphor further, from their setting, the baseness (or otherwise) of the 'metal' in which they reside.

For me, trying to make words sparkle like diamonds is almost a reason for being.

I'm thinking of taking a sabbatical from poetry. Giving it up for a while. A bit of 'detox'.

Why? Multiple reasons really. The easy one is to say that "I want to focus on my prose". Very little collateral damage in that one I suspect. And it also has the benefit of being true! I should be working on the final revisions of my up-coming novel "On Parliament Hill", and I am working on a first draft of a novel set in France (38k words in) - though I'm still not convinced I'm entirely persuaded by that one yet. Whether or not I see it through to conclusion, something will follow...

I'm also transcribing the contents of my old notebooks with the aim of turning them into some kind of non-fiction / diary / log / reflective naval-gazing tome. It's already over 200 pages long, so I think will be seen through to the bitter end (if only for my satisfaction!). This, of course, is also a project that takes time.

Interestingly, this exercise has also highlighted other things. The two stand-outs are 1) the number of solid ideas which have never seen the light of day, and 2) that "An Infinity of Mirrors" is probably the best and most complete novel I have ever written - and that I owe it to myself to come up with something new and equally comprehensive.

I could probably be forgiven for leaving it there - the excuses for taking a 'poetry break', that is. But there are two other reasons. The first is that I'm not sure I dedicate enough time to it. And the second is that I'm not convinced I'm good enough at it - or at least not as good as I want to be. I'm currently finalising another volume of poetry - "The Homelessness of a Child" - after which (unless the Muses are particularly generous) I may put down my quill. This is an important volume for me because so much of it is autobiographical and contains things from my past I feel the need to exorcise.

So that's the current plan:

· finish and publish "The Homelessness of a Child" (then decide...)
· finish and publish / have published "On Parliament Hill"
· finish and publish the 'notebooks' thing (I have a working title, but am not yet ready to share it!)
· start / conclude the next piece of fiction, whatever it might be

As ever, sounds so simple laid out like that, doesn't it?!

~~~~

Given his recent lauding of 'the language of diamonds', would it be fanciful to regard his proposal to 'give up' poetry as something of a bombshell? Was there a trigger for this sudden statement? It is difficult to distil the cause from what he had previously said in the notebooks; not only that, one might argue it runs counter to his expressed desire "to be a Writer" (and to be seen as such in his own eyes as much as in others'). Perhaps it had been brewing for a while, fermenting with his nagging notion that he's "not good enough at it".

But you could argue that such self-doubt is actually an intrinsic part of being a Writer; knowing one could be 'better' and have your words dance to a more melodious tune, self-doubt is surely one the key drivers. To be consistently dissatisfied is a common theme and a source of motivation, no matter what form one may choose to write in. But why not give up novel-writing rather than poetry? Is his statement no more than an exercise of choice? Given the finite nature of the time available to him, might the notion have been arrived at as the logical outcome of deciding to invest virtually all of it in just one genre? It is clear - in spite of his considerable output in that genre - that he has never regard himself as a 'Poet' first and foremost; nowhere in the notebooks does he label himself as such. Indeed, way back in 2017 he highlighted "that ancient question of 'Poet or Author?'". Was this suggestion of a "sabbatical" another attempt to definitively answer that question?

Logically, what follows is to ask whether or not he did indeed take a break from poetry. Presumably he would have made the suggestion not only to test out how it 'felt' as a statement of intent, but also recognising he did so in the face of practical difficulties. By early 2021 he has been running the Derbyshire Stanza group for over two years; if no longer writing poetry meant he had to walk away from that group - well, could he do that? An irregular member of the North Yorkshire Stanza, conversely he was the lynchpin of the Derby group. How could he possibly let that fold?

~~~~

27ᵗʰ March 2021 (w.com)

Imagine the scene.

The knock at the door. The delivery man. In his hands, an A4-sized box, the kind that contains those four-pack reams of paper you get for your inkjet printer. He smiles and hands you the box. "I'll go and get the other eight"... Once you have closed the front door, you turn to see the nine boxes staring blankly back at you from your hall floor; in each, 2000 sheets of paper; on each sheet, a poem. And taped to the the the lid of one box, the instruction: "PLEASE PICK A WINNER".

I don't envy the judges of the National Poetry Competition because this was the challenge they were set this year. How do you go about such an impossible task - especially if you make the assumption that at least 50% of entries will be 'decent'?

I can only assume that they would have to look for something that is 'different', that 'jumps off the page' at you. And if that's the case, then probably 90% of all entries are doomed before they are read...including my own!

On Thursday, the (virtual) event announcing the winners of the 2020 National Poetry Competition was held; c.309 people dialled into the meeting. Of these, about 20 knew the winners: the judges, members of the Poetry Society, the three winners and those commended. The other 289 of us were probably there more out of curiosity, to see what had beaten us. It was a session which a) led to my sympathy for the judges' task, and b) confirmed what you needed to produce to win such a competition.

One of the commended poets counselled us to keep the faith with poems we'd written that we believed in. He said his poem - now suddenly one of the top ten in the country? - had been rejected elsewhere on numerous occasions...

And surely that both proves a point and begs a question. It proves the outcomes of such competitions are subjective at best (and therefore on one level meaningless). And it begs the question, why bother entering them at all?

Of course, the real reason we do enter is that we hope next year we will be one of the 20, and not one of the 289...

30th March 2021 (w.com)

Over twenty years ago, a self-publishing company - BookSurge - was born in the US. Five years later the company was acquired by Amazon and came to trade as Create Space (now superseded by Kindle Direct Publishing (KDP)). According to Wikipedia, by the end of 2018 over 1.4 million titles from tens of thousands of authors were available on that platform alone, never mind the thousands more that flowed into the market via services such as Ingram Spark, Smashwords, Lulu and many others. I wonder how many books in Amazon's catalogue - especially in the Kindle format - are currently tagged as 'independently published' (which is essentially Amazon's phrase for self-published).

In parallel with this exponential expansion, on the 2020 Booker Prize shortlist (of six), four of the titles were produced by publishers either regarded as "Indie" or are members of the Independent Alliance. Indies also dominated the 17-strong longlist.

An "Indie Publisher"? Take your pick:

• "a publisher with annual sales below a certain level or below a certain number of titles published"

- "publishers that are not part of large conglomerates"

- in the US, "publishers with annual turnover of under $50 million, or those that publish on average 10 or fewer titles per year"

- publishers who focus on "genre fiction, poetry or limited-edition books, magazines, or niche non-fiction markets"

Importantly, Indie publishers normally offer pretty much the full range of services as the industry behemoths.

So for an Indie Publisher - alternatively known as the "Small Press" - size and capability is the thing. Undoubtedly there will be a line of some kind where once a threshold is crossed - turnover, number of books, number of employees - being tagged as an Indie might look less 'genuine'. For example, Faber & Faber is a core member of the Independent Alliance; how many writers would instinctively consider them an "Indie"? According to the Alliance's website, others members include Atlantic Books, Portobello Books, Canongate, Icon Books, Profile Books, Short Books, Granta Books, Serpent's Tail, Constable & Robinson, and David Ficking.

Considering these channels, the traditional route to publication - find an agent, find a publisher - has therefore ceased to be the only option for over two decades. Whilst it is still the 'Gold Standard' for an author, the spectrum now starts at DIY and runs all the way through to the majors. If there is a dividing line of some kind between an Indie and the Conglomerate (for want of a better phrase), what about the dividing line between self-publishers and Indies?

In my own case, I started out as a shameless self-publisher when I discovered KDP. In the distant past I had been through the painful experience of being rejected - quite rightly! - by traditional Agents, then suddenly I'd found a mechanism to get some of my more recent - and hopefully better - work into print. Not only was it an outlet pretty much in my control, but it actually spurred me on; I have never been as prolific as in the last few years. (Some might say that's a bad thing..!!)

Having become familiar with the system and process (though not using KDP any longer), in the last 12 months I have utilised those skills to collaborate with six people get their work into print, people who, like me, would most likely have struggled otherwise - not to mention the 70+ others included in two anthologies I've published. What does that make me now? Have I crossed that vague line between "Self" and "Indie"? I don't think so. I probably have a toe in some kind of purgatory between the two...

But that's an irrelevance. The key question for many revolves around the merits of self-publication. On the one hand you could argue that it's a brilliant thing, freeing people to be able to evidence their writing with a tangible (or virtual) book.

There's no feeling like it! It also allows new talent to reach the market and, like other modern-day technology (Facebook, Wordpress etc.) gives writers a voice. If in doing so these platforms encourage people to write more - and surely blogs, not publishing, is where that is most prevalent - then isn't that a great thing?

What do they say: "Never mind the quality, feel the width"?

Here's where the double-edged sword comes in. If traditional publishing through Penguin or Random House etc. represents the "gold standard", then self-publishing is surely "bronze" at best. Indeed, there is no standard. Anyone can publish anything; publishing democratised. This must mean, however, that a disproportionate volume of self-published work is not of "a standard" - both in terms of format (layout, proofreading etc.) as well as content. It may also flood the market to such an extent that it can be difficult for a potential reader to see the wood for the trees; how do they know what's good any more unless they stick to traditional and tried-and-tested publishers? But that doesn't necessarily mean that all self-published books will be rubbish. Why shouldn't something self-published be as good as a book from Vintage or MacMillan, or even - very rarely probably - better? In any event, self-publishing is also about pursuing "the dream", about self-esteem, about fulfilment if not reward, fuelled by the belief that our stuff is good, better than the next person's...

I suspect we may see the pendulum swing back towards traditional Agents and Publishers (Indie or otherwise) for that very reason. As a reader, I don't want to waste my hard-earned cash, and there are brands / 'names' I trust. As a writer, I want people to read my work because I actually think some of it is okay and because having a readership validates me and what I do - which also surely points me towards Literary Agents and 'proper' publishers. That is part of the dream too.

Conflicted? You might say that. I suspect it's a growing club...

30th March 2021 (PBS)

Idea for a novel: "Sleeping"

> "Don't you have anything - I don't know - stronger?"
> Dr. Fawcett looked at him with suspicion, as if he were disreputable, a major drug-dealer. His bow-tie - presumably worn to give him 'character' - twitched nervously. Perhaps he thought it lent him credibility.

Sleeping to forget, to remember?
He couldn't be sure.

> "I have been running away from things all my life," he said, "engaged in a perpetual game of truant."

In his fights with his daemons he would shout out incomprehensible things that required someone to translate them.

Q> Is the fact that she could not, be one of the reasons she left him?

Sympathy gradually bled from her to such an extent that in their last days together he had expected her to announce she had changed her name [Joy]. From her own perspective, of course, she was simply growing back into it.

First-person narrator exists in his dream state; 3rd person outside of that in the everyday world.

Q> is the first-person him or not (i.e. self-analysing)

Divorce. The large house with the extra bedroom, she sleeping apart from him. Took half his savings. (Divorce took half of the remainder.)

She abandoned the house and left him marooned once the kids had left home.
* This should give approximate ages - late 40s, early 50s.

The dreams could be about anything:
    remembering
    forgetting
    fantasising

Q> Is the story about his decline or his salvation?

? Buying more pills from the internet to supplement what the doctor had given him. (Cocktail that triggers the dreams?)

Question as to how much sleep he gets during the nights he dreams. And how does he feel in the morning after? Refreshed? Invigorated? Drained? Is he addicted?

Loneliness

If he is still playing truant, he now has no-one / no place to run to. Might the novel be about finding that 'thing' - or at the very least his search for it?

Does he find it?

What drives her away? Is it that he robs her of sleep too? Or the combination of restlessness, talking, farting, going to the toilet, sighing etc.

Presumably it needs to be something more fundamental than that? **->

❀

If he has been running from things, then what are they? They will need to be tangible. Are they also resurrected in his dreams to be resolved?

i.e.   to finally escape from (forget)   e.g. a recurring
          to run towards (remember)   dream that
          or to come to terms with   stops recurring

And if he is addicted, is it to the drugs or to the dreams, or to the sleep (promised or actual) - and how can he tell the difference?

If he has been running away from things, is that what the rest of his family does i.e. run away from him? Might there be a parallel sense of abandonment in his own life (caused by his truancy)?

**Q> Do we see this 'in real time' - i.e. Joy before she leaves him - or is it replayed via a dream? Actually this is a fundamental question about the 'now' in the story: when is it set? Is it a journey or is it all looking backwards, partly through dream and partly not? And for the 'not' part, what 'present' events take place which will enhance, colour, nuance, influence both his story and his dreams (or his lack of sleep)?

❀

Does he regard sleep as his comforter / solace, as his family would have been at some point in the past? If so, then his need for sleep is about more than a) simply resolving tiredness, or b) a mechanism to remember / forget / resolve.

What could those external 'events' be, past or present? Work. Relationship. Ambition of some kind. Wrong-doing. A 'dream' (probably not fulfilled - or dreaming of a dream fulfilled (like a lottery win)).

There is likely to be a blend here of past & present, real & dream.
Presumably there should be parallels with some of the things other characters are going through e.g. Joy.
Difference: he can 'structure' the present / real world and control (to some extent) how he moves through it, but he has no such control over a) his sleeping or b) his dreaming. Is there anything addictive in his lack of control &

abdication? Is he somehow liberated by not having to make decisions but rather simply react to circumstance?

This might tie-in well with his 'running away' e.g. he had been professionally successful to the point where he has too much responsibility & has to make too many decisions. The need to 'run away' from that costs his him his job possibly. The slippery slope toward being fired could be a thread throughout; he uses his lack of sleep as a medical argument for a) keeping his job, b) running away. Therefore it can have a positive impact in some circumstances.

Does he see a 'shrink' / have a confidant outside of any he creates for himself in his 'dream state'? Might the dream 'observer' be that person?

The opening needs to establish:
- his problem with sleep
- the means he has gone to / is prepared to go to in order to seek resolution
- some of the sources of his restlessness & something in his history
- an inkling into his state of mind (i.e. and possible futures)

Need him to have a name before I start, a 'peg' to hang the narrative on...
Will the name suit his condition of being contrary, surprising? Should it fit his day-time or night-time character? Should it be 'plain' - an Everyman name - or something outstanding? [I favour the former]

Harry? Robert/Bob? Will? Adam?

Dual names; one day, one night.

Henry / Harry	Joy
Robert / Bob	Dr Fawcett
William / Will *	
Edward / Ed	two names need to suggest different
Michael / Mike *	characters, temperaments, even ages...
David / Dave	
Maurice / Mo *	
Donald / Don	

For surname some kind of play on Hypnos?
Can Hypnos' parents/siblings help to provide some kind of structure (particularly to the dream-state) e.g. Thanatos / Death (brother), Nemesis (sibling)?

Hipnor or Hipner?

Joy's maiden name also becomes important?
Something the opposite of sleep perhaps: to suggest vitality e.g.
'Lively' (corny?), 'Fuller'?

❋

Had he once been a runner? (The parallel with running away from things…)
He had been good but never good enough.
Another essentially solitary experience that in a way removed him from things.

Why did he stop? In the end he ran away from that too.

It had been part of his family's legend. Joy had known him as a runner and his
kids had seen something of that until he gradually stopped. Consequently,
when everyone is gone, it is something else he doesn't have to fall back on; it's
only a memory for his dreams.

❋

Format of the book. Is it important the sequence in which the dreams occur?
i.e. the telling or the working out of a story. Do there need ∴ to be two parallel
plot lines: life & dream? If so, then middles and ends are required for both.

Presumably the first dream should only occur once he has taken his first
concoction of pills. We need to take it on trust that he's had bad dreams before;
that first dream needs to convince us of that…

Is his day-to-day life unravelling, falling apart? If so, then it will need to be
practical, mundane to a degree.

Need to decide early on if there is going to be a thread, a glimmer of hope, a
positive outcome - and where/how this is going to manifest itself.

Against this, how do the dreams 'progress'? As his real life falls apart do his
dreams permit him to resolve / reconcile his past? If so, how? A kind of
counterpoint. Or does the resolving of things in dreams provide him with the
tools he needs in order to sort his life out? i.e. what he had seen as debilitating
in the end proves to be his salvation…

At the end of the book, should he either stop dreaming or stop living? or start
living again?

If the journey is leading somewhere, then this is the question that needs to be answered.

~~~~

Although dated 30th March, the long entry above was probably written over a number of days leading up to the next entry which was dated fourteen days later.

There is a lot here regarding "Sleeping". Had he been considering this for some time in advance of his first notes on the subject, or if not, does the fact that he can apparently build and assimilate ideas so quickly further demonstrate of how far he has come over the decades? You might of course counter with the observation that many of the questions he asks himself (and, in a way, asks his characters) are the same as they have always been - i.e. at a fundamental level, "what happens?" - but he seems to get to the nub of things much more quickly these days. Remember how much going around the houses there had been with "Mirrors" thirty years earlier? Would that idea have suffered the same fate now?

~~~~

14th April 2021 (PBS)

I have started drafting "Sleeping" without any definitive plan in order to see if it has 'legs' in terms of establishing an emotional attachment to it. Thus far (about 5k words in) it seems to be going ok, though I can sense the need for a plan getting closer as I don't think I can play 'fast-and-loose' with this one...

Heard nothing in relation to P.Hill ARCs - maybe I didn't try hard enough - and the 3 month window for Agents to come back to me closes at the end of April. At that point it will be order an Ingram proof and publish around my birthday (unless I change my mind and have a second go at Agents).

Still annotating the notebooks. It's an exercise which seems to have established a life of its own, and it will be interesting to see how I feel about the whole once it is 'finished'. That's a question in itself of course; for example, do these entries make it into the book? Logically I think they should. Everything is fair game until the notebooks are published.

In this month's two Stanzas I have presented 'found poems'. The response has been interesting. I am happy with both pieces as 'poems', but their genesis worries me in terms of ownership of the language, stealing etc. The consensus seemed to be that attribution is key - which makes me worry about the found poems I have already published. Will I need to 'reissue' all of them with some kind of posthumous acknowledgement?

I'm also toying with the idea of seeing if National Geographic would be interested in a kind of formal/approved 'joint venture' where my poems are entirely sourced from their articles. I have a title for the volume already: "Lost & Found". I think that works on a number of levels.

Other than that I'm finding inspiration for poetry difficult[75], and re-editing my 'collected' poems is not a stimulating experience as I realise just how rough some of my earlier work was. Maybe there will be an argument for something more selective at some point, but my heart wouldn't be in it just at the minute.

16th April 2021 (w.com)

It seemed like a good idea. I mean, I had some free time on my hands after all. Not for right now you understand, but for some point in the future - just in case 'posterity' might ever need it...

Over the years I have written (thus far) a number of volumes of poetry, and I got to thinking: "If you put that lot together - essentially seven slim volumes - then you'd end up with maybe 500 poems. That would be a collection and a half! I wonder what it would look like..."

And then wondering turned to action, resulting in me pulling together all the aforementioned pieces into one document; pages of the stuff. Although I probably shouldn't have been, I was impressed. But if you are going to produce a true 'Collected Poems', then shouldn't you also take the opportunity to review the lot, if only to be able to say "completely revised" somewhere upfront? - because I've seen that more than once..!

You can debate whether that was my first or second mistake - or perhaps you've lost count! - but when I went back to the beginning, to those poems around the early 1980s (the ones I thought back then were great) more than once I found myself thinking disbelievingly "I wrote that?!". And I rarely said it in a good way... It was, quite frankly, a little demoralising.

There are two possible reasons for my reaction. The first is the knowledge that I don't write like that any more, and so the poems are of a time / era / sensibility. The second - and I'm being honest here - is that some of them may not be as good as I once thought. Of course, it could be a combination of both..!

Where did that hammer blow leave me? A pause on revisiting the old stuff - and the raising of a yet unanswered question as to whether a "Selected Poems" might not be a better option. You know, just the really good stuff...

Which all begs the question about the value of looking back too far into the past, the dangers inherent in turning over some of those old stones. Because - certainly

---

[75] Continuing the theme previously discussed.

in the case of poetry - I'm not sure you can win: leave the poems as they are and as an honest reflection of how you were / how you wrote at the time, or edit them to bring them right up-to-date with how you are / how you write now? The problem with the latter is that you effectively end up with completely different poems.

The great thing, of course - and here the glass is decidedly half-full - is that the exercise has already demonstrated that we move on, we develop, we begin to find our voice, our style; we learn what we want to write about, and how we want to do so. And hopefully the things we wrote this year are just a little better than what we came up up last year, even though that was a little better than the year before...

On that basis, I should already look forward to the next poem, the next story - and I do. If it's naïve being convinced the next volume, the next character, the next plot line is going to be a step up on the last, then guilty as charged. And thinking about it, isn't that a better place to be than finding out what you wrote yesterday is pretty much exactly the same as something you came up with twenty years ago?

So, for now, the project goes on the back-burner - after all, I assume (hope!) posterity won't come calling just yet.

~~~

Is "hammer blow" an extreme reaction to his discovery of a perceived inadequacy? Or is it rather a reality check, the validation that not everything can be as 'good' as he would wish it to be? In any event, surely the most important thing is what his does with such revelations; does he allow them to crush him (as is literally suggested by the term 'hammer blow') or to spur him on? Perhaps he has moved beyond the first of the two responses - the more juvenile of the two - confessing to "already look(ing) forward to the next poem, the next story". Even more pertinent is that, in spite of the self-inflicted disappointment, he has not totally dismissed the idea of a revised 'collected poems', recognising that it could be one which remains valid for some future point in time; demonstration of faith and belief, however misplaced these might prove to be.

~~~

18ᵗʰ April 2021 (PBS)

Letter sent to Nat. Geo…

In terms of "Sleeping", a decent enough start made, but without something concrete to aim at I'm concerned that I'll just start drifting through it. What's needed is the 'history' mapped out because without that I simply don't have sufficient context for the dreams and the danger becomes that William thinks something during the day then dreams about it at night in a kind of 'rinse -

repeat' cycle. The dreams need to be more random than that, more out of control.

Of course, I *could* follow that approach and then simply resequence the dreams in the final draft; that may keep up the momentum <u>and</u> ensure a decent link between them and William's history: what he 'thinks' and how he dreams it... If I'm going to do that I need <u>not</u> to title the segments 1, 2, 3, 4 etc. - and I still need to map out the historical events.

So, William's interactions are:
> William and Joy
> > and Josh
> > and Alex
> > and work
> > ...

These inflection points are what I need to define and work through.

<u>William & Joy</u>
> How they met / got together
> the process of getting married
> their first home
> + Josh
> + Alex
> how she reacts to his sleeping
> moving to a bigger house / how that works
> her decision to leave him
> William without Joy

Because the novel is William-centric (they are <u>his</u> dreams after all) there can be no element which does not contain him. True?

<u>William & Josh</u>
> Any childhood experiences
> do they drift apart / why Exeter?
> subsequent repercussions / home truths?

<u>William & Alex</u>
> Is this a similar relationship to Josh? William must have similar feelings, but presumably Alex is a different person. Josh (the elder) more bolshie? Alex a little more emotional / sympathetic?
> William with Alex & partner
> Alex after Joy has left William
> news of the baby?

William & work

something about his job (what it is, how he gets it)
how his sleeping starts to affect his work
relationship with work? incident with Ruth?
how his perception of his work and his standing differs from reality

William & others

Are there any third parties involved, either in his recent past (work?)
or in his distant past about whom he could dream? Opportunity for all
sorts of dreams here, including violence, fantasy etc.

Q> where is the balance to the book? i.e. do the dreams play the major part in
the narrative or is there a balance?
That seems to be a key question not only in terms of how the book is
structured…

19ᵗʰ April 2021 (PBS)

I need to address the 'biggest' question of all first: what is the trigger for
William's poor sleeping? Just about everything else is a consequence of that.
Yes, the bad sleeping triggers events etc. but it comes first. So why? As his
sleep disintegrates, so does his life; so what was it that caused the initial
decline?

Could be:

physical
emotional | assuming there's
psychological | a difference…

20ᵗʰ April 2021 (PBS)

William's problem with sleeping has to be a physical (mental?) manifestation
of something else; a shift, a change of balance, an imbalance. Or perhaps the
removal of an opportunity to correct / affect something. e.g. he has always felt
guilty about his parents over something, and had assumed that one day he
would 'right the wrong'. but when they died that opportunity was removed
which meant he had to live with his guilt / burden, unable to resolve it. In
consequence, would that disturb him enough to trigger dreams, restlessness?
No absolution.
Or did he do something wrong and fears discovery? If so, from who? [Can't
be Joy because her leaving him would solve his problems…]

William & his parents

…

What about the parallel stream of what William does in <u>real time</u> e.g. visit the P.O.?

If there are 30+ dreams (entirely possible) what are the 30+ events that are interspersed with them? Does it need to be balanced in that way? If so, assuming one dream per night, then that's a month in real time. What does William <u>do</u> in that month / what does he need to do? Would it be absurd for him to have more dreams than wakefulness - probably. But some of those past 30 could just be standard rememberings and not dreams at all... that might work.

Should I list the events/memories/dreams out in the document in order to give me something I could write against?

Undoubtedly some of the past events need to be remembered rather than dreamed (partly because we need to have William's conscious perspective on them).

❋

Need to factor in the events which represent his 'running away' - there need to be a few.

Ironic(?) that his family (one by one) run away from him...

~~~~

It would not be too fanciful to draw a parallel between his ideas for "Sleeping" and those relating to "This Time Tomorrow" from a few years earlier. In both cases it seems as if he had landed on a theme, a structure, some notions to explore, which had considerable interest and merit, yet in spite of that in both instances - in terms of skeleton for the narrative and some early drafting - the early progress ends up bearing little fruit. As has been suggested previously, do we have in "Sleeping" another example of a solid proposition being undermined by an inadequate plot? Or is it too early to say in this case?

In any event, we might argue that examples of such inadequacy should not to be confused with 'flimsiness' of writing; it is rather the failure of the scaffolding - in terms of complexity, sophistication - to be able to carry the load. If you think back to 'Mirrors', perhaps the greatest benefit to come out of the agonies of its exaggerated period of gestation was a rigorously tested plot, one that had been put together, dismantled and reassembled more than once. If that process represented his 'gold standard' for plot creation, could it be that he had reached a point when, were that benchmark not to be adequately met, it manifested itself in the consequent failure of both 'belief' and production? In relation to some of his earlier ideas, we might also legitimately ask whether any similar shortfall - if indeed these could be defined and proven - might have led to failure in delivering a suitable end product.

~~~~~

<div align="right">

27ᵗʰ April 2021 (PBS)

</div>

Having finished 'narrating' all the notebook + writeral entries to-date, I have now arrived at March '21 - which means the entries in *this* book need to be included next. The only question is when? Do I wait for a while or do I start adding them soon? If the latter I will quickly catch up and the narration of notebook entries will inevitably blend into one thing i.e. I am likely to write in the notebooks as if the entries are going straight into "Shrapnel". Maybe there's something logical or inevitable about that, me as author and editor blending into a single entity (which I am anyway, obviously!).

I remain unconvinced by the "Sleeping" idea even though I am about 9k words through. Perhaps that is why I have been unable to get my mind around a plan for the story, to articulate what happens. That and the question of belief I suppose…

Interesting conversation with Sarah yesterday about work and the possibility of going back to some kind of Mon-Fri away from home life. I don't think either of us are keen. Sarah suggested I should 'think outside the box' - not that either of us could define what the box looked like. The old life, I suppose.

Which effectively leaves just about everything on the table and possible. It was interesting today in editing the entries around the turn of the year, and the discussion about what kind of life it was I wanted to lead. Still to be shaped, obviously. And then committed to…

~~~~~

Which, in a way, is where all this started…

~~~~~

The following entries were written once editing the first draft of this volume was well under way. As such, they were produced in the knowledge that they would most likely find their way into this book. This gives them a slightly different status to just about everything previously written in the notebooks.

Eventually added to the draft just before the end of June 2021, to a certain extent they represent an amalgam (in style? content?) with the public posts on writeral.com. They also pose a challenge in the sense that they are too 'immediate' for comment i.e. there is insufficient post-entry activity and knowledge to inform any meaningful assessment of what was written. The passage of time will change this of course, but for now the entries are reproduced here without interpretation. (Ed - 5th July 2021)

29th April 2021 (PBB)

emailed the 'Gazette' today and asked them a) if I could write the odd book-related piece for them FOC, and b) whether they'd like to do a piece on Coverstory books… All part of the not-so-grand plan. We shall see.

Also tried to map out a few more of the 'sections'/vignettes for "Sleeping" based on the notes already made. That may help me put the proverbial pen-to-paper and keep up the momentum to see if it goes anywhere.

[Moved the notebook entries to here[76] for a change having copied everything else into the doc. When to stop??]

Oh, and also ordered the proof copy of "On Parliament Hill" - so we should see what that looks like next week.

Still waiting to hear from Nat. Geo. Unless I get something +ve from them it could be that I take my foot right off the poetry gas as per earlier entries - or at least leave just enough to keep the Derby Stanza going…

6th May 2021 (PBB)

OPH proof has arrived, so started the final 'on the page' review for minor tweaks / errors. Should take about a week and then we're good to go.

Also launched the submission window for NC2. Submittable seems to be working, I'll just need to decide the best way to keep on top of the entries (i.e. when to download them).

---

[76] The PBB notebook.

Struggling to keep up the momentum on the 'Sleeping' idea. I now think I may have got the use of tenses back-to-front, so my next task could be to reverse tenses in 10k or so words. A pain, but better now than later…

Struggling with sleeping per se. Not getting enough / too disturbed - and the tinnitus doesn't help when you wake up @ 4:30 in the morning. There is, I fear, no solution other than grinning and bearing - which is easier some times than others (increasingly not).

9th May 2021 (PBB)

Is there an argument to try and write a thriller, something commercial? Remaining unconvinced by 'Sleeping' and concerned that it could become just a rehash of old themes, is there any merit in doing something new?

The biggest carrot is probably the commercial one… (Does it count as "thinking outside of the box"?)

Whenever I've been through this in the past I've been stopped by two things: one, a lack of expertise in any typical 'thriller' area (e.g. I know nothing of murder, pathology etc.), and two, because it feels like a betrayal of some kind.

[Sudden thought: is the French thing a thriller of sorts?]

So if I did write something commercial it would have to be non-technical i.e. people-based. Rules out murder, technology, 'spying' (probably). But possibly not 'investigation' of some kind.

'Investigation' implies that there is a problem to be solved; something like the French thing is about a 'problem' being uncovered i.e. it's all a question of the starting point in terms of 'ignorance'. Or rather, knowing what the end goal is. Paul Rose is on a journey without an end point in mind (not really); events 'happen' to him. If you have a specific problem to solve to question to answer, then you know what the goal is. As does the reader. And there would be an assumption made (by the reader) that in the end the question will be answered. In a way their journey is a 'safe' one. But if you don't know where you are going, your experience as Reader is akin to that of your main character…

I can't believe I'm actually thinking of lifting the lid on the French thing again…!

Maybe all this is just food for thought at this stage. We'll see.

14th May 2021 (PBB)

Walking the walls of York this morning.

The flash of two opening sentences for a short story - and a wondering if that isn't what I need to focus on for a short while (at least while I edit 'Notebooks').

I suspect 'Sleeping' is both too random and too vague to be a viable option. And the French thing? Really?!

25th May 2021 (PBB)

Well those words from the York walk did indeed turn into a story - 'Kara' - which may prove the spur for a small collection, who knows? It was good writing something again after the slog of revision for OPH.

Of course still in the slog for the notebooks thing (about half-way through). One thing that has struck me on more than one occasion is that some of the ideas are pretty decent. For example the original thoughts on 'This Time Tomorrow' were good but seemed to get derailed when (I think) I settled on the wrong plot to support the idea. It's entirely possible that a different plot could have worked (could still work).

And the idea (so small I almost missed it) of writing about someone's thoughts as they lie in a coma... Offers all sorts of possibilities in terms of style and substance. Could be a short story perhaps?

Haven't picked up anything else (including the French thing).

On the non-writing front I have my first few submissions for NC2, and I may be on the verge of landing a monthly 'books' slot in the Ripon Gazette. I should have a better idea come the end of the week.

Last week was tough, navigating the challenge of being at home not 'working'. Nearly 8 months since I finished in Derby. Can't quite get my head around the 'not working' thing - though I am working of course. It's just that unsolved equation which seems to insist that work = income, and without income, how can it be work?

Sold 8 copies of OPH yesterday.

Whether conventional or not, I'd just like to recognise those people who have bought my latest novel, "On Parliament Hill", in the last week. So, "Thank you". It means a lot to me.

When you don't have some massive publishing behemoth behind you driving publicity, working with bookshops etc., your readers - inevitably in smaller numbers - become so much more important. And if you have a reader who likes your work, having them share that with their friends and connections is critical. If you're not backed by a Penguin or Vintage or Faber, word-of-mouth is the probably best publicity tool available to a writer.

So, thank you for buying "On Parliament Hill". Thank you for reading it - assuming you get through to then end! And thank you a third time if you like it and tell your friends...

3rd June 2021 (w.com)

With the exception of a couple of short stints in Europe and the Far East, I have lived in the UK all my life. This is where my - extended - family lives, and is home to the vast majority of my friends and ex-work colleagues. Two weeks ago I published my latest novel, "On Parliament Hill", and was pleased with its modest initial sales. Yesterday I had a breakdown form my distributor as to where those sales occurred, and guess how many of them were from the UK?

Not a single one! All the sales came from US dollar transactions, the majority directly from the US.

Inevitably this left me asking questions - including, most disturbingly perhaps, what does this say about me and my writing? None of which I propose to try and answer just now... Maybe I should just move to the US..!

But it does echo a post I made some time ago, which still seems to hold true...

In any event, to those of you who have bought the book, Thank you.

12th June 2021 (PBB)

First round of editing the Notebooks is now complete; I just need to type up the (many) amendments. There are also another couple of months' worth of these entries which should probably be included (though this once again begs the question about when to stop...).

Sales of OPH are now in the 20s with most of these coming outside the UK.

In terms of the next fiction project I am part-way through two short stories (one old, one new) and have parked the 'Sleeping' idea - though re-reading the notes for it as I edited the relevant notebook entries I was struck by how interesting some of the ideas were... I daresay I'll reread/refresh again soon and see what I think. A break from something can make all the difference. One way or another I'll need to settle on something.

Poetry is proving problematic. I've written virtually nothing for months, relying on a few 'found' pieces to see me through the Stanza groups (though I haven't been to the N. Yorks one for two+ months now).

Probably uppermost in my mind is the question of work. Nearly half-way through 2021 and not a sniff - though I'm hardly pushing. The news that Harry's going to get a full subsistence loan for his first year (based on my zero income) takes some of the pressure off - and I think he likes the idea of being independent from me / my income to a degree. But some work will probably happen. At this stage I feel half-committed to what's going on i.e. 'retirement' or not, writing or not. Maybe that's no surprise.

21st June 2021 (PBB)

Having drafted my third new short story yesterday, I feel invigorated by the way the medium offers me the chance to explore different characters in these compact vignettes. Driving back from Harrogate today, simply seeing someone walking along the road who I could 'steal' for the next one is an exciting and enticing prospect. Perhaps she will make her debut tomorrow...

Typing up the first revisions to 'Shrapnel' is going well, and I'm about ⅔ through. I need to decide whether to include all these new entries (I'm certain I will, in fact) plus any posted on Writeral in the interim. Then it will be down to producing a proof copy to review that. This time, of course, the process is different and can only be iterative to a degree. When, for example, will 'Shrapnel' be 'finished'? I think I am prepared for this one to have a longer gestation period and for me to pay for more than one proof copy along the way - there is no deadline, of course.

Afterword

Above all else, this is the story of a journey.

Over the last thirty-seven years or so, across a number of hand-written books, I have been keeping what might be termed a record; although, having said that, it is perhaps more instructional to say what the notebooks do *not* represent. They are neither 'diary' - as they lack the prerequisite structure - nor are they 'journals', primarily because of the nature of their subject matter. And on reflection, even the word 'record' is something of a misnomer.

The entries - almost exclusively relating to my ambition 'to be a Writer' - are a compendium of thoughts, ideas, plans, ruminations, decisions (needed, taken, and not taken), aspirations, failings and disappointments. And the occasional success! In some cases they chart the progress and development of an idea from inception all the way through to published work, most notably in relation to charting the gestation of my novel *Mirrors* (later *An Infinity of Mirrors*). All thirty-two years of it!

The contents of the notebooks also represent a search, a quest for that which always seems just within reach - but more often than not remains entirely elusive. So much so, that, were you to regard them as some kind of map, they would chart coastlines drawn before a continent's interior had been explored. Based on some of the entries, you could be forgiven for interpreting them as the ravings of a madman who still believed the world was flat.

If the entries are fragmentary, disjointed, inconclusive, why bother to take the trouble to not only transcribe them into a more persistent electronic record, but to do so in the format of a real physical book? Is it mere vanity run amok? Perhaps. But there are other reasons: the desire to capture as much of 'my writing life' as possible, before it is too late; the opportunity (albeit a selfish one, I grant you) to review and dissect prior thoughts and processes; perhaps to harvest old ideas to fuel new projects; and who knows, maybe one day others might find this scatter-gun trespassing on my literary dirty-washing illuminating, either for themselves or as an aid in the interrogation of my work. Another log thrown on the fire of posterity.

That's all well and good (if you'll indulge me for a moment longer), but these notebooks and their entries weren't designed to be 'read'. They are the more or less uncoordinated outpourings of a mind that was, at times, clearly frazzled! The challenge, therefore - and this with my editor's hat on - is how to architect the transition from the hand-written to the typed page. Not only that, given I now have years of hindsight with which to inform these prehistoric thoughts, to look back and say "this was spot on!" or "this was rubbish!", how do I insert my modern day self into the text without invalidating the integrity of what was written in 1984 or 1994 or 2004?

I started out with some rules. The first was to transcribe *exactly* what was written on the page. This posed difficulties where things were written in the margins or at jaunty angles, where words may have been crossed out or the text embellished with lines, arrows, and various other non-linguistic devices. Not wishing to shun the challenge, I used my keyboard as best I could to keep to the spirit of the original entry. The only editing I permitted myself during the first stage of transcription was to correct any obvious spelling mistakes.

The second rule was related to content. Was it all strictly necessary? If this is indeed an exposure of the 'shrapnel from a writing life', then anything that was irrelevant should surely be omitted. Filtering was, of course, easier said than done given how much of 'normal' intrudes upon the 'supra-normal'. Hence I have retained some passages which refer to my working life. Given how this sucked time from my writing, yet also to a degree funded it, I felt some of the non-writing material had to remain in order to provide a rounded picture of my overall experience at certain points in time. And then there were the more personal entries where the notes do, very occasionally, stray toward diary territory. The same rules had to apply: if something is directly relevant to the writing life, then reproducing it was valid.

The most difficult challenge of all came post-transcription; the question of how to interweave the me of 'now' into the me of 'then'...

Once again, there were a number of options. The first, obviously, was to do nothing; to leave the original text without any kind of embellishment at all and allow it to stand or fall on its own merits. Whilst this might have been a 'purist' approach, it didn't feel quite right as I couldn't help but recognise my duty to help the reader along and make the fragmentary a slightly easier pill to swallow.

So, if I was going to offer a helping hand - the second option - then there was the question as to how this should be done. A single summary at the beginning or end of each 'chapter' utilising what I know now in order to provide meaning and gloss? Or perhaps an even more intrusive approach where specific words or phrases were annotated in situ so that the reader could have a much more 'dynamic' experience of the present informing the past? And if I took that approach, then what format would these intrusions and clarifications take: small blocks of text in different fonts? Footnotes? Surely the danger with this would be that the 'new' might overwhelm the 'old', and the sense of journey and search which the whole should represent could be lost.

As an extreme option - but perhaps in many ways the most appropriate one - would be to turn the panoply of scribblings into a semi-fiction; take the notes as written, and morph them into the slightly more coherent ramblings of a 'fictional' writer. A blend of non-fiction and fiction, if you like; an attempt to turn myself into a character about whom I could write. A kind of tangential autobiography.

In the end, with the aim of drawing threads together and offering a gloss based on additional knowledge or insight, I opted for the insertion of paragraphs of 'editorial comment', brief footnotes where warranted, and, most importantly, to try and take a third-party view. Banishment of as much of the 'I' as possible - other than in the original notebook and website entries - felt an important component in being able to offer an oversight which, although informed, was as dispassionate as possible. I needed the 'editor' to not be the 'me' of the original material; in many ways the 'editor' is as much a fictional character as some of those about whom I wrote in the base material. Exercising what I hope proves to be an appropriate degree of self-control, I believe I have been able to achieve a sense of balance i.e. the voice of 'the editor' does not overwhelm the voice of 'the writer' - though obviously this proved a tricky challenge given both were me!

Drawing ever closer to the contemporary - i.e. where the time distance between original entry and when the editorial comments were being made - a further dilemma arose. Perhaps obtusely, passing judgement on something written thirty years earlier proved relatively easy, lots of water having passed beneath the literary bridge since then; but as the time gap shortened - thirty months, thirty weeks - so the job of acting as the 'disinterested interrogator' became harder. And when it got to thirty days? Indeed, the more general question of when to stop - given I was still adding to the notebooks in the background - came as something of a surprise. And what did 'stop' actually mean?

The conclusion drawn in the middle of 2021 was two-fold: firstly - and perhaps arbitrarily - that editorial comment should not be made against entries beyond April 2021; and secondly, that no further notebook entries should be included after mid-2021, which seemed a reasonable cut-off point. Who knows what might subsequently happen, or be *written*, which would force an extension to this deadline, one that is not only arbitrary but to which it is logically impossible to adhere.

So that is how it currently stands (as of 5th July, 2021). Of course, if there is a need to redraw that particular sand-line then I will need to modify not only the body of the book, but this afterword as well. Doing so would suggest that, in multiple senses, there is very little difference between this gloss, my editorial comments, and the original entries themselves. The blurring of such lines is - considering the nature of this endeavour - entirely appropriate.

Ian Gouge

Addenda

Residue

These brief notes were made at various points and in various notebooks, and were never dated. They are collected here as fragments which do not easily 'fit' elsewhere - largely because they cannot be located in time.

At an airport, people moving. A panoply, a parade of stories: of tragedy, of defeat, of minor victories. And all the voices unheard; all the perspectives unseen.

And the mythology extends through mobile phones. To whom do they talk (again unseen, unheard). And after that conversation, what do the unseen say to more unseen?

And where are the circles completed?

Because they must be, somewhere.

Somewhere invisible + unknown...

Recorded in notebook PBB at Philadelphia airport at some point in 2012 or 2013.

❁

[DREAM: Short story?]

<u>Vengeance for the Charioteers</u>

Starts lying on a green at the sea-side: ends being chained to a bed in hospital.

The dream.
Charioteers #3 and #5 help out someone who they think is unwell.
Become friends.
They show their chariots (part of a circus / fairground entertainment).
Gets close to #3.
Followed by two men on a couple of occasions.
Men attack the women in their 'shed', immobilise and then frame the man (hence the hospitalisation).

There is no-one left to tell the truth. The men have planted evidence (incl. DNA?)
What about security cameras?
Man escapes (car accident? freed while being transported?) - then vows vengeance.

Does he succeed?
Is he freed? e.g. camera footage.

✿

Idea

Series of 'verbal' interviews.

"These commentaries...are not the views of..." - taken from the Bond movie intro...

INTERESTING...!

Subject?

✿

Essentially monologues that allow the exploration of a wide range of topics from some specific perspectives (that can be unusual / challenging / upsetting / profound etc.)

Is there a need for a link between the subjects of all these communications - and if so, what is it?

Not necessary verbal. Perhaps a little more like someone leaving a tape recording running inside the brain. Structure and flow could therefore be 'loose' in some cases; almost stream on consciousness.

Recorded in notebook PBB at some point in 2015 or 2016.

✿

<u>Ideas for a 'professional' book</u>

- needs
  - to require no significant research
    ∴ personnel-based

  - to not be 'technical'
    ∴ Managemental
    people-oriented
    leadership
    'Authentic'

  - to follow some kind of structure or 'conceit' to aid creation
    e.g. Alphabet - months - etc.

  - not to be a random collection
    ∴ the A= , B= formula is out of the question

  - to be based around a new term / theory or
    a new way of looking at something
    e.g. Integrity, Authenticity

  - to possess a broader interpretation, shouldn't be about 'IT'

"Wrong time, wrong place"

Turn the ship around
       |
Management/Leadership
       ↳ how to change course
              ↳ could build a conceit here easily...
"BIG IDEA"
The power of moments   cf. nudge theory
       |
something about the impact of 'instants'
       ↳ small things, big change

coaching / mentoring
Governance
Culture
Change
'the Team'
Strategy

'Good enough'
Authenticity
Emotional Intelligence
Choice
Execution
'I'm not good at that!'
Measurement
How do you know…?
Cost - Price - Money
Values
Vision / Mission
Nudge Theory
Communication / Brand
'It's never about you'   "BIG IDEA"
'I wouldn't start from here'   "BIG IDEA"
    ↳ INTRO
'What we say isn't what we mean.'   "BIG IDEA"

Format will be key

Idea.
    Produce a 'typical' slide(s) on each topic / area that might easily be
used in a strategy doc, presentation, proposal - then 'debunk' the slide
    ↳ get to the truth of the matter

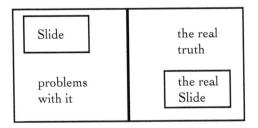

Intro   - some basic principles   "BIG IDEAS"
        - format of the book
        - contents summary
        - body

Cork -> Dublin   250km walk
                200-230 crow flies
                259 / 286/ 297 drive

Recorded in notebook PBB at some point in late 2017 or early 2018

"My Writing Diary"

One of the ideas for his Writeral website was to include a "writing diary", partly to allow his readers to keep track of what he was working on, and partly to keep himself honest. Between Spring 2017 and early 2021 (at which point it was removed from public view) entries to the diary were sporadic and often brief in the extreme.

In terms of our endeavour here, deciding how to integrate "My Writing Diary" posed challenges on a number of fronts. Whilst all entries are specifically dated, they are often the briefest summary of what he may have covered more expansively in the notebooks; as such, including them in amongst the main body of the work might simply re-confirm what we already knew, and potentially weaken the narrative of the journey we are trying to map out.

A few diary updates are substantial enough to be considered candidates for Writeral posts proper. This would seem to argue that they *should* be included in the chronology of this volume. Also, there are some cross-references in "the diary" to other blog entries, many of which *are* included in this analysis.

On balance, I have decided to subsume the "My Writing Diary" entries - regardless of length - into the main body of this book. Given how it grew organically on a single website page, its entries appeared in reverse chronological sequence, the most recent was always appended at the top of the page. By including each entry individually in the correct chronological sequence, I save my readers the chore of manually triangulating between a single reproduction of "My Writing Diary" and related notebook entries.

Note: his use of the term 'published' in the diary most often refers to the 'publishing' of the piece concerned on www.writeral.com, rather than the production of any physical volume.

Glossary

12th N	Shakespeare's *Twelfth Night*.
AUD	"An Unceremonious Departure".
BBG	'Biscuits Brun Grenoble', a notebook (purchased in Europe - possibly from the Pompidou Centre in Paris) with entries covering a period from 2014 to 2020.
CM	'Championship Manager', a massively successful football management game franchise for the PC.
CON	'Constable'; a notebook with part of John Constable's 'The Hay Wain' on the front cover. This contains the earliest notes on *Mirrors* (certainly pre-1983). The final entry was made in 1990.
CRC	No explanation for this abbreviation can be found.
DePuy	A medical device manufacturer (for example, of artificial knees and hips), and part of the Johnson & Johnson Group.
E²	Engeris Squared. This was a rebrand of the Planet Online internet service provider for whom he worked and which was eventually bought by Cable and Wireless (and later absorbed into Vodafone).
eMGMT	*eManagement*, his second professional book (and first published by Springer Verlag).
EMS	Edvard Munch 'The Scream', a notebook which contains two items: a first draft of the poem "St. Ives", and comprehensive notes relating to *Mirrors*, later to be re-titled as *An Infinity of Mirrors*.
GNR	The Great North Run, an annual multi-participant half-marathon run in Newcastle.
MB2000	Management Books 2000, a publishing company.
MSND	Shakespeare's *A Midsummer Night's Dream*.
MWD	My Writing Diary (see Addenda)
NC1	*New Contexts: 1*, a poetry anthology published by Coverstory books in January 2021.
NC2	*New Contexts: 2*, the follow on to *New Contexts: 1*, this time including some prose.
Nev	Short for Neville, hero of *The Big Frog Theory*.
Outokumpu	Previously known as British Steel Stainless and then Avesta Polarit; this was the steelworks in Meadowhall, Sheffield, where he worked as IT Director.
PBB	Paperblanks 'Ballad'; a notebook started in 2012 or 2013 with its final entry dated September 2017.
PBS	Paperchase, black squared; a notebook started in January 2001 with most entries from 2001 and 2002 apart from a few later entries in 2004, 2018 and 2021.
PDQ	Pretty Damned Quickly.
POV	Point of View.
PS	The Poetry Society.
PVR	Paperblanks 'Ventaglio Rosso'; a notebook started in late 2017 or early 2018, still in 'live' use at the time of the transposition into this document.
RBR	Ryman, black ruled; a notebook started in October 1992 with the last entry in December 2000.
Springer	Springer Verlag, a publishing imprint belonging to the Bertelsmann group.

Sun Alliance........ A UK insurer where he worked (in Bristol) for around 8 years until his move to DePuy and Leeds.

WBS................. Work Breakdown Structure, a standard mechanism for breaking work into specific individual tasks for ease of planning.

Writeral / w.com...www.writeral.com, his 'writing website' started in February 2017.

WTF................ "Walking Thru Fire".

UWE............... The University of the West of England.

Lightning Source UK Ltd.
Milton Keynes UK
UKHW021127060122
396705UK00007B/249